CONTENTS

Please note that all information in this publication
is correct up to and including 24 September 2013

MIX
From responsible
sources
FSC® C016961

G000269305

Ron Gourlay

DIRECTORS
(in alphabetical order)
Bruce Buck
Ron Gourlay
Marina Granovskaia
Eugene Tenenbaum

EXECUTIVE BOARD
Finance and Operations Director
Chris Alexander
Director/Club Secretary
David Barnard
Company Secretary
Alan Shaw

FOOTBALL CLUB BOARD
David Barnard
Bruce Buck
Ron Gourlay
Marina Granovskaia
Eugene Tenenbaum

LIFE PRESIDENT
Lord Attenborough CBE

VICE-PRESIDENTS
Peter Digby
Peter Harrison
Joe Hemani
John Leigh
Anthony Reeves
Alan Spence

FIRST-TEAM MANAGER
José Mourinho

ASSISTANT FIRST-TEAM COACH
Steve Holland

ASSISTANT FIRST-TEAM COACH
Silvino Louro

ASSISTANT FIRST-TEAM COACH
Rui Faria

ASSISTANT FIRST-TEAM COACH
José Morais

TECHNICAL DIRECTOR
Michael Emenalo

GOALKEEPER COACH
Christophe Lollichon

FIRST-TEAM FITNESS COACH
Chris Jones

chelseafc.com

MANAGING DIRECTOR Ken Rogers **SENIOR EDITOR** Steve Hanrahan **SENIOR ART EDITOR** Rick Cooke **SENIOR PRODUCTION EDITOR** Paul Dove
PROGRAMME EDITOR David Antill **FEATURES EDITOR** Dominic Bliss **FEATURES WRITER** Richard Godden **STAFF WRITER** James Sugrue
SUB EDITOR Gary Gilliland **DESIGNERS** Glen Hind and James Kenyon **STATISTICIAN** Paul Dutton
SALES & MARKETING MANAGER Elizabeth Morgan **BUSINESS DEVELOPMENT MANAGER** Will Beedles
PHOTOGRAPHY Darren Walsh, PA Photos, AP Images, Hugh Hastings, Chelsea FC Archive and Mirrorpix
PUBLISHED BY Sport Media **PRINTED BY** Bishops Printers **THANKS TO** Emma Wilkinson, John Barrett and Gareth Mills

CLUB CONTACTS: Address Chelsea Football Club, Stamford Bridge, London, SW6 1HS **CFC call centre** 0871 984 1905
PROGRAMME CONTACTS: Editorial 020 7958 2168 **Subscriptions** 0845 241 6210 **Email** cfc.programme@trinitymirror.com

Sport Media
A Trinity Mirror Business

WE'VE MADE HISTORY AND ARE NOW LOOKING TO GOALS FOR THE FUTURE

Becoming the first English team to have won all of UEFA's major club trophies is something to be proud of and is a fitting achievement to celebrate a decade of unparalleled success

After winning more European silverware in 2012/13, the return of José Mourinho as our manager in the summer has ensured there is much to look forward to for everybody associated with Chelsea Football Club.

José dubbed himself "The Happy One" at his press conference in June and we were equally happy to welcome him back. Of course, some of our players worked with him in his previous spell here. Along with them, we have a lot of experienced and up-and-coming talent within our squad and the ideal person to guide them in José.

Last term, our triumph in the Europa League was a memorable one as we became the first English club, and fourth overall, to win all three major UEFA competitions: the Champions League, the Cup Winners' Cup and Europa League. A strong finish in the Premier League then saw us take third place to secure automatic qualification for the Champions League once again.

In the summer, we celebrated the 10th anniversary of Roman Abramovich's arrival at Chelsea and our owner perfectly summed up how important the supporters are at this club. In a message to the fans on the front of our opening matchday programme of the season, he stated: "We have had a great decade together and the club could not have achieved it all without you. Thanks for your support, here's to many more years of success."

We have all experienced a wonderful decade since Mr Abramovich became the club's owner, with a remarkable haul of 11 major trophies, along with many off-field achievements. The goal now is to experience more success, both on and off the pitch, and I am confident that we are in a very strong position to do just that.

In August, we competed in the European Super Cup for the second season in succession. Although we were unfortunate to lose on penalties, I thought our performance was one which bodes well for the months ahead.

Before the competitive action got under way, we travelled to Asia for our Here To Play, Here To Stay tour. Wherever we go in the world, we always carry out grassroots work to ensure we leave a lasting legacy and this was the case in all three of the countries we visited, where we're seen as a community club.

It was evident that our fanbase is increasing all the time out there, with large attendances at all three of our matches. The biggest indicator of our growing popularity was the reception we received on our first-ever visit to Indonesia. Thousands of fans lined the streets on our arrival and a crowd in excess of 80,000 in the stadium, most of them wearing Chelsea shirts, was beyond our expectations.

As well as the Asia tour, we competed in the Guinness International Champions Cup in America, which formed a vital part of our preparation for the campaign ahead. Our Foundation coaches and Under-21s squad also travelled to the United States to launch an initiative with FC Harlem, once again demonstrating our commitment to developing football at a grassroots level all around the globe.

Our aim is to ensure the club continues to grow and we compete for trophies on all fronts. In order to do this, with the introduction of Financial Fair Play, commercial development is even more important then ever before. We welcomed a number of new partners from throughout the world during the summer and were delighted to extend our deal with adidas until 2023 after a highly successful first seven seasons. Both organisations share the same ethos and ambition and the new deal reaffirms adidas' belief in the club's status in world football.

Finally, let me thank you once more for your support and encourage you to get behind the team as we strive to make 2013/14 a season to remember.

The reception we received throughout the pre-season tour of Asia – such as here in Indonesia – was simply phenomenal

Chelsea Chief Executive Ron Gourlay congratulates Branislav Ivanovic, who scored the winning goal in the 2013 Europa League final as the Blues made history

MILESTONE SEASON FOR THE BLUES

A campaign of non-stop football saw the Blues play an incredible 69 competitive games, during which Frank Lampard became our top scorer of all time and Chelsea became the first English club to complete the set of major UEFA trophies

"When you win one trophy, you always want another. There is something in sport that keeps pushing you on."

Branislav Ivanovic's words after he had scored the winner in the 2012/13 Europa League final perfectly summarised the mentality within this Chelsea squad, who have made lifting silverware a bit of a habit over the last decade. In fact, with that 2-1 triumph over Benfica in Amsterdam, Chelsea became only the third club to have lifted all four UEFA club trophies – the Champions League, Europa League, European Cup Winners' Cup and Super Cup – in the company of Juventus and Ajax.

For a few fleeting days in May, a quirk of the football calendar meant that Chelsea were simultaneously holders of both the Champions League and the Europa League, becoming the first club to have achieved this honour.

In fact, it was a season of milestones. This was the year when the games just kept coming. By the time the final whistle was blown on the last fixture of the league campaign, Chelsea had played 69 competitive games in all competitions – a club record. In those matches, the Blues also scored more goals than ever before, netting 147 times (including eight in one game, against Aston Villa at Stamford Bridge).

As the club competed in a remarkable eight competitions – with Fernando Torres making Chelsea history by scoring in seven – there were away trips to Russia, Ukraine, Italy, Denmark, Romania, Switzerland, the Czech Republic and, of course, Amsterdam, not to mention the club's first-ever involvement in the FIFA Club World Championships in Japan and the European Super Cup in Monaco. Chelsea certainly racked up the air miles in 2012/13!

On the domestic front, we reached the semi-finals of both domestic cup competitions, but fell to Swansea City over two legs in the Capital One Cup and to Manchester City in the FA Cup, although some impressive form late in the season secured third place in the league.

The club also saw a change in management mid-season, as Roberto Di Matteo departed in November before the role was given to Rafa Benitez until the end of the campaign. For a team who looks to challenge for the title every season, finishing third was not the target at the outset of the campaign, but a combination of our mid-season blip and the competitiveness of Tottenham and Arsenal made it increasingly clear that a top-four finish would elude one of the three London clubs.

Key away wins at Manchester United and Aston Villa in May put Chelsea in the driving seat ahead of the final game with Everton, where another win – this time at Stamford Bridge – guaranteed third spot.

The 2-1 victory at Villa Park may have played a major part in securing a top-three finish, but it will surely be remembered more for the individual milestone reached by Frank Lampard, who scored both Chelsea goals. They were his

BARCLAYS PREMIER LEAGUE 2012/13

Team	Pld	HOME					AWAY					GD	Pts
		W	D	L	F	A	W	D	L	F	A		
1 Man Utd	38	16	0	3	45	19	12	5	2	41	24	+43	89
2 Man City	38	14	3	2	41	15	9	6	4	25	19	+32	78
3 Chelsea	38	12	5	2	41	16	10	4	5	34	23	+36	75
4 Arsenal	38	11	5	3	47	23	10	5	4	25	14	+35	73
5 Tottenham	38	11	5	3	29	18	10	4	5	37	28	+20	72
6 Everton	38	12	6	1	33	17	4	9	6	22	23	+15	63
7 Liverpool	38	9	6	4	33	16	7	7	5	38	27	+28	61
8 West Brom	38	9	4	6	32	25	5	3	11	21	32	-4	49
9 Swansea	38	6	8	5	28	26	5	5	9	19	25	-4	46
10 West Ham	38	9	6	4	34	22	3	4	12	11	31	-8	46
11 Norwich	38	8	7	4	25	20	2	7	10	16	38	-17	44
12 Fulham	38	7	3	9	28	30	4	7	8	22	30	-10	43
13 Stoke	38	7	7	5	21	22	2	8	9	13	23	-11	42
14 Southampton	38	6	7	6	26	24	3	7	9	23	36	-11	41
15 Aston Villa	38	5	5	9	23	28	5	6	8	24	41	-22	41
16 Newcastle	38	9	1	9	24	31	2	7	10	21	37	-23	41
17 Sunderland	38	5	8	6	20	19	4	4	11	21	35	-13	39
18 Wigan	38	4	6	9	26	39	5	3	11	21	34	-26	36
19 Reading	38	4	8	7	23	33	2	2	15	20	40	-30	28
20 QPR	38	2	8	9	13	28	2	5	12	17	32	-30	25

A brace at Aston Villa saw Frank Lampard become our top goalscorer of all time

202nd and 203rd strikes for the Blues, making him the club's highest scorer of all time, passing Bobby Tambling's 202 – a record that had stood since 1970.

In the days that followed, Lampard signed a one-year contract to stay at the club for the 2013/14 season and lifted the Europa League trophy. It was a week to remember for him and the supporters, who voted Juan Mata as their Player of the Year for the second consecutive season at the club's annual awards ceremony.

The team's strong finish meant the Bridge was brimming with positivity when the players set off on their traditional end-of-season lap of appreciation.

The return of José Mourinho as manager in the summer has increased that level of optimism further and one thing is certain – this group of players will be hungry to keep adding to their trophy collection.

MATA MAKES IT A DOUBLE

After being named Player of the Year in his debut season, the Spanish playmaker not only retained his award but added the Players' Player of the Year as well, becoming the first Blue to hold both titles

Juan Mata became the only person to be named the Blues' top performer in both of his first two seasons when he received the 2013 Chelsea Player of the Year award.

He is only the fourth person ever to retain the honour since it began in 1967 – alongside John Hollins (1970 and 1971), Ray Wilkins (1976 and 1977) and Mata's current team-mate Frank Lampard (2004 and 2005).

Our Spanish star even managed to improve on his impressive first season in west London, with 2012/13 bringing 20 goals, compared to 12 in the previous year, as well as ending the campaign as the Premier League's most prolific provider of assists with 17, one ahead of second-placed Eden Hazard.

Such great form meant it wasn't only the Chelsea supporters who were singing his praises, as Mata was also chosen by his Blues colleagues as the 2013 Players' Player of the Year, becoming the first person to win both awards in the same season.

"I am really, really happy and very proud – it is the best feeling in the world to feel loved by the supporters and my team-mates," said our No10. "It has made my year perfect.

"I can't choose between them. The players' one is very special because they are my team-mates and they see me every day. Together, we share the good and bad moments, so that makes it a big honour to be voted by them.

"The supporters' one, meanwhile, is from everybody who watches Chelsea from every part of the world. They are the heart of the club. To win both of them is perfect."

The Spaniard wasn't the only one picking up some silverware from hosts Vicky Gomersall and Ed Chamberlin, though. Ramires had won Goal of the

Season in the two previous campaigns and, while he couldn't make it a hat-trick, the trophy did stay with Chelsea's Brazilian contingent.

Oscar's strike against Juventus in the Champions League group stage came on his full debut for the Blues and just two minutes after he had scored his first goal for the club, making his exquisite touch past two defenders and pinpoint finish even more impressive.

"It was the best goal of my career so far. I was still surprised to win, but really happy for the award," explained the midfielder. "The other goals, they were amazing, and they chose one of mine as the best, so I am really happy.

"I was very pleased to score that goal and see a lot of good goals this season. I hope the next one is the same or even better."

Oscar marked his first term at the Bridge by picking up Goal of the Season

There was also a look to the future with the Young Player of the Year award, this time won by Dutchman Nathan Ake. The versatile defender and midfielder enjoyed a breakthrough campaign and was honoured for his progress in 2012/13.

Starting the season with the Under-18s, Ake was soon starring for the Under-21s before being called into the first-team squad on a regular basis. He went on to make his first six appearances at senior level and was named among the substitutes for the Europa League final in his native Holland.

The trophy was handed to the teenager by Lampard, who had earlier received his own gong on the stage. In a touching moment, he was given a Special Recognition Award by Bobby Tambling, whose all-time club scoring record he had overtaken six days earlier.

"It's been a good week," said the No8, who had also captained the Blues in the Europa League final victory the night before the awards ceremony. "Then, for Bobby to give me this award and to speak about me like he did, it made me emotional. I can only say thanks to him for that, it was brilliant."

ALL THE WINNERS

Player of the Year:
Juan Mata
Samsung Players' Player of the Year:
Juan Mata
adidas Young Player of the Year:
Nathan Ake
Chelsea TV Goal of the Season:
Oscar v Juventus (h) 19.09.12
Special Recognition:
Frank Lampard

Main: Juan Mata with his Player of the Year and Players' Player of the Year awards.
Above: Frank Lampard after receiving his Special Recognition award from Bobby Tambling.
Right: Nathan Ake, Young Player of the Year

IT'S BLUE.
WHAT ELSE MATTERS?

Players and fans go "all in" for kit campaign

The 2012/13 season ended with a second-consecutive European triumph for the Blues, thanks to the fantastic win against Benfica in the UEFA Europa League final, while a strong finish in the Premier League ensured third place and automatic qualification for this season's Champions League.

As last term reached a climax, adidas launched the innovative "It's blue. What else matters?" marketing campaign, which gave fans around the globe the chance to go "all in" and buy the 2013/14 home kit before it was revealed.

Soaked in a blue viscous liquid, the players took part and showed their commitment to the colour blue and the lengths they will go to in order to show their passion for the club and our fans.

Shot over two days, adidas created a film which featured some of our biggest stars and iconic imagery based on the belief that Chelsea is not just a football club, not just a team, but something deeper and more emotional.

Among those to take part in the shoot was Gary Cahill, who said: "It was crazy. They really thought outside the box and it was a mad thing we were doing, but the results look fantastic.

"When I came in, I could just see David Luiz sitting in a bath of blue paint – you can imagine what he looked like with his hair. He was covered in this paint. What they were doing with him looked good."

Our Brazilian No4 added: "It was a lot of fun, a great idea and all the world is now speaking about the Chelsea campaign. It was cold, but I do everything for this club."

The response from supporters was staggering, showing the love and commitment they have for the club. We hope the fans enjoyed the campaign as much as the players did being involved in it and we did creating it.

Later on in the summer, we were delighted to announce an extension to the existing contract with Chelsea for a further 10 years. We look forward to another successful decade working with this great football club.

We were also excited to see the return of José Mourinho to Stamford Bridge, which is certainly going to add further excitement to the Barclays Premier League, and we should be in store for a promising season in both domestic and European competitions.

Finally, we would like to extend our congratulations to Frank Lampard for breaking the club's goalscoring record in last season's penultimate league game. Frank has worn adidas boots his entire career and has been an outstanding professional to work with and sponsor.

To score that amount of goals from midfield shows that Frank is world-class and we look forward to seeing him and the rest of the Chelsea team go "all in" this forthcoming season.

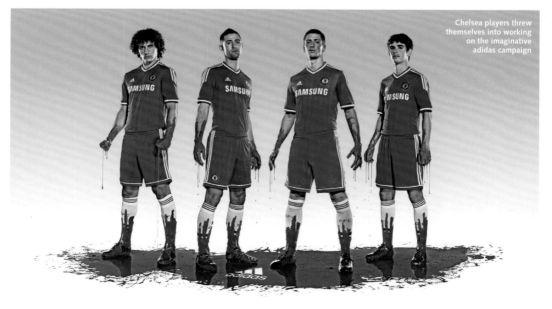

Chelsea players threw themselves into working on the imaginative adidas campaign

Part of the successful partnership between Samsung and Chelsea has been the Dream the Blues campaign

SAMSUNG AND CHELSEA
MAKING DREAMS TOGETHER

Samsung and Chelsea strengthened their partnership and engaged with fans through two youth football campaigns in the 2012/2013 season – the Dream the Blues and Samsung Free Kicks for Kids

The 2012/13 campaign was another unforgettable season for Chelsea, Samsung and Blues fans with the Europa League win writing another page in football history.

As an official sponsor, Samsung is proud to see the club continue to succeed and is happy to contribute to the club's reputation.

While that victory brought excitement, Samsung and Chelsea were working together to touch the hearts and minds of young kids from the UK and throughout the world, as well as their families and friends.

The Dream the Blues campaign, which spanned seven countries across three continents, demonstrated the power of football and sports to shape the stories of these youngsters and to encourage their dreams. Out of some 1,500 participants in the locally-held

Youth Football Camps, 14 lucky kids made it to the campaign's final destination. They got to take part in a clinic with the four Dream the Blues campaign ambassadors – Juan Mata, Victor Moses, Oscar, and Fernando Torres. They also played in a match against a Chelsea Foundation coaching group and watched our final game of 2012/13, which was against Everton at Stamford Bridge.

This campaign was one of the greatest ways to deliver on our commitment to youth and community as well as our brand ideal – to inspire and motivate people to expand their possibilities.

Samsung and Chelsea have teamed up for yet another youth football campaign in the UK – the Samsung Free Kicks for Kids. This is a nationwide campaign which aims to

attract more than 16,000 youngsters in the UK to a 32-week nationwide football coaching programme run by Chelsea Foundation coaches. The campaign has been very well-received and is still ongoing.

Like previous years, we are proud to have such a great partner along the journey, one who shares our vision and passion. We excitedly await our next project together. The ever-changing social and technological environment provides not a challenge, but an opportunity for both Samsung and Chelsea to collaborate on yet more meaningful campaigns.

Finally, we would like to thank everyone who made 2012/13 a successful campaign, and we would like to wish José Mourinho and the team another successful and exciting season for 2013/14.

CELEBRATING A DECADE OF SUCCESS

Roman Abramovich's work to transform Chelsea into one of the world's leading clubs both on and off the pitch has been an amazing achievement in his first 10 years at the helm

On 1 July 2003, Roman Abramovich became the owner of Chelsea Football Club, bringing an unprecedented level of achievement to Stamford Bridge.

When he bought the club 10 years ago, the Blues had not won the top-flight league title for almost 50 years, but that was put right as soon as his second season, when we lifted the Premier League trophy.

That was the first of 11 top-notch pieces of silverware that have arrived at Chelsea in the opening 10 years of Mr Abramovich's leadership, including our first back-to-back league titles, first domestic Double and first Champions League triumph.

Chelsea Chairman Bruce Buck said: "If it wasn't for all the help that Mr Abramovich has given us, then surely we wouldn't be here now celebrating such a wonderful 10 years.

"In 2003, he was a football fan who had seen some football and got enamoured with the game. Since then, and very quickly, he has become an honest-to-goodness football expert. He has spent a lot of time watching players, watching games and talking to experts – he really does know a lot."

Chief Executive Ron Gourlay added: "I think he just wants his football club to be successful. He wants it to be successful for the club, for the players and, importantly, for the fans. That's been his plan since day one.

"The success started, really, in the first season and we've continued that on in the last 10 years."

Of course, there has been far more to Mr Abramovich's tenure to date than just on-pitch success. Right from the start, there was a long-term vision to build strong foundations which have enabled us to remain a force, not only in English football, but on the continent as well.

An integral part of this plan was completed in 2007, when Chelsea opened a new training complex in Cobham, providing the team with the very best conditions in which to prepare for matches.

A year later, a state-of-the-art youth Academy was opened on the same site, bringing both the present and future of the Blues' on-pitch performance together at one world-class facility.

"There were two real key injections when Mr Abramovich took over the club," explained Gourlay. "One was into the playing side, to transform the team into one of the top clubs in Europe, almost overnight and certainly within one season. The plan was then set for the Academy, so it was always a long-term objective, it started at the same time as Mr Abramovich took over the club.

"These things are never quick fixes; it takes time and, I think, in the last three or four years we have started to see how successful our youth team has been and that is

We were crowned Premier League champions at the end of Mr Abramovich's second season

Building one of the most innovative training grounds in sport at Cobham has been key to our long-term development

Roman Abramovich has helped the club become one of the best in the world

the benefit of the Academy. With the challenges we have around Financial Fair Play, the key is to develop as many young players through the Academy as possible."

There are several other aspects of the club which have transformed beyond all recognition during the last 10 years.

The club's charity and community projects have increased dramatically, with our work at home in the UK now also replicated and expanded on, with programmes all around the world. All of this has been unified under one banner with the creation of our own charity, the Chelsea Foundation.

The Chelsea Ladies team has benefited in the last decade, becoming fully integrated into the club. As a result, they are now among

Mr Abramovich holds the Champions League trophy after our victory in 2012

the country's eight elite sides competing in the FA Women's Super League.

The players of the past have also been brought back into the fold, with the club reconnecting with our heritage. This was shown when the badge was altered in 2005 to be closer to the original crest, as well as the creation of the Past Players' Trust to offer support to those who have pulled on the Blue jersey in years gone by.

MAJOR TROPHIES WON IN 10 YEARS UNDER ROMAN ABRAMOVICH

Premier League (3): 2004/05, 2005/06, 2009/10
FA Cup (4): 2006/07, 2008/09, 2009/10, 2011/12
League Cup (2): 2004/05, 2006/07
UEFA Champions League: 2011/12
UEFA Europa League: 2012/13

CHELSEA FOOTBALL CLUB 2013/14

Back row, left to right: Silvino Louro (assistant first-team coach), Kevin De Bruyne, Tomas Kalas, Andre Schürrle, Demba Ba, Gary Cahill, Samuel Eto'o, John Mikel Obi, Ryan Bertrand, Christophe Lollichon (goalkeeper coach)

Middle row, left to right: José Morais (assistant first-team coach), Steve Holland (assistant first-team coach), Ramires, Marco van Ginkel, Henrique Hilario, Petr Cech, Mark Schwarzer, Jamal Blackman, Cesar Azpilicueta, Willian, Rui Faria (assistant first-team coach), Chris Jones (first-team fitness coach)

Front row, left to right: Juan Mata, Ashley Cole, Oscar, Fernando Torres, Frank Lampard, José Mourinho (first-team manager), John Terry, David Luiz, Branislav Ivanovic, Michael Essien, Eden Hazard

1.	PETR CECH	22.	WILLIAN
2.	BRANISLAV IVANOVIC	23.	MARK SCHWARZER
3.	ASHLEY COLE	24.	GARY CAHILL
4.	DAVID LUIZ	26.	JOHN TERRY
5.	MICHAEL ESSIEN	28.	CESAR AZPILICUETA
7.	RAMIRES	29.	SAMUEL ETO'O
8.	FRANK LAMPARD	33.	TOMAS KALAS
9.	FERNANDO TORRES	34.	RYAN BERTRAND
10.	JUAN MATA	46.	JAMAL BLACKMAN
11.	OSCAR		
12.	JOHN MIKEL OBI		
14.	ANDRE SCHÜRRLE		
15.	KEVIN DE BRUYNE		
16.	MARCO VAN GINKEL		
17.	EDEN HAZARD		
19.	DEMBA BA		

THIS IS THE SQUAD LIST SUBMITTED TO THE PREMIER LEAGUE AT THE START OF SEPTEMBER 2013

ALL CHELSEA PLAYER STATISTICS CORRECT TO THE END OF THE 2012/13 SEASON

PROFILES KEY
CAF: CONFEDERATION OF AFRICAN FOOTBALL
PFA: PROFESSIONAL FOOTBALLERS' ASSOCIATION
CWC: FIFA CLUB WORLD CUP
FWA: FOOTBALL WRITERS' ASSOCIATION
FIFPRO: WORLD PLAYERS' UNION

FACTS AND FIGURES

Born: Croydon, 27.10.93

Height: 1.99m (6ft 6in)

Weight: 92.5kgs (14st 8lb)

Source: Chelsea Academy

Chelsea scholarship: July 2010

Turned pro: July 2011

Trophies won with Chelsea: FA Youth Cup 2012

International caps won with Chelsea: England Under-20s, Under-17s, Under-16s

Reserve/U21s appearances: 26+1 games

U19s appearances: 3 games

U18s appearances: 50 games

JAMAL BLACKMAN

Although he is yet to appear in a competitive first-team fixture, Jamal regularly trains and travels with the squad and has seen action in friendly matches during the past two summers. He joined the club as a 13-year-old and has progressed through the ranks, including a starring role in our 2012 FA Youth Cup-winning campaign, while last term was largely spent representing the Under-21s. A sporting all-rounder as a youngster, excelling at rugby, basketball and cricket, even earning a trial with Surrey CCC – but not, as you might expect, as a wicketkeeper.

FACTS AND FIGURES

Born: Plzen, Czech Republic, 20.05.82

Height: 1.96m (6ft 5in)

Weight: 90kgs (14st 2lb)

Previous clubs: Viktoria Plzen, Chmel Blsany, Sparta Prague, Rennes

Signed: July 2004

Chelsea debut: Man Utd (h) 15.08.04. Won 1-0

Trophies won with Chelsea: UEFA Champions League 2012, Premier League 2005, 2006 and 2010, UEFA Europa League 2013, FA Cup 2007, 2009, 2010 and 2012, League Cup 2005 and 2007, FA Community Shield 2005 and 2009

Other Chelsea honours: Chelsea Player of the Year 2011, Chelsea Outstanding Achievement Award 2007, Premier League Golden Gloves award 2005 (21 clean sheets) and 2010 (17 clean sheets), UEFA's most valuable goalkeeper 2005, 2007 and 2008, Golden Ball Trophy for the best Czech Footballer 2005, 2006, 2007, 2008, 2010, 2011, 2012 and 2013, Czech Republic Footballer of the Year 2005, 2008, 2009, 2010, 2011 and 2012, International Sports Press Association Best Goalkeeper of the Year 2007, Chelsea's highest overseas appearance maker. Runners-up medals – UEFA Champions League 2008, FIFA Club World Cup 2012, UEFA Super Cup 2012, League Cup 2008, FA Community Shield 2007 and 2012

International honours: 2002 UEFA Under-21s Championship winner, named in UEFA's Euro 2004 All Star squad

Major international tournaments: Euro 2004 (4 games), 2006 World Cup (3 games), Euro 2008 (3 games), Euro 2012 (4 games)

International recognition: Czech Republic 101 caps, 51 clean sheets, Under-21s 15 caps, Czech Republic Youth

International caps won with Chelsea: Czech Republic 78 caps, 40 clean sheets

Captain: 29 games

Penalties faced: 40 (8 saved, 4 off target, 28 scored)

Penalty shoot-out faced: 27 (6 saved, 21 scored)

PETR CECH

The first overseas player to reach 400 appearances for the Blues, Cech has been a model of consistency during a Chelsea career that is now into its 10th season.

His propensity for pulling off world-class saves is allied to a command of the penalty area which leaves little room for uncertainty and once again helped us to a goals-against record that was among the best in the English top flight last term.

Cech, who won his 100th cap for the Czech Republic earlier this year, is one of only five keepers to be named Chelsea Player of the Year and his penalty-saving heroics in the 2012 Champions League final will live long in the memory.

CHELSEA CAREER

Appearances

Season	LGE	FAC	EUR	LC	CS	CWC	TTL
2004/05	35		11	2			48
2005/06	34		7		1		42
2006/07	20	6	8	2			36
2007/08	26	1	9	3	1		40
2008/09	35	6	12	1			54
2009/10	34	2	6		1		43
2010/11	38	3	9				50
2011/12	34	7	13	1+1			55+1
2012/13	36	5	16	3	1	2	63
TOTAL	**292**	**30**	**91**	**12+1**	**4**	**2**	**431+1**

Clean Sheets

Season	LGE	FAC	EUR	LC	CS	CWC	TTL
2004/05	24		4				28
2005/06	18		4				22
2006/07	13	3	2	1			19
2007/08	15		4	2			21
2008/09	19	1	5	1			26
2009/10	17	2	4				23
2010/11	15	1	4				20
2011/12	10	3	5	1			19
2012/13	14	3	2	1			20
TOTAL	**145**	**13**	**34**	**6**			**198**

FACTS AND FIGURES

Born: Sydney, Australia, 06.10.72

Height: 1.94m (6ft 4in)

Weight: 95kgs (15st)

Previous clubs: Marconi Stallions, Dynamo Dresden, Kaiserslautern, Bradford City, Middlesbrough, Fulham

Signed: July 2013

Honours with other clubs: Australian National League Championship 1993 (Marconi Stallions), German Cup 1996 (Kaiserslautern), League Cup 2004 (Middlesbrough), Fulham Player of the Year 2009, Australia Football Federation Footballer of the Year 2009 and 2010, Australian Football Media International Player of the Year 2009, Australia PFA Player of the Year 2010, Order of Australia Medal 2009 (for services to football) (Fulham)

International honours: 2004 OFC Nations Cup winners, 2011 AFC Asia Cup runners-up

Major international tournaments: 2004 OFC Nations Cup (2 games), 2006 World Cup (3 games), 2007 AFC Asia Cup (4 games), 2010 World Cup (3 games), 2011 AFC Asia Cup (6 games)

International recognition: Australia 108 caps, 44 clean sheets, Australia Youth. Holds the Australian record for caps, clean sheets, oldest player and longest career

MARK SCHWARZER

With the signing of Mark Schwarzer from neighbours Fulham, Chelsea could hardly have acquired a more experienced goalkeeper to provide competition between the sticks.

In the 21-year history of the Premier League, David James is the only shot-stopper to have appeared more times than Schwarzer, who became the first overseas player to play in 500 top-flight games. A goalkeeper similar in both build and style to Cech, Schwarzer is also the only Australian to reach the 100-cap mark for his country.

HENRIQUE HILARIO

The Portuguese shot-stopper put pen to paper on a one-year contract extension during the summer to take his stay at Stamford Bridge into an eighth season. Hilario moved to the club in 2006 as back-up to Petr Cech and Carlo Cudicini, keeping a clean sheet during an impressive debut against Barcelona in the Champions League group stage which immediately endeared him to the fans.

A likeable character with a dry sense of humour, he has found first-team opportunities limited in the past two seasons, although his experience is valuable to the squad.

FACTS AND FIGURES

Born: Sao Pedro da Cova, Portugal, 21.10.75

Height: 1.89m (6ft 2in)

Weight: 90kgs (14st 2lb)

Previous clubs: Porto, Naval (loan), Academica (loan), Estrela Amadora (loan), Varzim (loan), Academica (loan), CD Nacional

Signed: May 2006

Chelsea debut: Barcelona (h) Champions League 18.10.06. Won 1-0

Trophies won with Chelsea: FA Cup 2009 and 2010, League Cup 2007, FA Community Shield 2009

Other Chelsea honours: Runners-up medals – UEFA Champions League 2008, FIFA Club World Cup 2012, FA Community Shield 2006, 2007 and 2010

Honours with other clubs: Portuguese League Championship 1997 and 1998, Portuguese Cup 1998 and 2000, Best Young Talent in Portugal 1997 (Porto)

International recognition: Portugal 1 cap, Portugal B 1 cap, Under-21s 7 caps, Portugal Youth

International caps won with Chelsea: Portugal 1 cap

Penalties faced: 6 (1 saved, 5 scored)

Penalty shoot-out faced: 5 (1 saved, 4 scored)

Reserve appearances: 5 games

CHELSEA CAREER

Appearances

Season	LGE	FAC	EUR	LC	CS	TTL
2006/07	11	1	3	3		18
2007/08	2+1	1	0+1	1		4+2
2008/09	1					1
2009/10	2+1	4	0+1	3		9+2
2010/11					1	1
2011/12	2					2
2012/13						
TOTAL	**18+2**	**6**	**3+2**	**7**	**1**	**35+4**

Clean sheets

Season	LGE	FAC	EUR	LC	CS	TTL
2006/07	4		2	2		8
2007/08	0+1	1	0+1			1+2
2008/09	1					1
2009/10	1	3		2		6
2010/11						
2011/12						
2012/13						
TOTAL	**6+1**	**4**	**2+1**	**4**		**16+2**

FACTS AND FIGURES

Born: Pamplona, Spain, 28.08.89

Height: 1.78m (5ft 10in)

Weight: 75.5kgs (11st 12lb)

Previous clubs: Osasuna, Marseille

Signed: August 2012

Chelsea debut: Wolves (h) League Cup 25.09.12. Won 6-0

Trophies won with Chelsea: UEFA Europa League 2013

Other Chelsea honours: Runners-up medals – FIFA Club World Cup 2012

Honours with other clubs: Champions Trophy 2010 and 2011, French League Cup 2011 and 2012 (Marseille)

International honours: 2011 UEFA Under-21s Championship winner, 2007 UEFA Under-19s Championship winner, 2013 FIFA Confederations Cup runners-up

Major international tournaments: 2012 Olympics (1 game)

International recognition: Spain 4 caps, Under-23s 4 caps, Under-21s 19 caps, 1 goal, Spain Youth

International caps won with Chelsea: Spain 4 caps, 0 goals

CESAR AZPILICUETA

CHELSEA CAREER

Appearances

Season	LGE	FAC	EUR	LC	CS	CWC	TTL
2012/13	24+3	4+1	9	5		1+1	43+5

Goals: None

Affectionately referred to as "Dave" by Chelsea supporters, Azpilicueta highlighted his high level of fitness as one of his biggest attributes upon signing from Marseille in August 2012 and promptly went on to back up this claim by playing just shy of 50 games in his debut campaign. His reliability is up there with the last Spanish incumbent of the right-back role at Chelsea, Albert Ferrer, and earned him an international call-up. He will be looking to impress again in his second season with the Blues, to establish himself in Jose Mourinho's plans and perhaps help Spain retain the World Cup next year.

RYAN
BERTRAND

FACTS AND FIGURES

Born: Southwark, 05.08.89

Height: 1.79m (5ft 10in)

Weight: 75.5kgs (11st 12lb)

Source: Gillingham

Chelsea scholarship: July 2005

Turned pro: August 2006

Loans since signing: Bournemouth (2006/07, 7 games), Oldham (2007/08, 24 games), Norwich (2007/08, 19+1 games, 2008/09, 38+2 games), Reading (2009/10, 51 games, 1 goal), Nottingham Forest (2010/11, 19 games).

Chelsea debut: Birmingham (h) 20.04.11, substitute for Ashley Cole. Won 3-1.

Trophies won with Chelsea: UEFA Champions League 2012, UEFA Europa League 2013, FA Cup 2012, Premier Reserve League South 2011 and National Premier Reserve League 2011

Other Chelsea honours: Runners-up medals – FIFA Club World Cup 2012, UEFA Super Cup 2012, FA Community Shield 2012

Major international tournaments: 2012 Olympics (3 games)

International caps won with Chelsea: England 2 caps, 0 goals, Under-21s 16 caps, 0 goals, Under-20s, Under-19s, Under-18s, Under-17s, Great Britain Under-23s 4 caps, 0 goals

Reserve/U21s appearances: 21+6 games, 1 goal

U18s appearances: 29+4 games, 1 goal

It was always going to be tough for the homegrown left-back to top 2012 – after all, how many players make their European debut in the Champions League final and then follow that up by representing Great Britain at their home Olympic Games? It's testament to Bertrand, then, that he continued to show signs of improvement, with Ashley Cole tipping him to be England's left-back in the future.

His favourite book is Sun Tzu's The Art of War, of which he says: "Know your enemy. If I know everything about my opponent, there's nothing they can do to surprise me."

CHELSEA CAREER

Appearances

Season	LGE	FAC	EUR	LC	CS	TTL
2010/11	0+1					0+1
2011/12	6+1	3+1	1	3		13+2
2012/13	14+5	3+2	6+3	3+1	0+1	26+12
TOTAL	**20+7**	**6+3**	**7+3**	**6+1**	**0+1**	**39+15**

Goals

Season	LGE	FAC	EUR	LC	CS	TTL
2012/13				1	1	2
TOTAL				**1**	**1**	**2**

FACTS AND FIGURES

Born: Sheffield, 19.12.85

Height: 1.93m (6ft 4in)

Weight: 86kgs (13st 8lb)

Previous clubs: Aston Villa, Burnley (loan), Sheffield United (loan), Bolton Wanderers

Signed: January 2012

Chelsea debut: Man Utd (h) 05.02.12. Drew 3-3

Trophies won with Chelsea: UEFA Champions League 2012, UEFA Europa League 2013, FA Cup 2012

Other Chelsea honours: Runners-up medals – FIFA Club World Cup 2012, UEFA Super Cup 2012, FA Community Shield 2012

Honours with other clubs: Player of the Year and Young Player of the Year 2005 (Burnley). Bolton Players' Player of the Year 2009, Bolton Goal of the Season 2009/10

International recognition: England 15 caps, 2 goals, Under-21s 3 caps, England Youth

International caps won with Chelsea: England 8 caps, 1 goal

GARY CAHILL

CHELSEA CAREER

Appearances

Season	LGE	FAC	EUR	LC	CS	CWC	TTL
2011/12	9+1	3+1	4+1				16+3
2012/13	24+2	4	9	4		2	43+2
TOTAL	**33+3**	**7+1**	**13+1**	**4**		**2**	**59+5**

Goals

Season	LGE	FAC	EUR	LC	CS	CWC	TTL
2011/12	1	1					2
2012/13	2		2	2			6
TOTAL	**3**	**1**	**2**	**2**			**8**

Heroic performances in the Champions League against Barcelona and Bayern Munich endeared the wholehearted centre-back to Chelsea fans in his first six months with the Blues, but his calling card was soon to become spectacular strikes – none more so than his breathtaking volley in a memorable win at White Hart Lane, one of six goals to his name in 2012/13. Established at international level, Cahill missed England's European Championship campaign in 2012 through injury, so he will be hoping to ensure a safe passage, and a spot on the plane, to Brazil for next summer's World Cup.

FACTS AND FIGURES

Born: Stepney, 20.12.80

Height: 1.76m (5ft 9in)

Weight: 66.5kgs (10st 7lb)

Previous clubs: Arsenal, Crystal Palace (loan)

Signed: August 2006

Chelsea debut: Charlton (h) 09.09.06, substitute for Wayne Bridge. Won 2-1

Trophies won with Chelsea: UEFA Champions League 2012, Premier League 2010, UEFA Europa League 2013, FA Cup 2007, 2009, 2010 and 2012 (together with 3 won with Arsenal – the most won by any player in FA Cup history), League Cup 2007, FA Community Shield 2009

Other Chelsea honours: Chelsea Players' Player of the Year 2009 and 2011, 2009/10 Goal of the Season v Sunderland (h), best Premier League left back in "20 Year" awards in 2012. Runners-up medals – UEFA Champions League 2008, FIFA Club World Cup 2012, UEFA Super Cup 2012, FA Community Shield 2007, 2010 and 2012

Honours with other clubs: Premier League 2002 and 2004, FA Cup 2002, 2003 and 2005, FA Community Shield 2002 and 2004 (Arsenal)

International honours: England Player of the Year 2010, named in UEFA's Euro 2004 All-Star Squad

Major international tournaments: 2002 World Cup (5 games), Euro 2004 (4 games + 1 shoot-out goal), 2006 World Cup (5 games), 2010 World Cup (4 games), Euro 2012 (4 games). Most capped (22) England player in tournament football

International recognition: England 103 caps, England B 1 cap, Under-21s 4 caps, 1 goal, England Youth

International caps won with Chelsea: England 51 caps, 0 goals

Captain: 3 games

Penalty shoot-out goals: 2 from 3

Reserve/U21s appearances: 1 game

ASHLEY COLE

Another season and another set of milestones for one of the greatest left-backs in the history of the game. Last term, he became just the seventh man to win 100 caps for England and also passed the 300-appearance mark for the Blues.

A superb athlete and as natural a footballer as you are ever likely to find, Cole signed a one-year contract extension in 2013 and has established himself as a favourite with fans and team-mates alike, twice winning Chelsea's Players' Player of the Year award. He was also chosen as the best left-back in the first 20 years of the Premier League.

CHELSEA CAREER

Appearances

Season	LGE	FAC	EUR	LC	CS	CWC	TTL
2006/07	21+2	4+1	9	3			37+3
2007/08	27	1	10	1+1	1		40+1
2008/09	33+1	7	8				48+1
2009/10	25+2	2	4	0+1	1		32+3
2010/11	38	2	7		1		48
2011/12	31+1	4	11+1				46+2
2012/13	31	5	9	2+1	1	2	50+1
TOTAL	**206+6**	**25+1**	**58+1**	**6+3**	**4**	**2**	**301+11**

Goals

Season	LGE	FAC	EUR	LC	CS	CWC	TTL
2006/07							
2007/08	1						1
2008/09	1						1
2009/10	4						4
2010/11							
2011/12							
2012/13	1						1
TOTAL	**7**						**7**

FACTS AND FIGURES

Born: Sremska Mitrovica, Serbia, 22.02.84

Height: 1.85m (6ft 1in)

Weight: 91kgs (14st 5lb)

Previous clubs: SREM Sremska Mitrovica, OFK Beograd, Lokomotiv Moscow

Signed: January 2008

Chelsea debut: Portsmouth (a) League Cup 24.09.08. Won 4-0

Trophies won with Chelsea: UEFA Champions League 2012, Premier League 2010, UEFA Europa League 2013, FA Cup 2009, 2010 and 2012, FA Community Shield 2009

Other Chelsea honours: Serbia Footballer of the Year 2012. Runners-up medals – FIFA Club World Cup 2012, UEFA Super Cup 2012, FA Community Shield 2010 and 2012

Honours with other clubs: Russian Cup 2007 (Lokomotiv Moscow)

International honours: 2007 UEFA Under-21s Championship runners-up as captain and was named in UEFA's team of the tournament

Major international tournaments: 2010 World Cup (3 games)

International recognition: Serbia 61 caps (including 1 for Serbia and Montenegro), 7 goals, Under-23s 1 cap, Serbia and Serbia and Montenegro Under-21s and Serbia and Montenegro Youth

International caps won with Chelsea: Serbia 52 caps, 6 goals, Under-23s 1 cap, 0 goals

Reserve/U21s appearances: 2 games

CHELSEA CAREER

Appearances

Season	LGE	FAC	EUR	LC	CS	CWC	TTL
2008/09	11+5	3+1	4	2			20+6
2009/10	25+3	3	6	3	1		38+3
2010/11	32+2	3	10		1		46+2
2011/12	26+3	5	10	1			42+3
2012/13	33+1	6	12+1	3	1	2	57+2
TOTAL	127+14	20+1	42+1	9	3	2	203+16

Goals

Season	LGE	FAC	EUR	LC	CS	CWC	TTL
2008/09			2				2
2009/10	1						1
2010/11	4		2				6
2011/12	3		2				5
2012/13	5	1	1	1			8
TOTAL	13	1	7	1			22

BRANISLAV IVANOVIC

Ivanovic put the disappointment of missing the 2012 Champions League final behind him by scoring a dramatic late winner to secure our historic Europa League triumph. Like fellow defenders John Terry and Gary Cahill, goals are a big part of his game, and it was in this manner – with a brace against Liverpool in 2009 – that he announced himself to Blues fans. Once described by former team-mate Joe Cole as "the hardest man in football", Ivanovic's off-the-field persona couldn't be much different; a laugh and a joke are usually on the agenda when the Serbia captain is around.

TOMAS KALAS

FACTS AND FIGURES

Born: Olomouc, Czech Republic, 15.05.93

Height: 1.84m (6ft)

Weight: 75.5kgs (11st 12lb)

Previous club: SK Sigma Olomouc

Transfer completed: January 2011

Loans since signing: Vitesse Arnhem (2011/12, 37 games, 1 goal, 2012/13, 39+1 games, 1 goal)

Trophies won with Chelsea: Czech Republic Talent of the Year 2012, Premier Reserve League South 2011, National Premier Reserve League 2011

International caps won with Chelsea: Czech Republic 1 cap, 0 goals, Under-21s 10 caps, 0 goals, Under-19s

Reserve/U21s appearances: 11 games

U18s appearances: 4 games

The 20-year-old plays primarily as a centre-back but is also comfortable on the right side of defence. Athletic and calm on the ball, he has shown plenty of potential and made his senior international debut for the Czech Republic in November 2012. After arriving from Sigma Olomouc in January 2011, he joined up with the Blues reserves and helped them win the national title. He has spent the last two seasons on loan in Holland with Vitesse Arnhem, where he made 67 appearances and scored two goals. Kalas also won the 2012 Czech Talent of the Year award, which is given to the best young player from the country.

FACTS AND FIGURES

Born: Diadema, Brazil, 22.04.87

Height: 1.89m (6ft 2in)

Weight: 84kgs (13st 3lb)

Previous clubs: Esporte Clube Vitoria, Benfica

Signed: January 2011

Chelsea debut: Liverpool (h) 06.02.11, substitute for José Bosingwa. Lost 0-1

Trophies won with Chelsea: UEFA Champions League 2012, UEFA Europa League 2013, FA Cup 2012

Other Chelsea honours: Runners-up medals – FIFA Club World Cup 2012, UEFA Super Cup 2012, FA Community Shield 2012

Honours with other clubs: Bahia State Championship 2005 (Vitoria). Portuguese League Championship 2010, Portuguese League Cup 2009 and 2010, Portuguese League Footballer of the Year 2010, Benfica Breakthough Player of the Year 2007 (Benfica)

International honours: 2013 FIFA Confederations Cup winner

Major international tournaments: 2011 Copa America (0 games)

International recognition: Brazil 27 caps, Brazil Youth

International caps won with Chelsea: Brazil 23 caps, 0 goals

Penalties: 2 from 3

Penalty shoot-out goals: 2 from 2

DAVID LUIZ

CHELSEA CAREER

Appearances

Season	LGE	FAC	EUR	LC	CS	CWC	TTL
2010/11	11+1						11+1
2011/12	18+2	5+1	11	3			37+3
2012/13	29+1	5+1	14	3+1	1	2	54+3
TOTAL	58+4	10+2	25	6+1	1	2	102+7

Goals

Season	LGE	FAC	EUR	LC	CS	CWC	TTL
2010/11	2						2
2011/12	2		1				3
2012/13	2		4	1			7
TOTAL	6		5	1			12

As good a ball-playing centre-back as you'll find in the Premier League – not to mention brilliant from a set-piece – David Luiz is Chelsea's first No4 since Claude Makelele.

Last season, he was given the chance to replicate the Frenchman as a defensive-midfielder, which, in turn, had a positive effect on his regular role at the back. His leadership qualities came to the fore, too, for the second straight season in a European final and he took that form into the Confederations Cup as he led Brazil to a memorable triumph in front of their own supporters.

FACTS AND FIGURES

Born: Barking, 07.12.80

Height: 1.87m (6ft 2in)

Weight: 89.5kgs (14st 1lb)

Source: Chelsea Academy

Chelsea scholarship: July 1997

Turned pro: March 1998

Loan since signing: Nottingham Forest (1999/00, 5+1 games)

Chelsea debut: Aston Villa (h) League Cup 28.10.98, substitute for Dan Petrescu. Won 4-1

Trophies won with Chelsea: UEFA Champions League 2012, Premier League 2005, 2006 and 2010, UEFA Europa League 2013, FA Cup 2000, 2007, 2009, 2010 and 2012, League Cup 2005 and 2007, FA Community Shield 2005 and 2009

Other Chelsea honours: Chelsea Special Commitment Award 2009, Chelsea Player of the Year 2001 and 2006, PFA Player of the Year 2005, UEFA's most valuable defender 2005, 2008 and 2009, named in FIFA/FIFPro World Team of the Year 2005, 2006, 2007, 2008 and 2009, FWA Footballer of the Year runner-up 2005 and 2006, Chairman's Award 2002, Chelsea Young Player of the Year 1998, Chelsea's all-time top scoring defender, most appearances and most trophies as captain. Runners-up medals – UEFA Champions League 2008, FA Cup 2002, League Cup 2008, FA Community Shield 2006, 2010 and 2012

International honours: Named in FIFA's 2006 World Cup All-Star Squad

Major international tournaments: Euro 2004 (3 games + 1 shoot-out goal), 2006 World Cup (5 games), 2010 World Cup (4 games), Euro 2012 (4 games)

International caps won with Chelsea: England 78 caps, 6 goals, Under-21s 9 caps, 1 goal

Captain: 445 games

Penalty shoot-out goals: 1 from 2

Emergency goalkeeper: 1 game (2 minutes, shared clean sheet)

Reserve/U21s appearances: 35+11 games, 5 goals

U18s appearances: 36+5 games, 4 goals

JOHN TERRY

Although 2012/13 was an injury-interrupted campaign for Chelsea's "Captain, Leader, Legend", there was yet more silverware for our most successful skipper of all time as well as his 50th goal as a Blue, making him the first defender to reach that tally for the club.

Having risen through our ranks, JT's never-say-die attitude has been accompanied by an innate ability to read the play and excellent technical qualities, marking him out as one of England's finest centre-backs of the modern era.

CHELSEA CAREER

Appearances

Season	LGE	FAC	EUR	LC	CS	TTL
1998/99	0+2	2+1	1	0+1		3+4
1999/00	2+2	2+2		1		5+4
2000/01	19+3	3		1		23+3
2001/02	32+1	3+2	4	5		44+3
2002/03	16+4	5	1	3		25+4
2003/04	33	3	13	2		51
2004/05	36	1	11	5		53
2005/06	36	4	8	1	1	50
2006/07	27+1	4	10	2	1	44+1
2007/08	23	2	10	2		37
2008/09	35	4	11	1		51
2009/10	37	5	8	0+1	1	51+1
2010/11	33	3	8	1	1	46
2011/12	31	4	8	0+1		43+1
2012/13	11+3	3	8	1	1	24+3
TOTAL	**371+16**	**48+5**	**101**	**25+3**	**5**	**550+24**

Goals

Season	LGE	FAC	EUR	LC	CS	TTL
1998/99						
1999/00		1				1
2000/01	1					1
2001/02	1	2	1			4
2002/03	3	2	1			6
2003/04	2	1				3
2004/05	3	1	4			8
2005/06	4	2		1		7
2006/07	1					1
2007/08	1					1
2008/09	1		2			3
2009/10	2	1				3
2010/11	3		1			4
2011/12	6		1			7
2012/13	4	1	1			6
TOTAL	**32**	**11**	**11**	**1**		**55**

FACTS AND FIGURES

Born: Ghent, Belgium, 28.06.91

Height: 1.80m (5ft 11in)

Weight: 78.5kgs (12st 5lb)

Previous club: KRC Genk

Signed: January 2012

Loans since signing: KRC Genk (2011/12, 13 games, 2 goals), Werder Bremen (2012/13, 34 games, 10 goals)

Honours with other clubs: Belgian League Championship 2011, Belgian Cup 2009, Belgian Super Cup 2011 (KRC Genk). German League Young Player of the Year 2013 (Werder Bremen while on loan from Chelsea)

International recognition: Belgium 13 caps, 3 goals, Under-21s 2 caps, Belgium Youth

International caps won with Chelsea: Belgium 11 caps, 3 goals

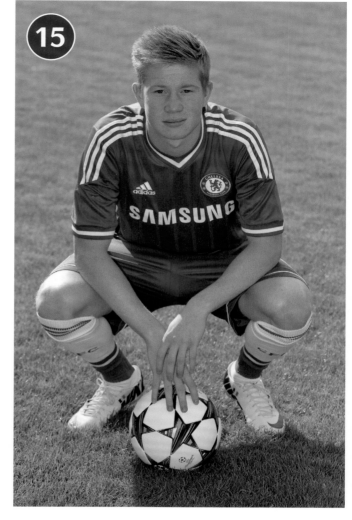

KEVIN DE BRUYNE

After signing for the club in January 2012, De Bruyne had two successful loan spells in Belgium and Germany respectively before joining up with Chelsea for this campaign. Last season, he was in eye-catching form for Bundesliga side Werder Bremen, scoring 10 goals in 33 league appearances and backing that up with nine assists – figures that ensure he returns to Stamford Bridge with great self-confidence.

Capable of playing wide on the left and in the hole behind the centre-forward, the Belgian international has bags of potential and joins an impressive collection of creative midfielders in the Blues ranks.

FACTS AND FIGURES

Born: Accra, Ghana, 03.12.82

Height: 1.77m (5ft 10in)

Weight: 87kgs (13st 10lb)

Previous clubs: Liberty Professionals (Ghana), Bastia, Lyon

Signed: August 2005

Chelsea debut: Arsenal (h) 21.08.05, substitute for Eidur Gudjohnsen. Won 1-0

Loan since signing: Real Madrid (2012/13, 31+4 games, 2 goals)

Trophies won with Chelsea: UEFA Champions League 2012, Premier League 2006 and 2010, FA Cup 2007, 2009 and 2012, League Cup 2007, FA Community Shield 2009

Other Chelsea honours: Named in CAF's Team of the Year 2005, 2006, 2008 and 2009, Chelsea Player of the Year 2007, 2006/07 Goal of the Season v Arsenal (h) and 2008/09 Goal of the Season v Barcelona (h). Runners-up medals – UEFA Champions League 2008, League Cup 2008, FA Community Shield 2006, 2007, 2010 and 2012

Honours with other clubs: French League Championship 2004 and 2005, French Champions Trophy 2003 and 2004, Lyon Player of the Year 2005, French League Player of the Year 2005, French League Team of the Year 2005 (Lyon)

International honours: Ghana Player of the Year 2008, 2010 Africa Cup of Nations runners-up, third in 2008 Africa Cup of Nations and named in the Best XI of the Tournament, 2001 FIFA Under-20s World Cup runners-up and Africa Under-20s Championship runners-up, 1999 Africa Under-17s Championship winner and third in 1999 FIFA Under-17s World Cup

Major international tournaments: 2002 Africa Cup of Nations (2 games), 2006 World Cup (3 games), 2008 Africa Cup of Nations (6 games, 2 goals), 2010 Africa Cup of Nations (0+1 game)

International recognition: Ghana 52 caps, 9 goals, Ghana Youth

International caps won with Chelsea: Ghana 41 caps, 7 goals

Penalty shoot-out goals: 1 from 1

Reserve appearances: 2 games, 1 goal

MICHAEL ESSIEN

Returning to the Chelsea fold after a loan spell at Real Madrid with José Mourinho last season, Essien remains a firm favourite among Blues supporters. One of the club's most significant signings over the last decade, the Ghanaian midfield dynamo has also shown his versatility, playing in a deep holding position, a marauding box-to-box role and also as a right-back. His solid build makes him a formidable physical force and he backs it up with the experience and tenacity to ensure that he is always at the heart of the action.

CHELSEA CAREER

Appearances

Season	LGE	FAC	EUR	LC	CS	TTL
2005/06	27+4	3+1	6	1		37+5
2006/07	33	4+1	10	6	1	54+1
2007/08	23+4	1+1	11+1	3+1	1	39+7
2008/09	10+1	2+1	5			17+2
2009/10	13+1		5+1	0+1	1	19+3
2010/11	32+1	1+1	7+1		1	41+3
2011/12	10+4	0+3	1+1			11+8
TOTAL	148+15	11+8	45+4	10+2	4	218+29

Goals

Season	LGE	FAC	EUR	LC	CS	TTL
2005/06	2					2
2006/07	2	1	2	1		6
2007/08	6					6
2008/09	1		2			3
2009/10	3		1			4
2010/11	3		1			4
2011/12						
TOTAL	17	1	6	1		25

FACTS AND FIGURES

Born: La Louviere, Belgium, 07.01.91

Height: 1.73m (5ft 8in)

Weight: 74.5kgs (11st 10lb)

Previous club: Lille

Signed: June 2012

Chelsea debut: Manchester City (Villa Park) FA Community Shield 12.08.12. Lost 2-3

Trophies won with Chelsea: UEFA Europa League 2013

Other Chelsea honours: Runners-up medals – FIFA Club World Cup 2012, UEFA Super Cup 2012, FA Community Shield 2012

Honours with other clubs: French League Championship 2011, French Cup 2011, French League Player of the Year 2011 and 2012, French League Team of the Year 2010, 2011 and 2012, French League Young Player of the Year 2009 and 2010 (Lille)

International recognition: Belgium 37 caps, 5 goals, Belgium Youth

International caps won with Chelsea: Belgium 9 caps, 3 goals

Penalties: 3 from 4

EDEN HAZARD

CHELSEA CAREER

Appearances

Season	LGE	FAC	EUR	LC	CS	CWC	TTL
2012/13	31+3	3+3	10+4	2+3	1	2	49+13

Goals

Season	LGE	FAC	EUR	LC	CS	CWC	TTL
2012/13	9	1	1	2			13

After a debut season that saw him shortlisted for the PFA Player of the Year and Young Player of the Year awards, Hazard is looking to build on that impact during his second Premier League campaign. Blistering pace and natural balance are backed up with unshakable confidence and a joy of playing that make the Belgian creator a nightmare to defend against. He scored an impressive 13 goals and created 25 more in 2012/13, and the fact that he made 62 appearances in his first year here demonstrated his importance to the team. Perhaps most excitingly of all, at just 22, Hazard looks to have many seasons ahead of him.

FRANK LAMPARD

The club's all-time record goalscorer began his 13th season as a Chelsea player with more than 600 appearances and 203 goals to his name after surpassing Bobby Tambling's long-standing tally last term.

He has reached double figures for goals from midfield in the past 10 campaigns, adding 17 in 50 appearances to his overall tally last term. Once again, he ended the season with silverware in his hands, lifting the Europa League trophy alongside captain John Terry in Amsterdam.

He now sits third in the club's all-time appearances table, behind only Ron Harris and Peter Bonetti.

FACTS AND FIGURES

Born: Romford, 20.06.78

Height: 1.84m (6ft)

Weight: 89kgs (14st 1lb)

Previous clubs: West Ham United, Swansea City (loan)

Signed: June 2001

Chelsea debut: Newcastle United (h) 19.08.01 Drew 1-1

Trophies won with Chelsea: UEFA Champions League 2012, Premier League 2005, 2006 and 2010, UEFA Europa League 2013, FA Cup 2007, 2009, 2010 and 2012, League Cup 2005 and 2007, FA Community Shield 2005 and 2009

Other Chelsea honours: Chelsea's all-time top scorer, FWA Footballer of the Year 2005, Premier League Player of the Year 2005, named in the FIFPro World Team of the Year 2005, UEFA's Most Valuable Midfielder 2008, FIFA World Player of the Year runner-up 2005, Ballon d'Or European Player of the Year runner up 2005, PFA Player of the Year runner-up 2004, 2005 and 2006, Chelsea Golden Boot winner 2005 (19 goals), 2006 (20 goals), 2008 (20 goals) and 2012 (16 goals), Chelsea Player of the Year 2004, 2005 and 2009, FWA Footballer of the Year runner-up 2004, Chelsea Special Achievement Award 2008 for 100 Chelsea goals, Chelsea Special Recognition Award 2013, FWA Tribute Award 2009. Runners-up medals - UEFA Champions League 2008, FIFA Club World Cup 2012, UEFA Super Cup 2012, FA Cup 2002, League Cup 2008, FA Community Shield 2006, 2007, 2010 and 2012

Honours with other clubs: Intertoto Cup winner 1999 (West Ham United)

International honours: England Player of the Year 2004 and 2005, named in UEFA's Euro 2004 All-Star Squad

Major international tournaments: Euro 2004 (4 games, 3 goals + plus 1 shoot-out goal), World Cup 2006 (5 games), World Cup 2010 (4 games)

International recognition: England 97 caps, 29 goals, England B 1 cap, Under-21s 19 caps, 9 goals, England Youth

International caps won with Chelsea: England 95 caps, 29 goals

Captain: 77 games

Hat-tricks: 5

Penalties: 48 from 55

Penalty shoot-out goals: 7 from 9

CHELSEA CAREER

Appearances

Season	LGE	FAC	EUR	LC	CS	CWC	TTL
2001/02	34+3	7+1	4	4			49+4
2002/03	37+1	5	1+1	3			46+2
2003/04	38	4	13+1	1+1			56+2
2004/05	38	0+2	12	3+3			53+5
2005/06	35	4+1	8	0+1	1		48+2
2006/07	36+1	7	11	3+3	1		58+4
2007/08	23+1	1	10+1	3	1		38+2
2008/09	37	7	11	1+1			56+1
2009/10	36	6	6+1	0+1	1		49+2
2010/11	23+1	3	4		1		31+1
2011/12	26+4	3+2	8+4	1+1			38+11
2012/13	21+8	3+1	11	2+1	1	1+1	39+11
TOTAL	**384+19**	**50+7**	**99+8**	**21+12**	**6**	**1+1**	**561+47**

Goals

Season	LGE	FAC	EUR	LC	CS	CWC	TTL
2001/02	5	1	1				7
2002/03	6	1	1				8
2003/04	10	1	4				15
2004/05	13		4	2			19
2005/06	16	2	2				20
2006/07	11	6	1	3			21
2007/08	10	2	4	4			20
2008/09	12	3	3	2			20
2009/10	22	3	1			1	27
2010/11	10	3					13
2011/12	11	2	3				16
2012/13	15	2					17
TOTAL	**141**	**26**	**24**	**11**	**1**		**203**

FACTS AND FIGURES

Born: Burgos, Spain, 28.04.88

Height: 1.72m (5ft 8in)

Weight: 66kgs (10st 5lb)

Previous clubs: Real Oviedo, Real Madrid, Valencia

Signed: August 2011

Chelsea debut: Norwich (h) 27.08.11. Won 3-1, substitute for Florent Malouda, scored the final goal

Trophies won with Chelsea: UEFA Champions League 2012, UEFA Europa League 2013, FA Cup 2012

Other Chelsea honours: Chelsea Player of the Year 2012 and 2013, Chelsea Players' Player of the Year 2013. Runners-up medals – FIFA Club World Cup 2012, UEFA Super Cup 2012, FA Community Shield 2012

Honours with other clubs: Spanish Cup 2008, Young Player of the Year 2008 (Valencia)

International honours: Euro 2012 winner, 2010 World Cup winner, 2011 UEFA Under-21s Championship winner and was named Golden Player and in Team of the Tournament, 2006 UEFA Under-19s Championship winner and was named Player of the Tournament, 2013 FIFA Confederations Cup runners-up.

Major international tournaments: 2010 World Cup (0+1 game), Euro 2012 (0+1 game, 1 goal), 2012 Olympics (3 games)

International recognition: Spain 29 caps, 8 goals, Under-23s 4 caps, Under-21s 19 caps, 5 goals, Spain Youth

International caps won with Chelsea: Spain 17 caps, 4 goals, Under-23s 4 caps, 0 goals

Penalties: 1 from 3

Penalty shoot-out goals: 0 from 1

JUAN MATA

CHELSEA CAREER

Appearances

Season	LGE	FAC	EUR	LC	CS	CWC	TTL
2011/12	29+5	7	11+1	0+1			47+7
2012/13	31+4	5+1	11+4	5	1	2	55+9
TOTAL	60+9	12+1	22+5	5+1	1	2	102+16

Goals

Season	LGE	FAC	EUR	LC	CS	CWC	TTL
2011/12	6	4	2				12
2012/13	12	1	4	2		1	20
TOTAL	18	5	6	2		1	32

In both of his first two seasons with the club, Mata has won the Chelsea Player of the Year award, such is his popularity with the Stamford Bridge faithful. His vision, technique and composure saw him score 20 goals and notch 37 assists from his position between the lines of midfield and attack last season and he also played in 64 games during 2012/13, making him joint top for appearances that term. His form in those games was enough to earn him a place alongside Eden Hazard in the PFA Premier League Team of the Year, as well as on the shortlist for the PFA Player of the Year award.

FACTS AND FIGURES

Born: Jos, Nigeria, 22.04.87

Height: 1.88m (6ft 2in)

Weight: 83kgs (13st 1lb)

Previous clubs: Plateau United, Ajax Cape Town, Lyn Oslo

Signed: June 2006

Chelsea debut: Liverpool (Millennium Stadium) FA Community Shield 13.08.06, substitute for Paulo Ferreira. Lost 1-2

Trophies won with Chelsea: UEFA Champions League 2012, UEFA Europa League 2013, Premier League 2010, FA Cup 2007, 2009, 2010 and 2012, League Cup 2007, FA Community Shield 2009

Other Chelsea honours: Chelsea Young Player of the Year 2007. Runners-up medals – UEFA Champions League 2008, FIFA Club World Cup 2012, UEFA Super Cup 2012, FA Community Shield 2006, 2007, 2010 and 2012

Honours with other clubs: CAF Young African Player of the Year and named in CAF's Team of the Year 2005 (Lyn Oslo)

International honours: 2013 Africa Cup of Nations winner, 2005 FIFA Under-20s World Cup runners-up and Silver Ball winner, third in the 2006 and 2010 Africa Cup of Nations and named Best Youth Player of the Tournament in 2006

Major international tournaments: 2006 Africa Cup of Nations (3+1 games + 1 shoot-out goal), 2008 Africa Cup of Nations (4 games, 1 goal), 2010 Africa Cup of Nations (5+1 games), 2013 Africa Cup of Nations (6 games)

International recognition: Nigeria 52 caps, 4 goals, Nigeria Youth

International caps won with Chelsea: Nigeria 47 caps, 3 goals

Penalty shoot-out goals: 0 from 1

Reserve appearances: 1 game

JOHN MIKEL OBI

Having finished the 2012/13 campaign as a Europa League champion and an Africa Cup of Nations winner, Mikel will once again be looking to recreate that winning feeling this season. Since joining Chelsea, the Nigerian midfielder has built up an enviable medal collection and established himself as a consistent and calming influence in the deep midfield position he regularly takes up. With an eye for a pass and a sensible head in possession, Mikel's positioning is one of his key attributes, with or without the ball. He will be delighted to work under José Mourinho again, after originally making his way into the first team under the Portuguese manager in 2006.

CHELSEA CAREER

Appearances

Season	LGE	FAC	EUR	LC	CS	CWC	TTL
2006/07	10+12	5+1	6+3	3+1	0+1		24+18
2007/08	21+8	2	1+3	3	1		28+11
2008/09	33+1	5	9	0+1			47+2
2009/10	21+4	3	4	2	1		31+4
2010/11	28	1+1	5+1		1		35+2
2011/12	15+7	5	7+2	0+1			27+10
2012/13	19+3	2+1	8+2	1	1	1	32+6
TOTAL	**147+35**	**23+3**	**40+11**	**9+3**	**4+1**	**1**	**224+53**

Goals

Season	LGE	FAC	EUR	LC	CS	CWC	TTL
2006/07		2					2
2007/08							
2008/09							
2009/10							
2010/11							
2011/12							
2012/13							
TOTAL		**2**					**2**

FACTS AND FIGURES

Born: Americana, Brazil, 09.09.91

Height: 1.79m (5ft 10in)

Weight: 67.5kgs (10st 9lb)

Previous clubs: Sao Paulo, Internacional

Signed: July 2012

Chelsea debut: Wigan (a) 19.08.12, substitute for Eden Hazard. Won 2-0.

Trophies won with Chelsea: UEFA Europa League 2013

Other Chelsea honours: 2012/13 Goal of the Season v Juventus (h). Runners-up medals – FIFA Club World Cup 2012, UEFA Super Cup 2012

Honours with other clubs: Brazil Serie A Championship 2008 (Sao Paulo), Rio Grande do Sul State Championship 2011 and 2012, Recopa Sudamericana winner 2011 (Internacional)

International honours: 2013 FIFA Confederations Cup winner, 2012 Olympic Silver medallist, 2011 FIFA Under-20s World Cup winner (scored a hat-trick in the final), 2011 South American Under-20s Championship winner

Major international tournaments: 2012 Olympics (5+1 games, 1 goal)

International recognition: Brazil 22 caps, 6 goals. Under 23s 7 caps, 1 goal. Brazil Youth

International caps won with Chelsea: Brazil 16 caps, 5 goals, Under-23s 6 caps, 1 goal

Penalties: 1 from 1

OSCAR

After an impressive debut season for the Blues and a starring role in Brazil's Confederations Cup triumph, Oscar's star is steadily rising. His 12 goals last term, including a spectacular Goal of the Season winner against Juventus in the Champions League, showed Chelsea supporters what the midfielder is capable of, but his excellent work rate would have been noted as well.

At the age of just 21, he finished the 2012/13 campaign with 64 appearances to his name in his first season in European club football, making him joint top in games for the Blues last term. In the build-up to Brazil's World Cup in 2014, this is an exciting time for the young Brazilian.

CHELSEA CAREER

Appearances

Season	LGE	FAC	EUR	LC	CS	CWC	TTL
2012/13	24+10	6+1	9+7	3+2		1+1	43+21

Goals

Season	LGE	FAC	EUR	LC	CS	CWC	TTL
2012/13	4	2	6				12

FACTS AND FIGURES

Born: Barra do Pirai, Brazil, 24.03.87

Height: 1.80m (5ft 11in)

Weight: 70kgs (11st)

Previous clubs: Joinville, Cruzeiro (loan), Cruzeiro, Benfica

Signed: August 2010

Chelsea debut: Stoke City (h) 28.08.10, substitute for Michael Essien. Won 2-0

Trophies won with Chelsea: UEFA Champions League 2012, UEFA Europa League 2013, FA Cup 2012

Other Chelsea honours: Chelsea Players' Player of the Year 2012, 2010/11 Goal of the Season v Man City (h) and 2011/12 Goal of the Season v Barcelona (a). Runners-up medals – FIFA Club World Cup 2012, UEFA Super Cup 2012, FA Community Shield 2012

Honours with other clubs: Santa Catarina State Championship 2005 and 2006 (both second level, Joinville). Minas Gerais State Championship 2008 and 2009, selected in the Brazil Football Federation Team of the Year 2008, Brazil league midfielder of the Year 2007 (Cruzeiro). Portuguese League and League Cup 2010 (Benfica)

International honours: 2009 FIFA Confederations Cup winner, 2008 Olympic Bronze medal winner

Major international tournaments: 2008 Olympics (1+2 games), 2010 World Cup (1+3 games), 2011 Copa America (4 games)

International recognition: Brazil 34 caps, 3 goals, Under 23s

International caps won with Chelsea: Brazil 17 caps, 1 goal

RAMIRES

Blessed with acceleration and a sense of anticipation, Ramires regularly turns 50-50 situations in his favour with a combination of sheer enthusiasm and raw athleticism.

The Brazilian, who reached 150 Chelsea appearances last season, also has an eye for the audacious, as he has proved with some spectacular and varied goals since arriving at the club in 2010.

Capable of playing in a compact midfield or in a wide-right position, his pace and awareness mean he is at his most dangerous on the counter-attack, where he can expose gaps in unprepared opposition defences.

CHELSEA CAREER

Appearances

Season	LGE	FAC	EUR	LC	CS	CWC	TTL
2010/11	22+7	3	7+1	1			33+8
2011/12	28+2	6	10	0+1			44+3
2012/13	28+7	6	15	3+1	1	1	54+8
TOTAL	78+16	15	32+1	4+2	1	1	131+19

Goals

Season	LGE	FAC	EUR	LC	CS	CWC	TTL
2010/11	2						2
2011/12	5	4	3				12
2012/13	5	2	1	1			9
TOTAL	12	6	4	1			23

FACTS AND FIGURES

Born: Amersfoort, Holland, 01.12.92

Height: 1.86m (6ft 1in)

Weight: 82kgs (12st 13lb)

Previous club: Vitesse Arnhem

Signed: July 2013

Honours with other clubs: Dutch Football Talent of the Year 2013 (Vitesse)

International recognition: Holland 1 cap, Under-21s 17 caps, 3 goals, Holland Youth

MARCO VAN GINKEL

A new signing who demonstrated his versatility during pre-season by operating in both a deep central midfield role and in the creative line between midfield and attack, Van Ginkel impressed in the Vitesse Arnhem side that finished fourth in Holland's Eredivisie last season. The 20-year-old has already represented Holland at senior level and, with his technical and physical strengths, he has all the attributes to fit right into the English game. With 12 goals to his name from 41 appearances last season, he certainly showed himself to be an attacking threat.

WILLIAN

FACTS AND FIGURES

Born: Ribeirao Pires, Brazil, 09.08.88

Height: 1.75m (5ft 9in)

Weight: 75kgs (11st 11lb)

Previous clubs: Corinthians, Shakhtar Donetsk, Anzhi Makhachkala

Signed: August 2013

Honours with other clubs: Sao Paulo Youth Cup 2005 (Corinthians), Ukrainian League Championship 2008, 2010, 2011, 2012, Ukrainian Cup 2008, 2011, 2012, Ukrainian Super Cup 2008, 2010, UEFA Cup 2009 (Shakhtar Donetsk)

International honours: 2007 South American Under-20s Championship winner

International recognition: Brazil 2 caps, Brazil Youth

Chelsea fans knew what they were getting when the Blues brought our sixth Brazilian to the club at the end of August, having seen Willian net twice in a virtuoso display for Shakhtar Donetsk at the Bridge in a Champions League game last term. Comfortable operating in any of the three attacking-midfield positions behind the main striker, he is quick, robust and perhaps at his best when cutting in from the left onto his stronger right foot, allowing his creativity to come to the fore. With a World Cup in his homeland also on the horizon, Willian will be hoping to catch the eye of Brazil's manager, former Blues boss Luiz Felipe Scolari.

FACTS AND FIGURES

Born: Sevres, France, 25.05.85

Height: 1.89m (6ft 2in)

Weight: 86kgs (13st 8lb)

Previous clubs: Rouen, Mouscron, Hoffenheim, West Ham, Newcastle

Signed: January 2013

Chelsea debut: Southampton (a) FA Cup 05.01.13. Won 5-1 and scored two goals

Honours with other clubs: Promotion to Bundesliga 2008 (Hoffenheim). Senegal Player of the Year 2012 (Newcastle)

Major international tournaments: 2012 Africa Cup of Nations (3 games)

International recognition: Senegal 17 caps, 4 goals

International caps won with Chelsea: Senegal 1 cap, 0 goals

DEMBA BA

Having scored 29 Premier League goals in one-and-a-half seasons for Newcastle United, Ba arrived to increase our attacking options in January 2013. He wasted no time in opening his account with the Blues, scoring twice on his debut at Southampton in the third round of the FA Cup – a competition he seemed to enjoy, as he also scored the quarter-final winner against Manchester United and in the semi-final versus Manchester City.

The French-born Senegal international also had previous spells in England with West Ham and, briefly, Watford. However, he made his name primarily with his goals in Germany for Hoffenheim, helping them earn promotion to the top flight and a seventh-place finish in their first Bundesliga campaign.

CHELSEA CAREER

Appearances

Season	LGE	FAC	EUR	LC	CS	CWC	TTL
2012/13	11+3	5+1		1+1			17+5

Goals

Season	LGE	FAC	EUR	LC	CS	CWC	TTL
2012/13	2	4					6

FACTS AND FIGURES

Born: Nkom, Cameroon, 10.03.81

Height: 1.80m (5ft 11in)

Weight: 75kgs (11st 11lb)

Previous clubs: Real Madrid, Leganes (loan), Espanyol (loan), Real Mallorca (loan), Real Mallorca, Barcelona, Inter Milan, Anzhi Makhachkala

Signed: August 2013

Honours with other clubs: Spanish Cup 2003, CAF African Player of the Year 2003, CAF Young African Player of the Year 2000 (Mallorca). Spanish League Championship 2005, 2006, 2009, Spanish Cup 2009, Spanish Super Cup 2005, 2006, Champions League 2006, 2009, CAF African Player of the Year 2004 and 2005, UEFA's most valuable forward 2006, FIFA World Player of the Year third 2005, named in the FIFPro World Team of the Year 2005 and 2006 (Barcelona). Italian League Championship 2010, Italian Cup 2010, 2011, Italian Super Cup 2010, Champions League 2010, FIFA Club World Cup 2010, FIFA Club World Cup Golden Ball winner 2010, CAF African Player of the Year 2010 (Inter Milan)

International honours: 2002 Africa Cup of Nations winner, 2000 Africa Cup of Nations winner, 2000 Olympic gold medallist, 2008 Africa Cup of Nations runners-up, named in the Best X1 of the 2006 Africa Cup of Nations, 2003 Confederations Cup runners-up

Major international tournaments: 1998 World Cup (0+1 game), 2000 Africa Cup of Nations (4+1 games, 4 goals), 2000 Olympics (6 games, 1 goal + 1 shoot-out goal), 2002 Africa Cup of Nations (6 games, 1 goal), 2002 World Cup (3 games, 1 goal), 2004 Africa Cup of Nations (4 games, 1 goal), 2006 Africa Cup of Nations (4 games, 5 goals, top scorer), 2008 Africa Cup of Nations (6 games, 5 goals, including 3 pens, top scorer), 2010 Africa Cup of Nations (4 games, 2 goals), 2010 World Cup (3 games, 2 goals)

International recognition: Cameroon 112 caps, 55 goals, Under-23s, Under-21s. Third most capped player and all-time top scorer for Cameroon.

SAMUEL
ETO'O

A record four-time African Player of the Year, Eto'o joined Chelsea from Russian side Anzhi Makhachkala this summer. That saw the striker reunited with manager José Mourinho, who signed him for Inter Milan in 2009, leading to the pair winning the Serie A title, Coppa Italia and Champions League in their first season together. That also gave Eto'o the rare distinction of winning a Treble in consecutive years in different countries, having previously won Europe's top trophy alongside Spain's domestic Double with Barcelona. The Champions League has proven to be a highly successful competition for Cameroon's all-time top goalscorer, as he has three winner's medals to his name and has found the net in two finals, as well as being named man of the match when Barcelona beat Arsenal in Paris in 2006.

FACTS AND FIGURES

Born: Ludwigshafen, Germany, 06.11.90

Height: 1.83m (6ft)

Weight: 72.5kgs (11st 6lb)

Previous clubs: Mainz, Bayer Leverkusen

Signed: June 2013

Honours with other clubs:
German Under-19s Championship 2009 (Mainz)

Major international tournaments:
Euro 2012 (1+1 games)

International recognition: Germany 24 caps,
7 goals, Under-21s 4 caps, 3 goals, Germany Youth

ANDRE SCHÜRRLE

A versatile forward, Schürrle has shown he poses a threat from either wing, as a centre-forward or playing off another striker. The German international, who jointly holds the honour of being the first player born in reunified Germany to represent the nation, became Chelsea's first summer signing of 2013 when he arrived from Bayer Leverkusen.

He started his career in the youth team of his local side Ludwigshafener before joining Mainz in 2006. He spent three years playing for the club's youth teams, where he won the national Under-19s Bundesliga in 2009. He scored his first two league goals for the team a few days before signing his first professional contract and set a club record of 15 Bundesliga goals in 2010/11 before departing for Bayer.

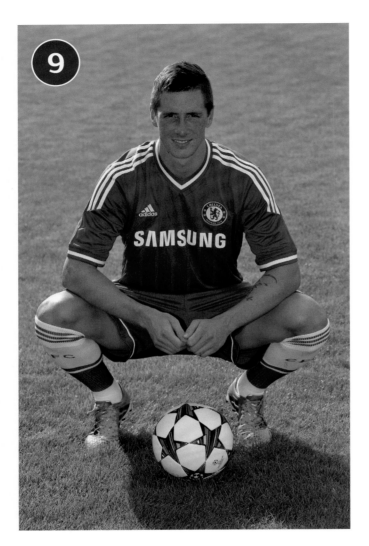

FACTS AND FIGURES

Born: Madrid, Spain, 20.03.84

Height: 1.86m (6ft 1in)

Weight: 81kgs (12st 11lb)

Previous clubs: Atletico Madrid, Liverpool

Signed: January 2011

Chelsea debut: Liverpool (h) 06.02.11. Lost 0-1

Trophies won with Chelsea: UEFA Champions League 2012, UEFA Europa League 2013, FA Cup 2012

Other Chelsea honours: Runners-up medals – FIFA Club World Cup 2012, UEFA Super Cup 2012, FA Community Shield 2012

Honours with other clubs: Spanish Second Division 2002 (Atletico Madrid). Liverpool Player of the Year 2008, named in FIFPro World Team of the Year 2008 and 2009, third in FIFA World Player of the Year 2008 and 3rd in Ballon d'Or European Player of the Year 2008, FWA Footballer of the Year runner-up 2008 (Liverpool)

International honours: Euro 2012 and Golden Boot winner, 2010 World Cup winner, Euro 2008 winner and named in UEFA's Team of the Tournament, 2002 UEFA Under-19s Championship winner, was top scorer and named in Team of the Tournament, 2001 UEFA Under-16s Championship winner, was top scorer and named in Team of the Tournament, 2013 FIFA Confederations Cup runners-up and Golden Boot winner.

Major international tournaments: Euro 2004 (1+2 games), 2006 World Cup (3+1 games, 3 goals (1 pen)), Euro 2008 (5 games, 2 goals), 2010 World Cup (4+3 games), Euro 2012 (2+3 games, 3 goals)

International recognition: Spain 106 caps, 36 goals, Under-21s 10 caps, 3 goals, Spain Youth

International caps won with Chelsea: Spain 24 caps, 10 goals

Penalties: 1 from 2

Hat-tricks: 1

FERNANDO TORRES

With 22 goals to his name, 2012/13 was Torres' most prolific season so far in a Blues shirt. He continued that run of goals at international level while representing Spain at the 2013 FIFA Confederations Cup, finishing as the tournament's top scorer, just as he had at Euro 2012.

With more than 100 international caps, he is also the third-highest scorer of all time for the world champions. He started his career with Atletico Madrid, where he became a club legend at a young age before moving to England with Liverpool. El Nino further established his credentials as one of Europe's top strikers at Anfield and caught Chelsea's eye with seven goals in as many games against the Blues.

CHELSEA CAREER

Appearances

Season	LGE	FAC	EUR	LC	CS	CWC	TTL
2010/11	8+6		3+1				11+7
2011/12	20+12	5+1	6+4	1			32+17
2012/13	28+8	2+3	15+1	3+1	1	2	51+13
TOTAL	**56+26**	**7+4**	**24+6**	**4+1**	**1**	**2**	**94+37**

Goals

Season	LGE	FAC	EUR	LC	CS	CWC	TTL
2010/11	1						1
2011/12	6	2	3				11
2012/13	8	1	9	2	1	1	22
TOTAL	**15**	**3**	**12**	**2**	**1**	**1**	**34**

ROBERTO DI MATTEO

Chelsea parted company with Roberto Di Matteo as first-team manager in November 2012.

The Italian became the first man in the club's history to lead us to Champions League glory. Prior to that, Di Matteo was a much-loved player at Stamford Bridge, scoring in our victorious 1997 and 2000 FA Cup finals as well as the 1998 League Cup triumph at Wembley.

He later embarked on a coaching career that took in spells with MK Dons and West Bromwich Albion before he returned to the Bridge as assistant to Andre Villas-Boas in 2011. When the Portuguese left the club in March 2012, Di Matteo stepped in for an 11-week interim spell which saw him leading the club to our seventh FA Cup success in the competition and that famous night in Munich.

Everyone at the club would like to thank Roberto for all he has done for Chelsea – we will never forget the huge contribution he has made to our history and he will always be welcome at Stamford Bridge.

PAULO FERREIRA

During nine years at the club, Paulo Ferreira became a fans' favourite thanks to his dedicated approach to the game and unswerving loyalty to the Blues.

The Portuguese right-back followed José Mourinho to Stamford Bridge in 2004 after winning the Champions League and played his part in Chelsea's first league title in 50 years, also helping set a Premier League defensive record of just 15 goals conceded.

Aside from the UEFA Super Cup, he added each and every major club-level honour to his collection, while rare goals came in the FA Cup against Colchester United and in the League Cup against Blackburn Rovers.

Ferreira appeared 217 times in our colours, 50 of those as a sub, and will be remembered as a likeable and reliable player who will remain a much-loved member of the Chelsea family.

FLORENT MALOUDA

Few wingers can match Malouda's 45-goal haul for the Blues.

It took the 2006 World Cup finalist time to settle at the Bridge following his move from Lyon in 2007, although he did play in the Champions League final in his first campaign, while assists, positive running and goals began to be regular facets of his game in 2009/10 as he was a key player in our Double triumph.

A year later, he finished as our leading scorer in the league, netting a career best of 13. The 2011/12 season would end in European glory, with Malouda celebrating at the end of the Champions League final this time. It was his 229th and final Chelsea appearance.

Now playing at Trabzonspor.

DANIEL STURRIDGE

Signed from Manchester City in 2009, the nephew of former Derby County striker Dean Sturridge took his time to make his mark at Stamford Bridge. However, while four FA Cup goals were netted in his first season as we won the Double, it wasn't until he returned from a prolific loan spell with Bolton in 2011 that he showed his best form.

Featuring from the right flank, he finished as our joint-leading Premier League scorer and ended the campaign as an unused substitute in the Champions League final. He completed a transfer to Liverpool in January 2013.

RAFAEL BENITEZ

Chelsea released Rafael Benitez in May when his contract with the club came to an end.

The Spaniard was appointed as the club's interim manager in November 2012, steering us to automatic Champions League qualification thanks to our third-place finish in the Barclays Premier League, while also leading us to the Europa League title in Amsterdam.

First-team fitness coach Paco De Miguel and first-team opposition analyst Xavi Valero also departed to join Napoli. Bolo Zenden, meanwhile, has linked up with PSV Eindhoven.

ROSS TURNBULL

Although the form of Petr Cech ensured Turnbull's four-year spell with the Blues was restricted to just 19 appearances, the likeable Geordie won numerous honours in his role as back-up goalkeeper.

Signed from Middlesbrough in the summer of 2009, he was on the bench for both of our European triumphs and also picked up an FA Cup winner's medal in 2012.

Now at Doncaster Rovers.

YOSSI BENAYOUN

Benayoun spent three years with the Blues, although during that time he made just seven starts.

The signing from Liverpool scored against Wigan Athletic on just his second appearance, but then suffered a torn Achilles tendon, which ruled him out for six months.

In the 2011/12 season, he went on loan to Arsenal, which was followed by a temporary transfer to former club West Ham last term. However, this was cut short in January and he returned to make 13 appearances for the Blues before the end of the campaign.

JEFFREY BRUMA

Having joined the club as a schoolboy in 2007, the Rotterdam-born centre-back went on to play a key role in our run to the 2008 FA Youth Cup final. He made his first-team debut as a 17-year-old in the 2009/10 campaign and featured 10 times in Chelsea colours during that and the next season.

A full international debut followed, as did loan spells with Leicester City and Hamburg, the latter spanning two seasons. Bruma now returns to his homeland with PSV, where he will link up with former Blue Boudewijn Zenden, who has been appointed in their Academy coaching staff.

AMIN AFFANE

The attacking midfielder, who could also feature out wide, was an ever-present in our victorious FA Youth Cup side of 2012 before heading on loan to Dutch side Roda JC.

However, the Swede was not retained by the Blues and is now playing at German club Energie Cottbus.

AZIZ DEEN-CONTEH

An attack-minded left-back, the Sierra Leone-born youngster was at Chelsea from the age of 13 and played his part in our FA Youth Cup success of 2010 before following that up with the National Premier Reserve League a year later.

Now with Greek side Ergotelis.

ARCHANGE NKUMU

Usually found at the heart of the defence or anchoring the midfield, Nkumu signed his first professional contract in 2011 and went on to make one start in our run to FA Youth Cup triumph. Last season, he went on loan to Yeovil Town and Colchester United, although the latter spell was hampered by injury.

JAMES ASHTON

The midfielder joined Chelsea at the age of eight and turned pro in 2010, but struggled with injuries for much of his time with the Blues.

ROHAN INCE

Another member of the victorious 2010 FA Youth Cup side, Ince joined the club as an eight-year-old and flitted between a midfield role and operating at the heart of the defence.
  Now at Brighton.

ANJUR OSMANOVIC

Osmanovic joined Chelsea during the 2010/11 season and became a Swedish youth international while representing the Blues Under-18s and reserves. The midfielder returned to his former club Larje-Angereds on loan last season, winning promotion to the Swedish Division Two. He parted company with Chelsea by mutual consent at the start of September.

CONOR CLIFFORD

Following his arrival in 2008, the Irish midfielder – capped all the way up to Under-21 level – became the first player to captain Chelsea to FA Youth Cup glory since Terry Venables in 1961, leading by example with the winning goal in the final of 2010.
  Spent time on loan with five different League One sides thereafter, before his release in January 2013.
  Now with Southend.

ADAM PHILLIP

Injuries halted the progress of the powerful centre-forward – who is now known by the name Adam Coombes – but, prior to that, his pace and goalscoring ability caused many a youth team problems.
  Now with Notts County.

BEN GORDON

Gordon joined the Blues from Leeds United as a schoolboy international and spent much of his time out on loan. The left-back's most successful spell was at Kilmarnock, where he lifted the Scottish League Cup.
  Now with Ross County.

The following scholars left the club during the last year:

SAM BANGURA

WALTER FIGUEIRA

ALASTAIR GORDON

TOM HOWARD

NORTEI NORTEY

ISMAIL SEREMBA

JESSE STARKEY

CHRISTIAN ATSU

The 21-year-old joined Chelsea from Porto on 1 September and will spend the 2013/14 season on loan at Vitesse Arnhem. Atsu made 31 appearances for the Dragoes last season as well as playing in all six of Ghana's matches at the Africa Cup of Nations. The winger won Rio Ave's Player of the Season award while on loan there in 2011/12.

FACTS AND FIGURES

Born: Ada Foah, Ghana, 10.01.92
Height: 1.72m (5ft 8in) **Weight:** 68kgs (10st 10lb)
Previous clubs: Cheetah FC, Porto, Rio Ave (loan)
Signed: September 2013
Loan since signing: Vitesse Arnhem (2013/14)
Honours with other clubs: Portuguese League Championship 2013, Portuguese Super Cup 2012, Porto Young Player of the Year 2011 (Porto). Rio Ave Player of the Year 2012
Major international tournaments: 2013 Africa Cup of Nations (5+1 games, 1 goal)
International recognition: Ghana 17 caps, 4 goals

PATRICK BAMFORD

The striker joined Chelsea from Nottingham Forest in January 2012, having made two first-team appearances, and scored nine goals in two FA Youth Cup games for his former club. Spending the first half of 2013/14 with MK Dons, where he got four goals during two loan spells last term.

FACTS AND FIGURES

Born: Grantham, 05.09.93
Height: 1.89m (6ft 2in) **Weight:** 81kgs (12st 11lb)
Previous club: Nottingham Forest
Signed: January 2012
Loans since signing: MK Dons (2012/13, 11+3 games, 4 goals, 2013/14)
International recognition: England Youth. Republic of Ireland Youth
International caps won with Chelsea: England Under-19s
Reserve/U21s appearances: 18 games, 9 goals (1 pen)
U19s appearances: 3 games, 1 goal
U18s appearances: 1 game, 1 goal

NATHANIEL CHALOBAH

Signed a new five-year deal with the Blues during the 2013 close season, then joined Nottingham Forest on loan until 15 January. Helped Watford reach 2012/13 Championship Play-off final.

FACTS AND FIGURES

Born: Freetown, Sierra Leone 12.12.94
Height: 1.87m (6ft 2in) **Weight:** 77kgs (12st 2lb)
Source: Chelsea Academy
Chelsea scholarship: July 2011
Turned pro: January 2012
Loans since signing: Watford (2012/13, 38+4 games, 5 goals), Nottingham Forest (2013/14)
Trophies won with Chelsea: FA Youth Cup 2012
International honours: 2012 England's Men's Youth Player of the Year, 2010 UEFA Under-17s Championship winner
International caps won with Chelsea: England Under-21s 7 caps, 0 goals, Under-19s, Under-17s, Under-16s
Reserve/U21s appearances: 30 games, 6 goals
U19s appearances: 1 game
U18s appearances: 30+3 games, 9 goals

THIBAUT COURTOIS

At the age of 21, Courtois is no stranger to silverware. He had already won the Belgian league title as well as the Belgian Goalkeeper of the Year and Genk Player of the Season awards before signing for Chelsea. In his first two years on loan at Atletico Madrid, where he will spend a third campaign in 2013/14, he has added the Europa League, UEFA Super Cup, Copa del Rey and the Zamora Trophy. He is also the youngest-ever goalkeeper to represent Belgium at senior international level.

FACTS AND FIGURES

Born: Bree, Belgium, 11.05.92
Height: 1.99m (6ft 6in) **Weight:** 91kgs (14st 5lb)
Previous clubs: KRC Genk
Signed: July 2011
Loans since signing: Atletico Madrid (2011/12, 52 games, 23 clean sheets, 2012/13, 46 games, 24 clean sheets, 2013/14)
Honours with other clubs: Belgian League Championship 2011, Belgian Goalkeeper of the Year 2011, KRC Genk Player of the Year 2011 (KRC Genk). UEFA Europa League 2012, UEFA Super Cup 2012, Spanish Cup 2013, Zamora Trophy 2013 for the lowest goals to games ratio in La Liga (Atletico Madrid while on loan from Chelsea)
International recognition: Belgium 10 caps, 6 clean sheets, Belgium Youth
International caps won with Chelsea: Belgium 10 caps, 6 clean sheets

CRISTIAN CUEVAS

One of several players spending 2013/14 on loan with Dutch club Vitesse Arnhem, Cuevas signed for the Blues in the summer. The Chilean can play anywhere down the left side.

FACTS AND FIGURES

Born: Rancagua, Chile, 02.04.95
Height: 1.73m (5ft 8in) **Weight:** 62.5kgs (9st 12lb)
Previous club: O'Higgins
Signed: July 2013
Loan since signing: Vitesse Arnhem (2013/14)
International recognition: Chile Youth

ULISES DAVILA

The 22-year-old attacker joined Chelsea from Chivas Guadalajara in 2011, signing a five-year deal. Spent his first term on loan at Vitesse Arnhem before moving to Spain with Sabadell for 2012/13. Now at Cordoba.

FACTS AND FIGURES

Born: Guadalajara, Mexico, 13.04.91
Height: 1.72m (5ft 8in) **Weight:** 68kgs (10st 10lb)
Previous club: Chivas Guadalajara
Signed: August 2011
Loans since signing: Vitesse Arnhem (2011/12, 3 games), Sabadell (2012/13, 24+13 games, 5 goals), Cordoba (2013/14)
International honours: 2011 CONCACAF Under-20s Championship winner, third in 2011 FIFA Under-20s World Cup
Major international tournaments: 2011 Copa America (0 games)
International recognition: Mexico Under-23s 2 caps, Mexico Youth

MATEJ DELAC

Delac is the youngest player ever to be called up for the Croatian national team, being named in the squad to face England and Belarus before joining Chelsea in August 2010. Last season saw him return to former club Inter Zaprelic on loan and he will spend 2013/14 with Vojvodina in Serbia.

FACTS AND FIGURES

Born: Gornji Vakuf-Uskoplje, Bosnia and Herzegovina, 20.08.92
Height: 1.90m (6ft 3in) **Weight:** 87kgs (13st 10lb)
Previous clubs: Inter Zaprešic
Signed: August 2010
Loans since signing: Vitesse Arnhem (2010/11, 0 games), SK Dynamo Ceske Budejovice (2011/12, 5 games), Vitoria Guimaraes (2012/13, 1 game), Inter Zaprešic (2012/13, 14 games, 4 clean sheets), Vojvodina (2013/14)
International recognition: Croatia Under-21s 5 caps, Croatia Youth

THORGAN HAZARD

Thorgan joined Chelsea in 2012, the same year as his older brother Eden Hazard. The younger of the siblings also plays as a winger and is currently on loan at Zulte Waregem in his native Belgium for a second season. He scored five goals in 37 games there in 2012/13 and started the current campaign by netting four times in their first six league fixtures.

FACTS AND FIGURES

Born: La Louviere, Belgium, 29.03.93
Height: 1.74m (5ft 8in) **Weight:** 71kgs (11st 2lb)
Previous club: Lens
Signed: July 2012
Loans since signing: Zulte Waregem (2012/13, 35+2 games, 5 goals, 2013/14)
International recognition: Belgium 1 cap, Under-21s 7 caps, Belgium Youth
International caps won with Chelsea: Belgium 1 cap, 0 goals, Under-21s 7 caps, 0 goals
Reserve/U21s appearances: 0+1 game
U19s appearances: 1 game

SAM HUTCHINSON

Chelsea Academy graduate Hutchinson first joined the club aged seven. Injuries forced his retirement in August 2010, but a year later he returned and made two appearances for the Blues towards the end of 2011/12, bringing his total number of first-team games to six. The defender spent last season on loan with Nottingham Forest and will play for Vitesse Arnhem this term.

FACTS AND FIGURES

Born: Slough, 03.08.89
Height: 1.83m (6ft) **Weight:** 77kgs (12st 2lb)
Source: Chelsea Academy
Chelsea scholarship: July 2005
Turned pro: August 2006
Loans since signing: Nottingham Forest (2012/13, 6+3 games, 1 goal), Vitesse Arnhem (2013/14)
Chelsea debut: Everton (h) 13.05.07, substitute for Wayne Bridge. Drew 1-1
International caps won with Chelsea: England Under-19s, Under-18s
First team appearances: 2+4 games
Reserve/U21s appearances: 38+3 games, 1 goal
U18s appearances: 40+8 games, 3 goals

TODD KANE

After impressing on a brief loan with Preston at the end of 2012, Kane joined Blackburn Rovers for the second half of last season. The right-back has returned to Ewood Park for the whole of 2013/14 and scored his first senior goal there in August.

FACTS AND FIGURES

Born: Huntingdon, 17.09.93
Height: 1.74m (5ft 8in) **Weight:** 68kgs (10st 10lb)
Source: Chelsea Academy
Chelsea scholarship: July 2010
Turned pro: July 2011
Loans since signing: Preston (2012/13, 5 games), Blackburn (2012/13, 13+1 games, 2013/14)
Trophies won with Chelsea: FA Youth Cup 2012, Premier Reserve League South 2011, National Premier Reserve League 2011
International caps won with Chelsea: England Under-19s
Reserve/U21s appearances: 39+4 games, 6 goals
U19s appearances: 2 games
U18s appearances: 43+2 games, 10 goals (1 pen)

GAEL KAKUTA

Now aged 22, Kakuta was voted the Chelsea Academy's Scholar of the Year by staff and team-mates in 2007/08. He was also named as Player of the Tournament at the 2010 European Under-19s Championship after helping France win the competition. The winger is at Vitesse Arnhem for a second year after previous loans at Fulham, Bolton and Dijon.

FACTS AND FIGURES

Born: Lille, France, 21.06.91
Height: 1.73m (5ft 8in) **Weight:** 70kgs (11st)
Source: Lens
Chelsea scholarship: July 2007
Turned pro: July 2008
Loans since signing: Fulham (2010/11, 2+5 games, 1 goal), Bolton (2011/12, 2+4 games, 1 goal), Dijon (2011/12, 13+3 games, 5 goals (1 pen), Vitesse Arnhem (2012/13, 25+1 games, 1 goal, 2013/14)
Chelsea debut: Wolves (h) 21.11.09, substitute for Nicolas Anelka. Won 4-0
International honours: 2010 UEFA Under-19s Championship winner and named UEFA's Golden Player of the Tournament, fourth in 2011 FIFA Under-20s World Cup
International caps won with Chelsea: France Under-21s 5 caps, 0 goals, Under-20s, Under-19s, Under-18s, Under-17s
Penalty shoot-out goals: 0 from 1
First team appearances: 5+11 games
Reserve/U21s appearances: 17+6 games, 4 goals
U18s appearances: 25+4 games, 14 goals

MILAN LALKOVIC

After previous loans with Doncaster Rovers, ADO Den Haag and Vitoria SC, Lalkovic has joined League One side Walsall until January 2014. The forward is a Slovakian Under-21 international and was part of the Blues sides that won the 2010 FA Youth Cup and 2011 national reserve title.

FACTS AND FIGURES

Born: Kosice, Slovakia, 09.12.92
Height: 1.72m (5ft 8in) **Weight:** 66kgs (10st 5lb)
Source: Chelsea Academy
Chelsea scholarship: July 2009
Turned pro: July 2010
Loans since signing: Doncaster Rovers (2011/12, 1+5 games), Den Haag (2011/12, 0+2 games), Vitoria Guimaraes (2012/13, 0+10 games), Walsall (2013/14)
Trophies won with Chelsea: FA Youth Cup 2010, Premier Reserve League South 2011, National Premier Reserve League 2011
International caps won with Chelsea: Slovakia Under-21s 16 caps, 1 goal, Under-19s, Under-17s
Reserve/U21s appearances: 45+2 games, 14 goals (1 pen)
U18s appearances: 37+9 games, 12 goals

ROMELU LUKAKU

The powerful striker was signed from Anderlecht in 2011, making 12 appearances for the Blues in his first season and another three at the start of the current campaign. His most successful year in England came on loan at West Brom last term, when he scored 17 Premier League goals, including a hat-trick against Manchester United. The Belgian international will be on loan in the top flight again in 2013/14, this time with Everton.

FACTS AND FIGURES

Born: Antwerp, Belgium, 13.05.93
Height: 1.91m (6ft 3in) **Weight:** 97kgs (15st 4lb)
Previous clubs: Lierse, Anderlecht
Signed: August 2011
Loans since signing: West Brom (2012/13, 23+15 games, 17 goals, 2 pens), Everton (2013/14)
Chelsea debut: Norwich (h) 27.08.11, substitute for Fernando Torres. Won 3-1
Honours with other clubs: Belgian League Championship 2010, Belgian League top scorer 2010 (15 goals), Belgium Super Cup 2010, Belgian Ebony Shoe 2011 (Anderlecht), West Brom Young Player of the Year 2013 (while on loan from Chelsea)
International recognition: Belgium 21 caps, 3 goals, Under-21s 5 caps, 1 goal, Belgium Youth
International caps won with Chelsea: Belgium 11 caps, 1 goal
First team appearances: 4+8 games
Reserve/U21s appearances: 9 games, 7 goals (1 pen)

MARKO MARIN

Marin made 16 appearances for Chelsea last term, his one goal coming in the 4-1 win over Wigan. The winger joined the Blues from Werder Bremen in 2012, having previously represented Borussia Monchengladbach, and will spend 2013/14 in Spain with Sevilla. He was born in Bosnia and Herzegovina but plays his international football with Germany, including two games at the 2010 World Cup.

FACTS AND FIGURES

Born: Bosanska Gradiska, Bosnia and Herzegovina, 13.03.89

Height: 1.70m (5ft 7in) **Weight:** 67.5kgs (10st 9lb)

Previous clubs: Borussia Monchengladbach, Werder Bremen

Signed: July 2012

Loan since signing: Sevilla (2013/14)

Chelsea debut: Wolves (h) League Cup 25.09.12, substitute for Juan Mata. Won 6-0

Trophies won with Chelsea: UEFA Europa League 2013

Other Chelsea honours: Runners-up medals – FIFA Club World Cup 2012

Honours with other clubs: German Second Division Champions 2008, Under-18s German Player of the Year 2007 (Borussia Monchengladbach)

International honours: Third in the 2010 World Cup, 2009 UEFA Under-21s Championship winner

Major international tournaments: 2010 World Cup (0+2 games)

International recognition: Germany 16 caps, 1 goal, Under-21s 12 caps, 1 goal, Germany Youth

International caps won with Chelsea: None

First team appearances: 5+11 games, 1 goal

Reserve/U21s appearances: 3 games, 2 goals

JOSH MCEACHRAN

The central midfielder joined Chelsea aged eight and made his first-team debut in the Champions League at 17. He made a total of 22 appearances for the Blues before moving on loan to Swansea in January 2012. The 20-year-old impressed with Middlesbrough last season, playing 38 times for the Championship side, and joined Watford on loan in September until 2 January.

FACTS AND FIGURES

Born: Oxford, 01.03.93

Height: 1.80m (5ft 11in) **Weight:** 71kgs (11st 2lb)

Source: Chelsea Academy

Chelsea scholarship: July 2009 **Turned pro:** July 2010

Loans since signing: Swansea (2011/12, 2+3 games), Middlesbrough (2012/13, 35+3 games), Watford (2013/14)

Chelsea debut: MSK Zlina (a) Champions League 15.09.10, substitute for Daniel Sturridge and became our youngest Champions League debutant at 17 years 198 days. Won 4-1

Trophies won with Chelsea: Premier Reserve League South 2011, National Premier Reserve League 2011 and FA Youth Cup 2010

Other Chelsea honours: Chelsea Young Player of the Year 2011

International honours: 2010 UEFA Under-17s Championship winner

International caps won with Chelsea: England Under-21s 13 caps, 1 goal, Under-19s, Under-17s, Under-16s

First team appearances: 7+15 games

Reserve/U21s appearances: 19+2 games, 1 goal

U18s appearances: 38+8 games, 7 goals

VICTOR MOSES

Moses moved to Stamford Bridge from Wigan in 2012 and scored 10 goals in 43 games in his debut season, including four strikes in the Europa League en route to lifting the trophy in Amsterdam. Despite representing England at youth level, the versatile forward is a full international with Nigeria, scoring twice for the Super Eagles as they won the 2013 Africa Cup of Nations. He will play for Liverpool on loan this term.

FACTS AND FIGURES

Born: Kaduna, Nigeria, 12.12.90

Height: 1.77m (5ft 10in) **Weight:** 76kgs (11st 13lb)

Previous clubs: Crystal Palace, Wigan Athletic

Signed: August 2012

Chelsea debut: QPR (a) 15.09.12, substitute for Ryan Bertrand. Drew 0-0

Loan since signing: Liverpool (2013/14)

Trophies won with Chelsea: UEFA Europa League 2013

Other Chelsea honours: Runners-up medals – FIFA Club World Cup 2012, UEFA Super Cup 2012

International honours: 2013 Africa Cup of Nations winner, Golden Boot winner in the 2007 UEFA Under-17s Championship

Major international tournaments: 2013 Africa Cup of Nations (5 games, 2 pens)

International recognition: Nigeria 13 caps, 4 goals. England Under-21s 1 cap. England Youth

International caps won with Chelsea: Nigeria 9 caps, 4 goals

First team appearances: 27+16 games, 10 goals

JHON PIREZ

The Uruguayan striker scored two goals in 10 games for Leganes last season after recovering from an injury and will spend a second term with the Spanish side. He had previously been with Defensor Sporting, from where he had originally signed for Chelsea, and has represented his country at Under-17s and Under-20s level.

FACTS AND FIGURES

Born: Montevideo, Uruguay, 20.02.93

Height: 1.89m (6ft 2in) **Weight:** 74kgs (11st 9lb)

Previous club: Defensor Sporting

Signed: August 2011

Loans since signing: CD Leganes (2012/13, 3+7 games, 2 goals, 2013/14)

International recognition: Uruguay Youth

STIPE PERICA

Striker Perica arrived at the Bridge in the summer from Zadar, where he scored 10 goals in 24 games last season. The 18-year-old represented Croatia at the 2013 Under-20s World Cup and will spend this season with Dutch side NAC Breda.

FACTS AND FIGURES

Born: Zadar, Croatia, 07.07.95

Height: 1.91m (6ft 3in) **Weight:** 74.5kgs (11st 10lb)

Previous club: NK Zadar

Signed: August 2013

Loan since signing: NAC Breda (2013/14)

International recognition: Croatia Under-21s 1 cap, Croatia Youth

DANIEL PAPPOE

With Chelsea since Under-12s level, Ghanaian-born Pappoe was a member of the 2010 FA Youth Cup-winning side and captained the Under-18s in that competition the next year, although he missed the end of both seasons through injury. He has joined Colchester United on loan until January 2014.

FACTS AND FIGURES

Born: Accra, Ghana, 30.12.93

Height: 1.92m (6ft 3in) **Weight:** 94kgs (14st 11lb)

Source: Chelsea Academy

Chelsea scholarship: July 2010

Turned pro: July 2011

Loan since signing: Colchester (2013/14)

Trophies won with Chelsea: Premier Reserve League South 2011, National Premier Reserve League 2011, FA Youth Cup 2010

International caps won with Chelsea: Ghana Under-20s

Reserve/U21s appearances: 21+5 games, 1 goal

U19s appearances: 4 games

U18s appearances: 32+3 games, 1 goal

LUCAS PIAZON

The midfielder joined Chelsea from Sao Paulo. In 2012, he won the FA Youth Cup with the Blues, his performances earning him our Young Player of the Year award. Made three first-team appearances last season before joining Malaga on loan and will play for Vitesse Arnhem in 2013/14.

FACTS AND FIGURES

Born: Sao Paulo, Brazil, 20.01.94
Height: 1.83m (6ft) **Weight:** 69.5kgs (10st 13lb)
Previous club: Sao Paulo
Signed: August 2011
Loans since signing: Malaga (2012/13, 4+10 games), Vitesse Arnhem (2013/14)
Chelsea debut: Wolves (h) League Cup 25.09.12. Won 6-0
Trophies won with Chelsea: FA Youth Cup 2012
Other Chelsea honours: Chelsea Young Player of the Year 2012. Runners-up medals – FIFA Club World Cup 2012, FA Community Shield 2012
International honours: 2011 South American Under-17s Championship winner, 2009 South American Under-15s Championship runners-up, was top scorer with 10 goals, fourth in 2011 FIFA Under-17s World Cup
International recognition: Brazil Youth
International caps won with Chelsea: None
Penalties: 0 from 1
First team appearances: 2+1 games
Reserve/U21s appearances: 14+1 games, 6 goals (1 pen)
U19s appearances: 2 games, 1 goal
U18s appearances: 13 games, 3 goals

PATRICK VAN AANHOLT

The Dutch left-back will play for Vitesse Arnhem again this season, having spent last term and the second half of 2011/12 there. He has also had loans in England as well as eight games for Chelsea, scoring one goal.

FACTS AND FIGURES

Born: 's-Hertogenbosch, Holland, 29.08.90
Height: 1.78m (5ft 10in) **Weight:** 72kgs (11st 5lb)
Source: PSV Eindhoven
Chelsea scholarship: July 2007
Turned pro: September 2007
Loans since signing: Coventry (2009/10, 19+1 games), Newcastle (2009/10, 7 games), Leicester (2010/11, 12 games, 1 goal), Wigan (2011/12, 4 games), Vitesse Arnhem (2011/12, 10+1 games, 2012/13, 39 games, 2 goals, 2013/14)
Chelsea debut: Portsmouth (a) 24.03.10, substitute for Yury Zhirkov. Won 5-0
Chelsea honours: Runners-up medals – FA Community Shield 2010
International caps won with Chelsea: Holland Under-21s 16 caps, 0 goals, Under-21s B 1 cap, 0 goals, Under-19s, Under-18s
First team appearances: 3+5 games, 1 goal
Reserve/U21s appearances: 37+1 games, 4 goals
U18s appearances: 14+1 games, 1 goal

ORIOL ROMEU

Romeu arrived at Chelsea in 2011 from Barcelona. The Spanish midfielder played in 24 matches in his first season with the Blues and a further nine last term before injury ruled him out for the second half of the campaign. For 2013/14, he has returned to his homeland to play for Valencia.

FACTS AND FIGURES

Born: Ulldecona, Spain, 24.09.91
Height: 1.84m (6ft) **Weight:** 84kgs (13st 3lb)
Previous club: Barcelona
Signed: August 2011
Loan since signing: Valencia (2013/14)
Chelsea debut: Sunderland (a) 10.09.11, substitute for Nicolas Anelka. Won 2-1
Trophies won with Chelsea: UEFA Champions League 2012
Other Chelsea honours: Runners-up medals – UEFA Super Cup 2012
Honours with other clubs: Spanish Super Cup 2010 (Barcelona)
International honours: 2008 UEFA Under-17s Championship winner, 2010 UEFA Under-19s Championship runners-up
Major international tournaments: 2012 Olympics (1+1 games)
International caps won with Chelsea: Spain Under-23s 5 caps, 0 goals, Under-21s 10 caps, 0 goals, Under-20s
Penalties: 1 from 1
First team appearances: 24+9 games, 1 goal

SAM WALKER

Goalkeeper Walker has rejoined Colchester United until January 2014, having helped the League One side avoid relegation at the end of last season. He has previously represented Bristol Rovers, Northampton, Yeovil and Barnet during loan spells.

FACTS AND FIGURES

Born: Gravesend, 02.10.91
Height: 2m (6ft 7in) **Weight:** 98kgs (15st 6lb)
Source: Millwall
Chelsea scholarship: July 2008
Turned pro: July 2009
Loans since signing: Barnet (2010/11, 7 games), Northampton (2011/12, 25 games), Yeovil (2011/12, 20 games), Bristol Rovers (2012/13, 14 games), Colchester (2012/13, 19 games, 2013/14)
Trophies won with Chelsea: Premier Reserve League South 2011, National Premier Reserve League 2011, FA Youth Cup 2010
International recognition: England Youth
International caps won with Chelsea: None
Reserve/U21s appearances: 9 games
U18s appearances: 37+1 games

GEORGE SAVILLE

Having made three appearances on loan with Millwall last season, Saville has joined another London club, Brentford, until January 2014. The 20-year-old midfielder joined the Blues from Reading at Under-13s level and featured in our run to win the 2010 FA Youth Cup.

FACTS AND FIGURES

Born: Camberley, 01.06.93
Height: 1.83m (6ft) **Weight:** 73.5kgs (11st 8lb)
Source: Chelsea Academy
Chelsea scholarship: July 2009
Turned pro: July 2010
Loans since signing: Millwall (2012/13, 2+1 games), Brentford (2013/14)
Trophies won with Chelsea: Premier Reserve League South 2011, National Premier Reserve League 2011, FA Youth Cup 2010
Other Chelsea honours: Runners-up medals – FIFA Club World Cup 2012
Reserve/U21s appearances: 35+11 games, 3 goals
U19s appearances: 3 games, 1 goal
U18s appearances: 46+3 games, 1 goal

WALLACE

The 19-year-old right-back signed for Chelsea in January 2013 after winning the Brazilian national championship, as well as Rio State's league and cup titles, with Fluminense, where he remained on loan until the summer. He also helped Brazil triumph at the South American Under-17s Championship in 2011. Wallace will spend 2013/14 on loan in Italy with Inter Milan.

FACTS AND FIGURES

Born: Rio de Janeiro, Brazil, 01.05.94
Height: 1.74m (5ft 8in) **Weight:** 77.5kgs (12st 3lb)
Previous club: Fluminense
Signed: January 2013
Loans since signing: Fluminense (2012/13, 3+2 games), Inter Milan (2013/14)
Honours with other clubs: Brazil Serie A Championship 2012, Rio de Janeiro State Championship 2012, Rio de Janeiro State Cup 2012 (Fluminense)
International honours: 2011 South American Under-17s Championship winner
International recognition: Brazil Youth
International caps won with Chelsea: Brazil Under-20s

JOSE MOURINHO

José Mourinho returned for his second spell in charge of Chelsea with some emotive words for Blues supporters.

"I am in a position which is new to me," he told the official Chelsea magazine. "This is at the same time being a manager and a fan – it's the first time this has happened to me when I have started a job. I feel this club deeply, in the professional way and in the emotional way.

"I want very much, more than ever, to do well. I want to do it because I am a professional and I want to do it because I am a supporter and this is the highest motivation I could feel in my career."

The hunger, the drive and the ambition that have seen Mourinho establish himself as one of the all-time managerial greats continue to burn brightly as he makes his return to the Premier League with the club he loves and it is easy to see why the mutual appreciation between the fans and manager is so apparent.

In 2004/05, Mourinho arrived in England for his first spell as Blues manager and immediately charmed the faithful in the stands with his charisma and unshakable confidence in his methods. They were even more enamoured when he led the club to the league title for the first time in 50 years, having won the League Cup earlier in the season.

A year later, Chelsea defended their Premier League crown before lifting both domestic cup competitions in 2006/07 – the FA Cup triumph being sealed with a 1-0 win over

Manchester United in the first final at the new Wembley Stadium.

Mourinho's success in England was a continuation of a managerial career that had been on a sharp upward trajectory since he began coaching the juniors at hometown club Vitoria Setubal, where his father Felix had enjoyed a successful career as a goalkeeper.

In the years that followed, Mourinho moved to Estrela Amadora and, in 1992, to Lisbon giants Sporting, where he coached under Bobby Robson. He continued to work with the Englishman at Porto and then Barcelona, where he stayed on after Robson's departure as assistant to legendary Dutch manager Louis van Gaal.

In 2000, Mourinho made the decision to strike out on his own, taking up his first managerial post with Benfica. After falling victim to a change in president, though, he made his name with minor Portuguese side UD Leiria, transforming them into something of a force.

In 2002, Porto called again for their former coach and asked him to take over as manager. He took the opportunity and transformed the club's fortunes over the next two-and-a-half years. Two league titles and a domestic cup were backed up with incredible wins in Europe – the UEFA Cup in 2003 and the Champions League in 2004.

The world was watching and Mourinho was quickly chosen as the next manager of Chelsea, as owner Roman Abramovich looked to install the right man to lead the club to glory. As you will know by now, he succeeded.

Since laying that all-important groundwork for success at Chelsea, Mourinho has gone on to achieve great things in both Italy and Spain, reinforcing his reputation across the continent.

At Inter Milan, he won consecutive Serie A titles and in his second season completed a remarkable Treble as the Nerazzurri won the Champions League,

Mourinho overseeing training on the pitches at Cobham

JOSE MOURINHO – THE SUCCESS STORY

CLUB HONOURS

Porto (2002-04)
- Champions League (2003/04)
- UEFA Cup (2002/03)
- Primeira Liga (2002/03, 2003/04)
- Portuguese Cup (2002/03)
- Portuguese Super Cup (2003)

Chelsea (2004-07)
- Premier League (2004/05, 2005/06)
- FA Cup (2006/07)
- League Cup (2004/05, 2006/07)
- Community Shield (2005)

Inter Milan (2008-10)
- Champions League (2009/10)
- Serie A (2008/09, 2009/10)
- Coppa Italia (2009/10)
- Italian Super Cup (2008)

Real Madrid (2010-13)
- La Liga (2011/12)
- Copa del Rey (2010/11)
- Spanish Super Cup (2012)

INDIVIDUAL HONOURS
- FIFA World Coach of the Year (2010)
- UEFA Manager of the Year (2002/03, 2003/04)
- UEFA Team of the Year (2003, 2004, 2005, 2010)
- Premier League Manager of the Year (2004/05, 2005/06)
- Portuguese Primeira Liga Manager of the Year (2002/03, 2003/04)
- Italian Serie A Manager of the Year (2008/09, 2009/10)
- Miguel Munoz Trophy, Spain (2010/11, 2011/12)

the league and the Coppa Italia in 2009/10.

It was the perfect way to bid farewell to Italy as he took up his next challenge with Real Madrid.

At the Estadio Santiago Bernabeu, Mourinho took on the task of reining in a dominant Barcelona side and immediately set about achieving his aim. Real lifted the Copa del Rey in his first season in charge before running away with the league in 2011/12.

With 100 points and 121 goals to their name, Real broke national records that year and Mourinho began the following season by completing the set of domestic silverware with the Supercopa de Espana (a success that also made him the first manager to have won the equivalent competition in four different countries).

By the end of last season, however, the team had fallen short of the final target – the Champions League.

"Everything was perfect, except we didn't win the Champions League, which was a bit of a frustration," Mourinho explained. "However, it is so difficult to do it that I cannot be frustrated.

"I learned a lot with these experiences – different players, different personalities, different cultures, different media, different structures in the club – but I think you still have to learn and improve every day."

Now, he is back at Stamford Bridge, the place where he says he is not just the manager, but also one of the supporters. No wonder he declared himself to be "The Happy One" as he was revealed once again as Chelsea manager in June.

STEVE HOLLAND
Assistant first-team coach

This is Holland's third season as assistant first-team coach at Chelsea. In his previous role here, as reserve-team manager, he led a young side to the Premier Reserve League trophy in 2010/11. His coaching career began in the renowned Crewe Alexandra youth set-up under former Chelsea coach Dario Gradi. Over 15 years, Holland progressed to the point where he took responsibility for the Crewe first team in 2007. He departed Gresty Road in late 2008 and joined Stoke City's Academy set-up in April 2009, from where he was offered the role of reserve-team manager by Chelsea four months later. Assisted coaching with England's Under-21s in September 2013.

SILVINO LOURO
Assistant first-team coach

An experienced coach who has worked with José Mourinho for several years – at Porto, Chelsea, Inter Milan and Real Madrid. Prior to linking up with Mourinho, he was also part of the Portuguese national team coaching staff. As a player, Silvino made more than 400 appearances, with his goalkeeping career continuing into his 40s. During a long spell with Lisbon giants Benfica, he played in two European Cup finals (1988 and 1990), captaining the side in the latter, while he also earned 23 international caps for Portugal. Having previously been a goalkeeper coach, Silvino is now working solely as assistant first-team coach.

RUI FARIA
Assistant first-team coach

As a sports science graduate from Porto University, Faria initially met José Mourinho while doing research and work experience at Barcelona in the 1998/99 season. Then, when Mourinho became manager of Portuguese club UD Leiria in 2001, he took Faria on as his assistant methodology coach. During that time, the methodology he and Mourinho worked on revolutionised coaching in Portugal. They have worked together ever since, winning league titles in four different countries – at Porto, Chelsea, Inter and Real Madrid – as well as two Champions League titles (with Porto and Inter Milan) and the UEFA Cup (also with Porto).

JOSE MORAIS
Assistant first-team coach

Having initially met José Mourinho when they worked together at Benfica in 2000, Morais was reunited with his friend at Inter Milan in 2009. In between those roles, Morais coached on several continents, picking up invaluable experience in countries as diverse as Sweden, Saudi Arabia, Tunisia, Germany and Yemen. After being reunited with Mourinho at Inter, Morais was part of the coaching staff as the Milanese club won the first-ever Italian Treble (Serie A, Coppa Italia and Champions League) in 2009/10. He then moved with his manager to join Real Madrid before arriving at Chelsea for the first time this season.

MICHAEL EMENALO
Technical director

Previously head opposition scout and assistant first-team coach at the club, Emenalo has been on the Chelsea backroom staff since 2007. In 2011/12, he took up the position of technical director, working closely with the manager, leading the club's scouting structure and helping to drive the technical programmes both of our Academy and international youth network. Emenalo's career in football began following his graduation from Boston University with a degree in international relations with political sciences. As a player, he enjoyed stints with clubs in Belgium, Germany, Spain, Israel and the USA, not to mention a short spell with Notts County.

CHRISTOPHE LOLLICHON
Goalkeeper coach

An innovative and very active coach, Lollichon has been putting Chelsea's senior goalkeepers through their paces since November 2007. Prior to that, the Frenchman had been working with the shot-stoppers at Ligue 1 club Rennes for eight years, in which time he coached Petr Cech before the keeper's move to Chelsea. Lollichon has been coaching since his early 20s, has a keen eye for detail and puts great stock in communicating and discussing ideas with his goalkeepers and fellow coaches.

CHRIS JONES
First-team fitness coach

After joining the club in 2006, Jones initially worked with our Academy and reserve teams, moving up to join the first-team coaching staff ahead of the 2009/10 campaign. The Loughborough University graduate joined Chelsea from west London neighbours Fulham, where he spent three years, and has also worked with the England Under-19s and Under-21s. Previously a semi-professional footballer, Jones has also represented Chelsea's reserves as a substitute in the past.

FOOTBALL CLUB BOARD

DAVID BARNARD

BRUCE BUCK

RON GOURLAY

MARINA GRANOVSKAIA

EUGENE TENENBAUM

ADMINISTRATION

DAVID BARNARD
Director/Club secretary

CLAIRE HEMBROW
Assistant club secretary

JANE FITZGERALD
PA to the manager/
Football administrator

KIM MALL
PA to the club secretary

SAMANTHA POWELL
PA to the technical director

KEVIN CAMPELLO
Head of player welfare

LINDA EDSTRÖM
Training ground operations manager

JASON GRIFFIN
Head groundsman. Responsible for
both Stamford Bridge and Cobham.

GARY STAKER
Player liaison officer

NICOLA MITCHEISON
Scouting logistics co-ordinator

TECHNICAL, PERFORMANCE AND SCOUTING

SCOTT MCLACHLAN
Head of international scouting
Arrived at the start of the 2011/12
season to head up the club's
international scouting programme.
Previously worked at Fulham as a
technical scout. He has also been head
of performance analysis at
Southampton.

MICK MCGIVEN
Senior opposition scout
An experienced opposition scout, Mick
previously coached Chelsea's reserves
for 10 years and managed Ipswich
Town. As a player, he represented West
Ham and Sunderland.

PAUL MCGIVEN
Opposition scout
Provides match analysis on
our opponents.

JAMES MELBOURNE
Head of match analysis/Scout
Measures our own team performances
and helps to assess and dissect
opposition displays, producing video
footage for the management.

CHRISTY FENWICK
First-team match analyst
Works alongside James Melbourne
and the first-team technical
department. He analyses match action
and produces statistical feedback and
videos for the coaching staff.

GIOVANNI CERRA
Visual designer
Analyses match action and works
alongside the first-team match
analysis department, producing visual
reports and infographics that illustrate
relevant data and strategies.

MATT HALLAM
Advanced player recruitment analyst
Co-ordinates scouting reports and
technical statistics to help develop
integrated reports on players and
analyse the club's scouting network.

PAUL QUILTER
Match analysis/Recruitment assistant
Assists first-team match analysis
department and produces recruitment
videos for the scouting department.

TIM HARKNESS
Club psychologist
Sports psychologist who joined Chelsea
in 2009. He has a positive psychology
background, with a focus on learning and
sharing common sense people skills such
as balance, perspective, resilience,
communication and change.

STAFF

KIT DEPARTMENT

GARRY GREY
Senior kit manager
Now in his fourth full season here, having previously worked at Fulham for 11 years.

MICK ROBERTS
Assistant kit manager
Long-standing kitman who previously worked for the reserves and Academy here.

RUSSELL HARVEY
Head ball boy

RICKY DOWLING
Ball boy

MALCOLM SHENTON
Kit assistant

JULIE SAY
Kit assistant

FRANK STEER
Players' assistant

ALAN BARRATT
Players' assistant

MEDICAL DEPARTMENT

DR PACO BIOSCA
Medical director
Heads up the medical department. Arrived at Chelsea in 2011, after working for Ukrainian side Shakhtar Donetsk and, previously, Lleida in his native Spain. A specialist in orthopaedic surgery, he is a former president of both the European Federation of Orthopaedic and Sports Trauma and the Spanish Society of Sports Trauma.

DR EVA CARNEIRO
First-team doctor
Sports medicine specialist who previously worked at the British Olympic Medical Institute and with England Women's Football and UK Athletics. Joined Chelsea in February 2009.

JASON PALMER
Physiotherapist
Arrived at Chelsea in 2007, having previously headed up the medical department at Fulham and, prior to that, within the Australian national team set-up and private practice.

MEDICAL DEPARTMENT CONT.

THIERRY LAURENT
Physiotherapist
Specialist rehabilitation physio who has worked at Chelsea since 2005, having previously worked with the French national team.

JON FEARN
Physiotherapist
Joined Chelsea in January 2010 from Reading, where he was head of sports medicine for nine years. Previously first-team physiotherapist at West Ham.

STEVE HUGHES
Physiotherapist
First joined the club as an Academy physio in 2001 and went full-time in 2004. Works closely with those players who are out on loan.

IVAN ORTEGA
Sports therapist
Joined our medical department in 2011 after two years with Liverpool.

BILLY MCCULLOCH
Massage therapist
Has worked at the club for more than a decade now, having also worked with both the English and Scottish national teams in that time.

STUART SULLIVAN
Massage therapist
Joined Chelsea in 2004, having worked at Watford, Reading and then with the Republic of Ireland squad in 2004/05. Part of the England medical team during the 2010 World Cup.

SIMON MORRIS
Massage therapist
Previously with the English Institute of Sport and UK Athletics. Joined Chelsea in 2009.

MANOEL RIBEIRO
Massage therapist
In his fifth season with Chelsea, Manoel previously worked at West Ham and Fulham, as well as for the Cirque du Soleil and the Royal Ballet.

JO CLUBB
Sports science officer
Sport scientist to the club since 2009, having graduated from Loughborough University.

MEDICAL DEPARTMENT CONT.

CLARE REID
Senior nurse
Started work at Chelsea last season as the club's first full-time nurse.

PAMELA JORDAN
Practice manager
Manages the day-to-day running of the department.

ACADEMY MANAGEMENT

NEIL BATH
Head of youth development
Having joined the youth coaching staff in 1993, worked his way through the ranks to become Academy manager in 2004, and subsequently took on his current role overseeing the work of the Academy at all levels from Under-21s down.

JIM FRASER
Assistant head of youth development
Head of Academy recruitment
Assists Neil Bath in the running of the Academy, overseeing Under-9s to Under-16s and heading up recruitment for Under-15s to Under-19s.

EDDIE NEWTON
Technical coach
Responsible for the management and monitoring of loan players. He also works with coaches across the youth programme.

ACADEMY COACHING

DERMOT DRUMMY
Under-21s manager
FA Youth Cup-winning former youth-team manager who led an Under-19s side to the NextGen Series final last season. As a youngster, he was on the books at Arsenal and also played for Blackpool. He coached in the Arsenal Academy before moving to Chelsea in 2007, initially as Under-16s coach.

ADI VIVEASH
Youth-team manager
Former Walsall, Reading and Swindon defender who joined the Chelsea Academy coaching staff four years ago and took charge of the youth team in 2011/12, winning the FA Youth Cup in his first season and reaching the final again the following year.

ACADEMY COACHING CONT.

ANDY MYERS
Under-21s assistant coach

Former Chelsea defender who made more than 100 appearances for the club, Andy previously coached the Under-15s before making the step up to join Dermot Drummy's Under-21s coaching team last season.

MARK BEENEY
Under-21s and Academy goalkeeper coach

Formerly a goalkeeper with Leeds United, Mark has coached the Academy shot-stoppers for several years and is now a key part of the Under-21s coaching set-up. His son, Mitchell, is among the goalkeeping options for the Under-21s and youth team.

JOE EDWARDS
Under-16s coach and Under-18s assistant coach

A former Chelsea Academy player, Joe has quickly progressed since becoming a coach at a young age, managing the Under-16s team as well as assisting Adi Viveash with the Under-18s team.

BILL THOMPSON
Under-18s goalkeeper coach

FRANK O'BRIEN
Under-15s coach and safeguarding assistant

JON HARLEY
Academy coach

TORE ANDRE FLO
Academy coach

MATT BIRNIE
Head of Academy physical fitness and Under-21s conditioning coach

ELLIOT AXTELL
Under-18s conditioning coach

SAM BOWHAY
Under-16s conditioning coach

ACADEMY PERFORMANCE AND RECRUITMENT

BEN SMITH
Head of development performance systems

DARREN GRACE
Head of local recruitment

ED BRAND
Assistant recruitment officer and Under-12s coach

BEN KNIGHT
Development centre co-ordinator and Under-11s coach

ACADEMY MEDICAL DEPARTMENT

DR DAVID PORTER
Under-21s doctor

DR CHRIS HUGHES
Academy doctor

DR JULIAN REDHEAD
Academy doctor

STUART VAUGHAN
Physiotherapist

SIMON DICKIE
Physiotherapist

KATE YOXALL
Physiotherapist

EMMA PATRICK
Physiotherapist

WILL TULLETT
Movement specialist

JACK CHRISTOPHER
Sports scientist

ACADEMY ADMINISTRATION

BOB OSBORN
Youth development officer

GERRY HARVEY
Head of education

JACK FRANCIS
Head of lifestyle and mentoring

PAUL WALDRON
Education officer and Under-9s to Under-11s coach co-ordinator

SAMPA CHIBULU
Lifestyle and mentoring assistant

HAYLEY PRIOR
Academy operations manager

EMMA THOMAS
Academy administrator

FIONA ARMFIELD
Scout co-ordinator

ANNA LINEHAN
Academy and training ground receptionist

ACADEMY KIT DEPARTMENT

CRAIG BROWN
Under-21s kit manager

ERIC ASIEDU
Academy kit manager

Video analysis is just one aspect of the training and development carried out by staff at Chelsea

THE MATCHES
2012/13

FA Community Shield
Villa Park, 12.08.12, 1.30pm

CHELSEA 2
Torres 39, Bertrand 79

MANCHESTER CITY 3
Y Toure 52, Tevez 58, Nasri 64

Eden Hazard has an attempt at goal

Chelsea were narrowly beaten by Manchester City in an entertaining Community Shield at Villa Park.

The Blues deservedly went ahead through Fernando Torres. Ramires was the provider, dropping the shoulder to deceive his marker and make space to find Torres with a precise pass, allowing our No9 to dink the ball home.

Joy turned to frustration as Branislav Ivanovic was shown a red card for lunging in on compatriot Aleksandar Kolarov and, unfortunately, the 10 men couldn't hold out for long, as a burst of three goals in 12 second-half minutes put City in control.

Ryan Bertrand later came off the substitutes' bench to tap in his first senior goal for the Blues, but it proved to be little more than a consolation, as last season's Premier League winners held on.

Chelsea (4-2-3-1): Cech; Ivanovic, David Luiz, Terry (c), Cole; Mikel, Lampard; Ramires, Mata (Sturridge 74), Hazard (Bertrand 71); Torres **Unused subs:** Turnbull, Cahill, Essien, Meireles, Piazon **Booked:** Ramires, Mikel, Lampard, Cole, Bertrand **Sent off:** Ivanovic (41) serious foul play

Manchester City (3-4-1-2): Pantilimon; Savic (Clichy h/t), Kompany (c), Zabaleta; Milner, Y Toure, De Jong, Kolarov; Nasri (Silva 77); Tevez (Dzeko 88), Aguero **Unused subs:** Johansen, K Toure, Razak, A Johnson **Booked:** Savic, Kompany, Pantilimon

Referee: Kevin Friend **Att:** 36,394

UEFA Super Cup
Stade Louis II (Monaco), 31.08.12, 7.45pm

CHELSEA 1
Cahill 74

ATLETICO MADRID 4
Falcao 6, 18, 44, Miranda 60

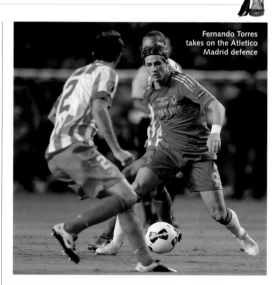

Fernando Torres takes on the Atletico Madrid defence

Chelsea's hopes of winning the UEFA Super Cup were ended by Atletico Madrid, who recorded a 4-1 win in Monaco thanks to Radamel Falcao's hat-trick.

The Blues lifted the trophy 14 years ago against Real Madrid – city rivals of Atletico – but, on this occasion, we were on the backfoot from the sixth minute, when Falcao strode clear to clip the ball past Petr Cech.

The Colombian made it 2-0 before 20 minutes had gone, this time curling a left-footed effort into the far corner, and he completed his treble just before half-time with another cool finish.

Despite trailing 3-0, Chelsea were enjoying the better of the possession without really testing keeper Thibaut Courtois, on loan at Atletico from the Blues.

We did eventually make the breakthrough – although not before Miranda had added a fourth – when Gary Cahill lashed home from inside the box for a consolation goal.

Chelsea (4-2-3-1): Cech; Ivanovic, Cahill, David Luiz, Cole (Bertrand 89); Mikel, Lampard (c); Ramires (Oscar h/t), Hazard, Mata (Sturridge 81); Torres **Unused subs:** Turnbull, Romeu, Meireles, Moses **Booked:** Ivanovic

Atletico Madrid (4-2-3-1): Courtois; Juanfran, Miranda, Godin, Filipe Luis; Gabi (c), Mario Suarez; Arda Turan, Koke (Raul Garcia 81), Adrian Lopez (Rodriguez 56); Falcao (Emre 87) **Unused subs:** Asenjo, Silvio, Cata Diaz, Costa

Referee: Damir Skomina (Slovenia) **Att:** 14,312

Barclays Premier League
DW Stadium, 19.08.12, 1.30pm

WIGAN ATHLETIC 0

CHELSEA 2
Ivanovic 2, Lampard 6 (pen)

Team-mates swarm to congratulate Branislav Ivanovic

A superb Premier League debut from Eden Hazard was the catalyst for a perfect start to the campaign at the DW Stadium.

The Blues took the lead with just over a minute gone when the Belgian youngster superbly turned his marker, Ivan Ramis, just inside the Wigan half before slipping a slide-rule pass through for Branislav Ivanovic to drive a low finish past Ali Al Habsi.

Things got even better for Chelsea and, once again, it was a moment of magic from Hazard, who jinked past one Latics defender before Ramis mistimed his challenge. Referee Mike Jones pointed to the spot and Frank Lampard drilled a low shot beyond Al Habsi.

The home side rallied well after a disastrous start, but Petr Cech was rarely troubled and the best chance of the second half fell to Fernando Torres, who was unlucky to see his shot cleared off the line by Ramis.

Wigan Athletic (3-4-3): Al Habsi; Alcaraz, Caldwell (c), Ramis; Boyce, McCarthy, McArthur (Watson 80), Figueroa; Moses, Di Santo (Kone 66), Maloney (Gomez 48). **Unused subs:** Pollitt, Jones, Crusat, Boselli. **Booked:** Caldwell, McArthur

Chelsea (4-2-3-1): Cech; Ivanovic, David Luiz, Terry (c), Cole; Mikel, Lampard; Mata (Meireles 82), Hazard (Oscar 64), Bertrand; Torres. **Unused subs:** Turnbull, Cahill, Ferreira, Essien, Sturridge.

Referee: Mike Jones **Att:** 19,738

Barclays Premier League
Stamford Bridge, 22.08.12, 7.45pm

CHELSEA 4
Lampard 18 (pen), Cahill 69, Torres 81, Ivanovic 90+5

READING 2
Pogrebnyak 24, Guthrie 29

Chelsea came from behind to defeat Reading in a thrilling game at Stamford Bridge.

Although Frank Lampard put the Blues ahead from the penalty spot early on, the Royals turned the game around in the space of five first-half minutes. Pavel Pogrebnyak grabbed the equaliser with a powerful header before Danny Guthrie's free-kick found a way past Petr Cech.

The 2011/12 Championship winners defended resolutely, but they were finally undone by a long-range effort from Gary Cahill, who burst out of defence to fire a rasping drive that skipped up off the turf and beat Adam Federici.

Then, with nine minutes remaining, a superb passing move culminated in Ashley Cole crossing for Fernando Torres to tap-in at the far post. There was still one more goal in Chelsea as, with Federici up for a Reading corner in stoppage time, Hazard burst clear and squared to Branislav Ivanovic for a simple finish.

Gary Cahill fires home

Chelsea (4-2-3-1): Cech; Ivanovic, Cahill, Terry (c), Cole; Mikel (Sturridge 68), Lampard; Ramires (Oscar 57), Hazard, Mata (Meireles 84); Torres **Unused subs:** Turnbull, Bertrand, Essien, Romeu

Reading (4-4-1-1): Federici; Gunter, Pearce, Gorkss, Harte; McCleary (Robson-Kanu 85), Karacan (Le Fondre 71), Leigertwood, McAnuff (c); Guthrie; Pogrebnyak (Hunt 77) **Unused subs:** Tabb, Mariappa, McCarthy, Cummings **Booked:** Karacan, Pogrebnyak

Referee: Lee Mason **Att:** 41,733

Barclays Premier League
Stamford Bridge, 25.08.12, 5.30pm

CHELSEA 2
Hazard 22 (pen), Torres 45+2

NEWCASTLE UNITED 0

Eden Hazard puts away a penalty to open the scoring

Chelsea secured a first Premier League home win over Newcastle United since 2007 thanks to first-half goals from Eden Hazard and Fernando Torres.

The Blues were quick out of the blocks against Alan Pardew's side and were given the perfect opportunity to open the scoring when Torres was carelessly tripped by Vurnon Anita. This allowed Hazard to step up and fire home from the penalty spot for his first Premier League goal for the club.

There was a role reversal on the stroke of half-time, with the Belgian turning provider for our No9's third goal of the season.

A brilliant exchange saw Hazard back-heel the ball into Torres' path for a fierce drive that left goalkeeper Tim Krul grasping at thin air.

A 2-0 lead was the least our performance deserved. However, while the second half featured little goalmouth action of note, Petr Cech was called upon to make a smart stop from Demba Ba with less than 10 minutes remaining.

Chelsea (4-2-3-1): Cech (c); Ivanovic, Cahill, David Luiz, Cole; Meireles (Lampard 87), Mikel; Mata (Ramires 67), Hazard, Bertrand; Torres
Unused subs: Turnbull, Essien, Romeu, Oscar, Sturridge
Booked: Torres

Newcastle United (4-4-2): Krul; Simpson (R Taylor 63), S Taylor, Coloccini (c), Santon (Marveaux 74); Ben Arfa, Cabaye (Perch 77), Anita, Gutierrez; Ba, Cisse
Unused subs: Harper, Williamson, Obertan, Amalfitano

Referee: Phil Dowd **Att:** 41,718

Barclays Premier League
Loftus Road, 15.09.12, 3pm

QPR 0

CHELSEA 0

Ryan Bertrand holds the ball

The first west London derby of the season finished goalless as the Blues were denied a Premier League victory for the first time in 2012/13.

Chelsea had hammered QPR 6-1 in our previous meeting in April 2012 and there were signs that we could be in for a goal-filled afternoon early on when Eden Hazard, enjoying another bright start, was denied by Julio Cesar.

The Belgian was unfortunate not to win a penalty, too – as Shaun Wright-Phillips looked to have tripped him in the box – which came after another spot-kick claim from John Terry had been waved away by the referee.

The home side came into it more after the interval, with Ji-Sung Park and Bobby Zamora spurning opportunities, but there was almost a perfect ending for the Blues when substitute Victor Moses squared for an unmarked Hazard. Unfortunately, the finish was off target and the game finished all square.

QPR (4-4-2): Cesar; Bosingwa, Ferdinand, Nelsen, Fabio (Onuoha 18); Wright-Phillips (Cisse 69), Granero, Faurlin, Park (c); Zamora, Johnson (Mackie 32) **Unused subs:** Green, Dyer, Hoilett, Taarabt

Chelsea (4-2-3-1): Cech; Ivanovic, David Luiz, Terry (c), Cole; Mikel, Lampard; Ramires, Hazard, Bertrand (Moses 58); Torres (Sturridge 80) **Unused subs:** Turnbull, Azpilicueta, Cahill, Romeu, Oscar **Booked:** Ramires, Bertrand

Referee: Andre Marriner **Att:** 18,271

Ashley Cole acknowledges the crowd after scoring

Barclays Premier League
Stamford Bridge, 22.09.12, 3pm

CHELSEA 1

Cole 84

STOKE CITY 0

Ashley Cole netted his first goal since May 2010 to earn Chelsea a well-deserved win over Stoke City.

The Potters arrived here having lost all four of their Premier League visits to Stamford Bridge and a fifth looked to be on the cards as we piled on the pressure in the early stages.

However, the visitors had arguably the best chance of the opening half, with Jon Walters heading against the crossbar from a Charlie Adam free-kick.

The Blues pushed the Potters deep into their own half for much of the final 45 minutes, but Asmir Begovic kept out a couple of Oscar efforts, while our intricate passing game was unable to split through the dogged rearguard of the visitors.

However, with six minutes left on the clock, Branislav Ivanovic's pass was brilliantly turned into the path of Cole by an audacious Juan Mata flick and the full-back showed great composure to clip it over Begovic to take all three points.

Chelsea (4-2-3-1): Cech (c); Ivanovic, Cahill, David Luiz, Cole; Ramires, Mikel (Lampard 81); Mata (Terry 88), Oscar, Hazard (Moses 61); Torres **Unused subs:** Turnbull, Azpilicueta, Bertrand, Romeu **Booked:** Oscar, David Luiz

Stoke City (4-2-3-1): Begovic; Cameron, Shawcross (c), Huth, Wilson; Nzonzi, Whelan; Walters, Adam (Owen 63), Kightly (Etherington 71); Crouch (Jones 75) **Unused subs:** Sorensen, Upson, Shotton, Whitehead **Booked:** Adam

Referee: Michael Oliver **Att:** 41,112

Barclays Premier League
Emirates Stadium, 29.09.12, 12.45pm

ARSENAL 1

Gervinho 42

CHELSEA 2

Torres 19, Mata 53

Fernando Torres and Juan Mata scored to maintain our lead at the top of the Barclays Premier League.

An action-packed game saw the Blues get off to a flier, courtesy of a wonderful piece of improvisation from our No9.

Mata's free-kick just evaded the head of David Luiz and found Torres at the far post, who – despite being held off by Laurent Koscielny – superbly guided home a volley.

The Gunners then drew level on the stroke of half-time. A cross from out wide was well controlled by Gervinho, who turned and struck a powerful shot past Petr Cech. Early in the second half, though, a set-piece once again proved to be Arsenal's undoing. Mata clipped his free-kick into a dangerous area at the far post and past keeper Vito Mannone via the slightest touches off Koscielny.

Cech was called into action to make a couple of superb saves and showed he was well up to the task as we sealed the three points.

Fernando Torres after getting our first goal

Arsenal (4-2-3-1): Mannone; Jenkinson, Koscielny, Vermaelen (c), Gibbs; Diaby (Oxlade-Chamberlain 17), Arteta; Ramsey (Walcott 66), Cazorla, Podolski (Giroud 66); Gervinho **Unused subs:** Martinez, Santos, Mertesacker, Djourou **Booked:** Ramsey, Vermaelen

Chelsea (4-2-3-1): Cech; Ivanovic, David Luiz (Cahill 81), Terry (c), Cole; Mikel, Ramires; Mata (Bertrand 84), Oscar (Moses 73), Hazard; Torres **Unused subs:** Turnbull, Azpilicueta, Romeu, Lampard **Booked:** Oscar, David Luiz, Ramires

Referee: Martin Atkinson
Att: 60,101

Barclays Premier League
Stamford Bridge, 06.10.12, 3pm

CHELSEA 4
Torres 14, Lampard 21, Hazard 30,
Ivanovic 76

NORWICH CITY 1
Holt 10

Eden Hazard after finding the target against the Canaries

Chelsea recovered from conceding an early goal to overcome Norwich City thanks to a virtuoso attacking display.

Following a Grant Holt strike for the Canaries, the score was level just four minutes later when Branislav Ivanovic put a cross onto the head of Fernando Torres, who finished past John Ruddy.

Frank Lampard, doing what he does best, arrived on the edge of the box to send a controlled half-volley home and then the swiftest of counter-attacks saw us take a two-goal lead into half-time. Juan Mata won the ball back in his own half and carried it deep into Norwich territory before slipping a delightful pass to Eden Hazard for a smart finish.

However, arguably the best strike of the game came from Chelsea right-back Ivanovic.

Mata was the creator again, skilfully flicking the ball into the defender's path for a vicious volley that Ruddy couldn't keep out.

Chelsea (4-2-3-1): Cech; Ivanovic (Azpilicueta 78), David Luiz, Terry (c), Cole; Mikel (Romeu 82), Lampard (Ramires 67); Mata, Oscar, Hazard; Torres **Unused subs:** Turnbull, Cahill, Bertrand, Moses

Norwich City (4-4-1-1): Ruddy; R Martin, Barnett, Bassong (R Bennett 78), Garrido; E Bennett, Howson, Tettey, Johnson (Pilkington 68); Hoolahan; Holt (c) (Morison 77) **Unused subs:** Bunn, Snodgrass, Turner, Jackson

Referee: Anthony Taylor **Att:** 41,784

Barclays Premier League
White Hart Lane, 20.10.12, 12.45pm

TOTTENHAM HOTSPUR 2
Gallas 46, Defoe 54

CHELSEA 4
Cahill 17, Mata 66, 69, Sturridge 90

Juan Mata inspired Chelsea in a six-goal thriller against Tottenham Hotspur that gave us our first Premier League victory at White Hart Lane since 2005.

The Blues took the lead when Gary Cahill, showing the technique of a centre-forward, crashed a volley past keeper Brad Friedel.

Spurs turned the tie on its head within 10 minutes of the restart, though – William Gallas with a close-range finish before Jermain Defoe clipped a shot past Petr Cech.

Juan Mata hits his second of the afternoon

Their advantage didn't last long, as Mata got us back on level terms with a fine drilled finish. The Spaniard was then at it again three minutes later, collecting Eden Hazard's wonderful slide-rule pass to shoot past Friedel.

Cech was called upon to make a superb save from Kyle Walker's long-range effort, but the Spurs right-back was caught on the ball in stoppage time, allowing Mata to pick out substitute Daniel Sturridge for a tap-in.

Tottenham Hotspur (4-2-3-1): Friedel; Walker, Gallas (c), Caulker, Vertonghen; Sandro, Huddlestone (Livermore 67); Lennon, Sigurdsson, Dempsey (Adebayor 74); Defoe **Unused subs:** Lloris, Dawson, Naughton, Falque, Townsend **Booked:** Huddlestone, Gallas, Walker

Chelsea (4-2-3-1): Cech (c); Ivanovic, Cahill, David Luiz, Cole; Mikel, Ramires; Mata, Oscar (Sturridge 83), Hazard (Lampard 89); Torres **Unused subs:** Turnbull, Azpilicueta, Bertrand, Romeu, Moses **Booked:** Ivanovic, Ramires

Referee: Mike Dean **Att:** 36,060

Ramires in action during this intense encounter

Barclays Premier League
Stamford Bridge, 28.10.12, 4pm

CHELSEA 2

Mata 43, Ramires 53

MANCHESTER UNITED 3

David Luiz (og) 3, Van Persie 12, Hernandez 75

▶▶ Chelsea's unbeaten start to the Premier League season came to an end in this intense encounter.

The visitors were two-up early on, with Robin van Persie instrumental in both goals – his shot rebounding off the post and against David Luiz for the opener before a crisp strike for the second.

The response from Chelsea came in the moments leading up to the interval as Juan Mata curled home a sumptuous free-kick, while the Blues drew level just after the break through a powerful Ramires header. However, the game was turned in the space of three minutes just past the hour mark. Branislav Ivanovic was given a straight red for bringing down Ashley Young when the winger was through on goal and then Fernando Torres was sent off for two bookable offences, the second of which was for diving, despite Jonny Evans making contact with his trailing leg.

United's winner came from sub Javier Hernandez, who appeared to have come from an offside position to tap home.

Chelsea (4-2-3-1): Cech (c); Ivanovic, Cahill, David Luiz, Cole; Ramires, Mikel; Mata (Bertrand 71), Oscar (Azpilicueta 66), Hazard (Sturridge 82); Torres
Unused subs: Turnbull, Romeu, Marin, Moses
Booked: Mikel **Sent off:** Ivanovic (62) denying a goalscoring opportunity, Torres (68) two yellows

Manchester United (4-2-3-1): De Gea; Rafael, Ferdinand, Evans, Evra (c); Carrick, Cleverley (Hernandez 64); Valencia, Rooney (Giggs 73), Young; Van Persie
Unused subs: Lindegaard, Anderson, Scholes, Nani, Welbeck
Booked: Rooney, Valencia

Referee: Mark Clattenburg
Att: 41,644

Barclays Premier League
Liberty Stadium, 03.11.12, 3pm

SWANSEA CITY 1

Hernandez 87

CHELSEA 1

Moses 60

▶▶ Chelsea were denied victory at the Liberty Stadium after a late equaliser by Pablo Hernandez cancelled out Victor Moses' maiden Premier League goal for the Blues.

Moses and Cesar Azpilicueta both started their first league game for the club, but the early stages of the match were slow, with little goalmouth action.

That all changed after the break, though, and the Blues came out with far more zip in our attacking play. Despite that, it required a set-piece to break the deadlock, along with the improvised intervention of Moses.

Gary Cahill, as he has done so often this season, rose highest to meet a corner from Oscar and the Nigerian winger was in the right place to flick a header in off the post.

Petr Cech, wearing the captain's armband, looked to have consolidated the points with good stops from Jonathan de Guzman and Nathan Dyer, but the Swans nicked an equaliser with three minutes remaining.

Swansea City (4-2-1-3): Tremmel; Rangel, Monk (c), Williams, Davies; Britton (Graham 64), Ki Sung-Yueng; De Guzman; Hernandez, Michu (Shechter 79), Routledge (Dyer 64)
Unused subs: Cornell, Tate, Tiendalli, Agustien
Booked: Britton, De Guzman, Ki Sung-Yeung, Shechter

Chelsea (4-2-3-1): Cech (c); Azpilicueta, Ivanovic, Cahill, Cole; Mikel, Romeu (Ramires h/t); Moses (Sturridge 72), Oscar (Bertrand 79), Hazard; Torres
Unused subs: Turnbull, Ferreira, Marin, Piazon
Booked: Azpilicueta

Referee: Kevin Friend **Att:** 20,527

Victor Moses celebrates finding the net

Barclays Premier League
Stamford Bridge, 11.11.12, 4pm

CHELSEA 1
Terry 19

LIVERPOOL 1
Suarez 72

John Terry gets his landmark 50th goal

John Terry became the first defender to score 50 goals for Chelsea, but the Blues skipper's early header wasn't enough to see off Liverpool, Luis Suarez bagging a late equaliser.

The visitors struggled to deal with the movement of our attacking quartet in the early stages and it came as no surprise when the opening goal went Chelsea's way. Terry rose unmarked to direct a powerful header past Brad Jones from a superb Juan Mata corner.

However, the captain's game was ended before the half-time break when an unfortunate collision with

Luis Suarez forced him off on a stretcher.

The Blues did look to be in control of the game for much of the second half, but Suarez was in the right place to head home from close range after Jamie Carragher flicked a corner into his path.

Both sides had chances to take all

the points in the remaining minutes, but it finished honours even.

Chelsea (4-2-3-1): Cech; Azpilicueta, Ivanovic, Terry (c) (Cahill 39), Bertrand; Mikel, Ramires; Mata, Oscar (Moses 76), Hazard; Torres (Sturridge 81) **Unused subs:** Turnbull, Ferreira, Romeu, Marin **Booked:** Mikel

Liverpool (3-4-1-2): Jones; Wisdom, Carragher, Agger; Johnson, Allen, Sahin (Suso 59), Enrique; Gerrard (c); Sterling, Suarez **Unused subs:** Gulacsi, Coates, Henderson, Downing, Cole, Assaidi **Booked:** Allen, Johnson, Gerrard

Referee: Howard Webb **Att:** 41,627

Eden Hazard evades the West Brom players

Barclays Premier League
The Hawthorns, 17.11.12, 3pm

WEST BROMWICH ALBION 2
Long 9, Odemwingie 50

CHELSEA 1
Hazard 39

Chelsea slipped to a narrow defeat against a West Bromwich Albion side managed by Blues legend Steve Clarke.

The Throstles took an early lead, Shane Long the scorer after peeling off his marker at the back stick to head past Petr Cech.

The Blues drew level before half-time when Eden Hazard played a one-two with Cesar Azpilicueta, whose return pass was a superb cross onto

the Belgian's head, although a slight deflection off the defender was crucial.

Our hard work was undone early in the second period and – for the third time in the game – a header proved to be pivotal. This time, it was a near-post effort from Peter Odemwingie that beat Cech and the Blues were facing a tricky task to come back against a side with a strong home record.

There were chances, though, but

Daniel Sturridge, in particular, was met by an immovable object in the form of Boaz Myhill between the sticks for the Baggies.

West Bromwich Albion (4-2-3-1): Myhill; Jones, Tamas, Olsson (c), Ridgewell; Mulumbu, Yacob; Odemwingie, Morrison (Dorrans 70), Gera (Brunt 70); Long (Rosenberg 80) **Unused subs:** L Daniels, Reid, Popov, Fortune

Chelsea (4-2-3-1): Cech; Azpilicueta, Cahill, David Luiz, Bertrand; Romeu (Oscar 62), Mikel (Ramires 80); Sturridge, Hazard, Moses; Torres (Mata 62) **Unused subs:** Turnbull, Ivanovic, Cole, Marin

Referee: Michael Oliver **Att:** 25,933

Fernando Torres drives forward with the ball

Barclays Premier League
Stamford Bridge, 25.11.12, 4pm

CHELSEA 0

MANCHESTER CITY 0

Chelsea were held to a goalless draw by Manchester City at Stamford Bridge in Rafael Benitez's first game as interim first-team manager.

Chances were slim in a meeting between the kings of Europe and the champions of England as both rearguards were on top, but there were positive signs for the Blues as we kept our first clean sheet since a 4-0 win over Nordsjaelland at the start of October.

The best chances of the first half fell City's way, though, and Petr Cech did particularly well to keep out Pablo Zabaleta when the Argentine full-back was well placed to finish off a sweeping move.

However, we came into the game more after the break and Fernando Torres had arguably our best effort of the game when he sent a fizzing left-footed drive just over Joe Hart's crossbar after the hour mark.

A late piledriver from Ashley Cole called the England No1 into action for a smart stop, but there was to be no breakthrough for either side at the Bridge.

Chelsea (4-2-3-1): Cech (c); Azpilicueta, Ivanovic, David Luiz, Cole; Mikel (Romeu 79), Ramires; Mata, Oscar, Hazard (Moses 70); Torres
Unused subs: Turnbull, Ferreira, Cahill, Bertrand, Marin

Manchester City (4-4-2): Hart; Zabaleta, Kompany (c), Nastasic, Kolarov; Silva, Y Toure, Barry, Milner; Aguero (Balotelli 85), Dzeko (Tevez 68)
Unused subs: Pantilimon, Maicon, K Toure, Garcia, Nasri
Booked: Zabaleta, Kolarov, Balotelli

Referee: Chris Foy
Att: 41,792

Barclays Premier League
Stamford Bridge, 28.11.12, 7.45pm

CHELSEA 0

FULHAM 0

Chelsea were held to a second consecutive goalless draw at Stamford Bridge, with our neighbours Fulham returning home with a point after a solid defensive display.

Clear-cut chances in the opening half proved to be few and far between, with both sides unable to find a way through rearguards which were solid and well-drilled, resulting in a stalemate for much of the first 45 minutes.

The one highlight was a neat turn and shot from Fernando Torres, albeit an effort that never really troubled Mark Schwarzer.

The second period followed a similar pattern in the early part, although Fulham were required to make some last-ditch tackles while also looking more dangerous on the counter-attack, Petr Cech twice called upon to make excellent saves.

Torres arguably had the Blues' best chance of the half, with his chest control followed by an acrobatic volley able to beat Schwarzer, only for Aaron Hughes to intervene.

Oscar breaks through Fulham's lines

Chelsea (4-2-3-1): Cech (c); Azpilicueta, Ivanovic, David Luiz, Cole; Ramires, Romeu; Hazard (Marin 82), Oscar, Bertrand (Mata 63); Torres
Unused subs: Turnbull, Ferreira, Cahill, Mikel, Moses
Booked: Ivanovic, Romeu, David Luiz

Fulham (4-4-1-1): Schwarzer; Riether, Senderos, Hughes, Riise; Duff, Diarra (Baird 63), Sidwell, Rodallega (Petric 83); Karagounis (Frei 73); Berbatov (c)
Unused subs: Etheridge, Kelly, Kasami, Dejagah

Referee: Anthony Taylor
Att: 41,707

Barclays Premier League
Boleyn Ground, 01.12.12, 12.45pm

WEST HAM 3
Cole 63, Diame 85, Maiga 90+1

CHELSEA 1
Mata 12

Chelsea let a one-goal lead slip against West Ham to lose at the Boleyn Ground for the first time since May 2003.

The Blues looked bright in the opening stages in east London and deservedly took the lead through a composed finish by Juan Mata. Victor Moses was involved in the build-up, feeding Fernando Torres, who pulled the ball back for his fellow countryman to neatly sidefoot a shot past Jussi Jaaskelainen.

The opening half was all Chelsea and we were picking apart the home side at will, only for the finishing touch to prove elusive.

We were made to pay for our wastefulness on the hour mark when former Blues striker Carlton Cole climbed all over Branislav Ivanovic before heading in an equaliser.

It proved to be the turning point, as the Hammers netted twice late on to win the tie.

Half-time substitute Mohamed Diame drilled home from the edge of the box and Modibo Maiga delivered the killer blow in stoppage time to make it a miserable afternoon for the boys in blue.

Ramires challenging for the ball

West Ham United (4-1-4-1): Jaaskelainen; Demel, Collins, Reid, O'Brien; Tomkins (Diame h/t); O'Neil (Taylor h/t), Noble, Nolan (c), Jarvis; C Cole (Maiga 87) **Unused subs:** Spiegel, Spence, Fanimo, Moncur **Booked:** Noble

Chelsea (4-2-3-1): Cech (c); Azpilicueta, Cahill, Ivanovic, Cole; Mikel, Ramires; Moses (Marin 78), Mata, Hazard (Oscar 72); Torres **Unused subs:** Turnbull, Ferreira, Romeu, Bertrand, Piazon **Booked:** Cech, Mikel

Referee: Martin Atkinson **Att:** 35,005

Barclays Premier League
Stadium of Light, 08.12.12, 3pm

SUNDERLAND 1
Johnson 65

CHELSEA 3
Torres 11, 45+2 (pen), Mata 48

A first-half brace from Fernando Torres helped to extend Chelsea's winning streak at the Stadium of Light to eight in a row.

Torres struck after just 11 minutes, steering a low cross from Eden Hazard past Simon Mignolet.

Although a bright start quietened heading into the interval, we doubled our lead on the stroke of half-time when Sebastian Larsson clumsily brought down Ramires in the box and Torres stepped up to confidently convert from 12 yards.

If that goal came at a crucial time, then the third – just three minutes into the second half – knocked the stuffing out of Sunderland. It came from the boot of another of our Spanish contingent, Juan Mata, who was nicely placed to finish after Torres had crashed a shot off the bar. Although Adam Johnson pulled one back

Juan Mata cuts the ball back past keeper Simon Mignolet

for the Black Cats with a splendid strike, the Blues took all three points.

Sunderland (4-2-3-1): Mignolet; Bardsley (Colback 66), O'Shea (c), Cuellar, Rose; Larsson (Saha 81), Gardner; Johnson, Sessegnon, McClean; Wickham **Unused subs:** Westwood, Bramble, Vaughan, Kilgallon, Campbell **Booked:** Gardner

Chelsea (4-2-3-1): Cech (c); Ivanovic, Cahill, David Luiz, Cole; Ramires, Romeu (Oscar 19); Moses (Bertrand 61), Mata, Hazard (Lampard 79); Torres **Unused subs:** Turnbull, Ferreira, Azpilicueta, Marin **Booked:** Ivanovic, Ramires, Mata

Referee: Mark Halsey **Att:** 39,273

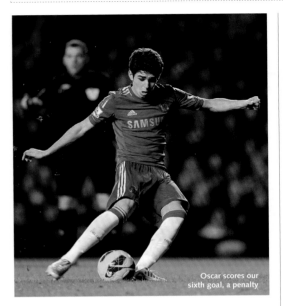

Oscar scores our sixth goal, a penalty

Barclays Premier League
Stamford Bridge, 23.12.12, 4pm

CHELSEA 8

Torres 2, David Luiz 28, Ivanovic 34, Lampard 58, Ramires 75, 90+1, Oscar 78 (pen), Hazard 83

ASTON VILLA 0

Chelsea smashed eight goals past Aston Villa to equal our biggest-ever league victory.

The scoring started after just two minutes when Cesar Azpilicueta delivered a superb cross to Fernando Torres, who powered home a header from the edge of the penalty area.

The visitors looked to be getting a foothold in the game, but a quick-fire double either side of the half-hour mark proved to be critical. First, David Luiz curled home an exquisite free-kick and then Branislav Ivanovic was perfectly placed to head home after Gary Cahill's shot deflected into his path.

Frank Lampard, making his 500th Premier League start, put away a fizzing half volley – a milestone goal, as it took him above Bobby Tambling as our all-time leading league scorer in the top flight.

Lucas Piazon then teed up Ramires for the fifth and Oscar won a penalty, which he converted.

The pick of the goals, however, came from Eden Hazard's left boot as he lashed home a stunner. Although Piazon missed a penalty soon after, the scoring wasn't finished, with Ramires finding the net again.

Chelsea (4-2-3-1): Cech; Azpilicueta, Cahill, Ivanovic, Cole; David Luiz, Lampard (c) (Ramires 60); Moses, Mata (Piazon 74), Hazard; Torres (Oscar 67) **Unused subs:** Turnbull, Ferreira, Ake, Marin

Aston Villa (3-5-2): Guzan; Herd, Clark (c), Baker; Lowton, Westwood (Ireland 56), Holman (Bowery 79), Bannan, Lichaj (Bennett 56); Weimann, Benteke **Unused subs:** Given, El Ahmadi, Albrighton, Delph

Referee: Phil Dowd **Att:** 41,363

Barclays Premier League
Carrow Road, 26.12.12, 3pm

NORWICH CITY 0

CHELSEA 1

Mata 38

Juan Mata marked his 50th Premier League appearance with the only goal of the game against Norwich City as Chelsea picked up three points from our Boxing Day trip to Carrow Road.

The Blues were full of confidence heading into this fixture, having put eight past Aston Villa three days earlier, but both defences were on top in the early stages in Norfolk and it took a moment of brilliance from Mata to put us in front.

With half-time approaching, Oscar's patient build-up play was rewarded when he found the Spanish maestro, whose sweetly-struck shot left Mark Bunn with no chance and gave us a deserved advantage against a side who had won five home games on the spin.

Although there was to be no second goal to kill off the game, the Blues looked comfortable in defence as the game wore on, with the Canaries' only real opportunity coming from Sebastien Bassong's downward header that cleared the bar in stoppage time.

Chelsea fans were given further reason to cheer when youngster Nathan Ake was brought on in the closing stages for his senior debut.

Norwich City (4-4-1-1): Bunn; R Martin, Turner, Bassong, Garrido; Snodgrass, Tettey, Johnson (Howson 81), Pilkington (Morison 78); Hoolahan (E Bennett 88); Holt (c) **Unused subs:** Rudd, Jackson, R Bennett, Barnett **Booked:** Johnson

Chelsea (4-2-3-1): Cech (c); Azpilicueta, Cahill, Ivanovic, Cole; David Luiz, Mikel (Lampard 73); Moses (Hazard 78), Mata (Ake 90+1), Oscar; Torres **Unused subs:** Turnbull, Ferreira, Marin, Piazon **Booked:** Hazard

Referee: Jonathan Moss **Att:** 26,831

Juan Mata scored on his 50th Premier League appearance

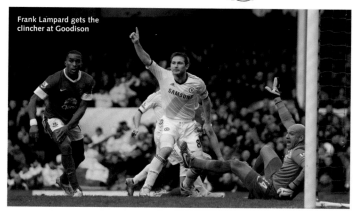

Frank Lampard gets the clincher at Goodison

Barclays Premier League
Goodison Park, 30.12.12, 1.30pm

EVERTON 1
Pienaar 1

CHELSEA 2
Lampard 41, 71

Frank Lampard netted twice as Chelsea came from behind to secure a win at Goodison Park.

The Blues conceded a goal in the first minute when Petr Cech was left helpless as Victor Anichebe's header hit the post and the ball fell into the path of Steven Pienaar, who netted from the rebound.

The deficit could soon have been worse, though, as Nikica Jelavic curled a free-kick against the upright.

However, we drew level just before half-time through Lampard, who was perfectly placed to head home Ramires' left-footed cross. Then, Cech, who was making a milestone appearance as the first foreign player to represent the club 400 times, did not return after the interval due to an injury and was replaced by Ross Turnbull.

The match remained tight, but we eventually got the breakthrough with 20 minutes remaining, Lampard slotting home the rebound from Juan Mata's saved shot. The goal took Lampard to within one strike of Kerry Dixon, our second-highest scorer of all time, and gave us a hard-fought victory.

Everton (4-4-1-1): Howard; Jagielka (c), Heitinga, Distin, Baines; Naismith (Vellios 76), Hitzlsperger (Barkley 78), Osman, Anichebe; Pienaar (Oviedo, 80); Jelavic **Unused subs:** Mucha, Browning, Duffy, Gueye **Booked:** Pienaar, Distin

Chelsea (4-3-3): Cech (Turnbull h/t); Azpilicueta, Cahill, Ivanovic, Cole; Ramires, David Luiz, Lampard (c); Mata (Oscar 85), Torres, Hazard (Moses 73) **Unused subs:** Ferreira, Ake, Marin, Piazon **Booked:** Cahill, David Luiz, Cole

Referee: Howard Webb **Att:** 39,485

Barclays Premier League
Stamford Bridge, 02.01.13, 7.45pm

CHELSEA 0

QUEENS PARK RANGERS 1
Wright-Phillips 78

Cesar Azpilicueta challenges for the ball

Former Blues winger Shaun Wright-Phillips scored the only goal of a subdued west London derby as Queens Park Rangers picked up their first win at the Bridge since 1983.

There was a full Premier League debut for Marko Marin, while Ross Turnbull was making his first full top-flight appearance of the season in place of the injured Petr Cech.

After a quiet opening period, the action picked up after the interval and we looked the likelier team to grab the breakthrough goal. Victor Moses was inches away from turning in a threatening cross by Marin and the Nigerian also sent two powerful shots just off the target, while Julio Cesar made a superb reaction save to deny Fernando Torres.

The opener looked to have come in the 66th minute when Frank Lampard fired a crisp half-volley into the bottom corner, only to be deemed offside. Instead, the visitors snatched the points, and it was a fine effort from Wright-Phillips which beat Turnbull.

There was still time for Branislav Ivanovic to glance a header over the goal from substitute Juan Mata's inviting cross, but that proved to be the last action of the game.

Chelsea (4-2-3-1): Turnbull; Azpilicueta, Cahill, Ivanovic, Bertrand; David Luiz, Lampard (c) (Ramires 78); Marin (Hazard 59), Oscar, Moses (Mata 74); Torres **Unused subs:** Hilario, Ferreira, Cole, Piazon **Booked:** Marin

QPR (4-1-4-1): Julio Cesar; Onuoha, Nelsen, Hill (c), Fabio; Derry; Mackie, Granero (Park 89), Mbia, Hoilett (Wright-Phillips 15); Taarabt (Dyer 90+2) **Unused subs:** Green, Ferdinand, Faurlin, Cisse **Booked:** Hill

Referee: Lee Mason **Att:** 41,634

Barclays Premier League
Britannia Stadium, 12.01.13, 3pm

STOKE CITY 0

CHELSEA 4

Walters (og) 45+2, (og) 62,
Lampard 65 (pen), Hazard 72

Frank Lampard became Chelsea's second-highest scorer of all time at Stoke

Chelsea recorded our biggest-ever win at Stoke City, thanks to an impressive display at the Britannia Stadium.

The Potters, unbeaten at their home ground in nearly a year, put the Blues under some intense early pressure. However, the game changed when Jonathan Walters headed into his own net from Cesar Azpilicueta's cross on the stroke of the interval.

Stoke thought they would have the chance to draw level from the penalty spot just after the half-time break, only for the referee to reverse his decision to penalise Azpilicueta due to an offside call. Then, moments later, it was 2-0. Incredibly, it was that man Walters – making his 100th top-flight appearance – who was on target for the Blues again.

Frank Lampard made it 3-0 from the spot after Juan Mata was felled in the area, taking the Blues No8 clear as our second-highest scorer of all time, before Eden Hazard scored the goal of the game with a wonderful shot from all of 30 yards.

There was still time for Walters to complete his miserable afternoon, skimming the crossbar with a penalty.

Stoke City (4-2-3-1): Begovic; Cameron, Shawcross (c), Huth, Wilkinson; Whelan, Nzonzi; Walters, Adam (Whitehead 78), Etherington (Kightly 86); Jones (Jerome 78) **Unused subs:** Sorensen, Upson, Crouch, Shotton **Booked:** Wilkinson

Chelsea (4-2-3-1): Cech; Azpilicueta (Ferreira 82), Ivanovic, David Luiz, Cole; Lampard (c), Ramires; Hazard, Mata (Terry 79), Bertrand; Ba (Torres 71) **Unused subs:** Turnbull, Ake, Oscar, Marin

Referee: Andre Marriner **Att:** 27,348

Barclays Premier League
Stamford Bridge, 16.01.13, 7.45pm

CHELSEA 2

Ba 25, Hazard 45

SOUTHAMPTON 2

Lambert 57, Puncheon 74

Demba Ba's athletic strike

Chelsea let a two-goal lead slip as Southampton staged a strong second-half fightback to leave Stamford Bridge with a point.

The two sides had met less than a fortnight earlier in the FA Cup third round, with the Blues recording a 5-1 victory, and it looked like another high-scoring game could be on the cards as we went in at half-time with a commanding lead.

Demba Ba got the ball rolling with his first goal in front of the Stamford Bridge faithful, showing superb awareness and athleticism to fire a half volley past Artur Boruc.

The advantage was doubled on the stroke of half-time through Eden Hazard. After Ramires had hammered a shot against the woodwork, the ball fell to the Belgian to steer home a left-footed shot.

However, the introduction of striker Rickie Lambert helped the Saints force their way back into the game after the break and he headed home just before the hour mark. Jason Puncheon then lashed home with less than 20 minutes remaining to earn his side a draw.

Chelsea (4-2-3-1): Cech; Azpilicueta, Cahill, David Luiz, Cole; Ramires, Lampard (c) (Torres 79); Oscar, Mata, Hazard; Ba **Unused subs:** Turnbull, Ferreira, Ivanovic, Terry, Bertrand, Marin **Booked:** David Luiz

Southampton (4-1-4-1): Boruc; Clyne, Yoshida, Hooiveld, Shaw; Cork; Puncheon, S Davis (Chaplow 66), Schneiderlin (c), Do Prado (Ramirez 73); Rodriguez (Lambert 54) **Unused subs:** K Davis, Fox, Ward-Prowse, Seaborne

Referee: Michael Oliver **Att:** 38,484

Juan Mata is congratulated on his early goal

Chelsea recorded a first home win of 2013 thanks to a lightning-quick start against Arsenal.

The Blues made light of the snowfall at Stamford Bridge to take the lead after just five minutes through Juan Mata. The Spaniard was picked out by an inch-perfect pass from Cesar Azpilicueta, showing a sublime first touch before firing a left-footed shot past Wojciech Szczesny.

The lead was doubled soon after, Mata once again instrumental as he jinked inside his man before finding Ramires in the penalty area. The Brazilian was brought down by Szczesny and the resulting penalty was converted by Frank Lampard.

Chelsea could have been further ahead by the interval but for a combination of good goalkeeping and wasteful finishing, and our nerves were tested shortly after the break as Theo Walcott cut the deficit with a clinical finish.

However, the Blues defended heroically to ensure we completed the double over Arsenal for the first time since 2009/10.

Barclays Premier League
Stamford Bridge, 20.01.13, 1.30pm

CHELSEA 2
Mata 5, Lampard 16 (pen)

ARSENAL 1
Walcott 57

Chelsea (4-2-3-1): Cech; Azpilicueta, Cahill, Ivanovic, Cole; Ramires, Lampard (c); Hazard (Marin 88), Mata, Oscar (Bertrand 71); Torres (Ba 80) **Unused subs:** Turnbull, Ferreira, Terry, Ake **Booked:** Mata, Cole

Arsenal (4-2-3-1): Szczesny; Sagna, Mertesacker, Vermaelen (c), Gibbs; Diaby (Arshavin 75), Coquelin (Ramsey 58); Walcott, Wilshere, Cazorla; Giroud **Unused subs:** Mannone, Santos, Koscielny, Jenkinson, Frimpong **Booked:** Szczesny

Referee: Martin Atkinson **Att:** 41,784

Barclays Premier League
Madejski Stadium, 30.01.13, 8pm

READING 2
Le Fondre 87, 90+4

CHELSEA 2
Mata 45+1, Lampard 65

Reading fought back from two goals down to snatch a point after a late double from Adam Le Fondre.

The Blues had dominated proceedings for all but the final five minutes, although the opening goal didn't come until virtually the last kick of the first half.

It was a strike made in Spain, with the finishing touch being applied by Juan Mata for his ninth league goal of the campaign. The playmaker clipped the ball to Fernando Torres, who played a superb return pass for his fellow countryman to fire home.

The second half began with Chelsea in control and we extended the

advantage through Frank Lampard's emphatic header from Mata's left-wing corner.

Oscar was then denied by Adam Federici – and Reading took advantage by pulling a goal back through Le Fondre. There was then a sense of deja vu about the equaliser, as another Federici save was followed up by another Le Fondre goal.

Reading (4-1-4-1): Federici; Kelly, Pearce, Mariappa, Harte; Leigertwood; Kebe, Karacan (Akpan 76), Guthrie (McCleary 58), McAnuff (c) (Le Fondre 66); Pogrebnyak **Unused subs:** Taylor, Shorey, Morrison, Robson-Kanu **Booked:** McAnuff

Chelsea (4-2-3-1): Turnbull; Azpilicueta, Cahill, Ivanovic, Cole; Ramires, Lampard (c); Oscar, Mata (Benayoun 76), Bertrand; Torres (Ba 90+2) **Unused subs:** Hilario, Ferreira, Terry, Ake, Marin **Booked:** Ramires, Azpilicueta

Referee: Mark Halsey **Att:** 24,097

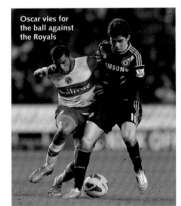

Oscar vies for the ball against the Royals

A focused Fernando Torres keeps an eye on the ball

Barclays Premier League
St James' Park, 02.02.13, 3pm

NEWCASTLE UNITED 3
Gutierrez 40, Sissoko 67, 89

CHELSEA 2
Lampard 54, Mata 61

Stunning goals from Frank Lampard and Juan Mata weren't enough to maintain Chelsea's fine record at Newcastle United.

The Blues hadn't lost on Tyneside since 2006, but that was under threat in the first half as the home side went ahead shortly after Demba Ba had almost netted against his former club.

The Senegalese striker was, however, caught in the face by Fabricio Coloccini's boot in attempting to score and he returned to the pitch just in time to see Jonas Gutierrez glance home.

Chelsea's response after the break was swift, as Lampard controlled a throw-in before smashing a shot past Tim Krul.

The turnaround was complete just past the hour as Mata curled home an exquisite effort from Fernando Torres' lay-off.

It proved to be a short-lived lead, as Moussa Sissoko bagged his first United goal on the break, before doubling his tally late on to condemn the Blues to defeat.

Newcastle United (4-2-3-1): Krul; Debuchy, S Taylor, Coloccini (c), Santon; Perch, Cabaye; Gutierrez; Sissoko (Yanga-Mbiwa 90+2), Gouffran (Marveaux 84); Cisse
Unused subs: Elliot, Anita, Bigirimana, Obertan, Shola Ameobi
Booked: Perch, Cisse

Chelsea (4-2-3-1): Cech; Ivanovic, Cahill, Terry (c), Cole; Ramires, Lampard; Oscar, Mata, Bertrand; Ba (Torres 42) **Unused subs:** Turnbull, Ferreira, Azpilicueta, Ake, Benayoun, Marin
Booked: Ramires, Cole, Oscar

Referee: Howard Webb **Att:** 52,314

Barclays Premier League
Stamford Bridge, 09.02.13, 3pm

CHELSEA 4
Ramires 23, Hazard 55, Lampard 86, Marin 90+1

WIGAN ATHLETIC 1
Maloney 57

Chelsea got back to winning ways in the Barclays Premier League with a 4-1 victory over Wigan Athletic.

The Blues were boosted by the return of Eden Hazard and David Luiz, with the latter's deployment in central midfield allowing Ramires to move to the right-hand side – and it was from this position that our No7 opened the scoring.

Fernando Torres was the provider, slotting a delightful pass through the Wigan defence for the Brazilian to slot home.

Hazard doubled the lead early in the second half, tucking home a neat finish from Cesar Azpilicueta's pull-back. However, the Latics responded almost immediately through Shaun Maloney's goal to set up a tense finale.

There was to be no comeback from the visitors, though, as Hazard teed up Frank Lampard for a trademark strike

Marko Marin celebrates his first Chelsea goal

from the edge of the box which put the game out of Wigan's reach. There was still time for Marko Marin to get his first-ever Chelsea goal, though, as he executed a perfect diving header, turning in the rebound after Azpilicueta's powerful drive was stopped by Ali Al Habsi.

Chelsea (4-2-3-1): Cech; Azpilicueta, Cahill (Benayoun 87), Ivanovic, Cole; David Luiz, Lampard (c); Ramires, Oscar (Mata 77), Hazard (Marin 90); Torres **Unused subs:** Turnbull, Ferreira, Bertrand, Ba **Booked:** Marin

Wigan Athletic (3-5-2): Al Habsi; Scharner, Caldwell (c), Figueroa; Stam (Jones 82), McArthur, McCarthy, Espinoza (Kone 58), Beausejour; Di Santo, Maloney **Unused subs:** Robles, Golobart, Gomez, McManaman, Henriquez **Booked:** Scharner, Figueroa

Referee: Mike Dean **Att:** 41,562

Eden Hazard makes a break against the Citizens

and had the chance to go ahead early on when the referee pointed to the penalty spot for a foul by Joe Hart on Demba Ba. That gave Frank Lampard the opportunity to become just the second player to score 200 goals for the Blues, but Hart produced a superb save to deny him.

The momentum shifted back towards City and they went ahead courtesy of a trademark driving run by Yaya Toure, although the Ivorian's side-foot finish may not have beaten Cech without the aid of a deflection off Gary Cahill.

Rafa Benitez shuffled his pack in a bid to get back on level terms, but the game was put to bed by substitute Carlos Tevez's unstoppable drive from 25 yards.

Barclays Premier League
Etihad Stadium, 24.02.13, 1.30pm

MANCHESTER CITY 2

Y Toure 62, Tevez 85

CHELSEA 0

Chelsea slipped seven points behind second-place Manchester City in the Barclays Premier League table after falling to defeat at the Etihad Stadium.

The game only truly came to life in the second half after a goalless opening 45 minutes, although the home side were frustrated not to be ahead following a string of excellent stops by Petr Cech.

However, it was Chelsea who began the second period brightest

Manchester City (4-3-2-1): Hart; Zabaleta (c), K Toure, Nastasic, Clichy; Milner, Javi Garcia, Rodwell (Tevez 54); Silva (Lescott 90+2), Y Toure, Aguero (Nasri 90) **Unused subs:** Pantilimon, Kolarov, Sinclair, Dzeko **Booked:** Rodwell, Y Toure, Zabaleta

Chelsea (4-2-3-1): Cech; Ivanovic, Cahill, David Luiz, Cole; Mikel (Torres 81), Lampard (c); Ramires, Mata, Hazard (Oscar 68); Ba **Unused subs:** Turnbull, Azpilicueta, Terry, Bertrand **Booked:** Ramires

Referee: Andre Marriner **Att:** 47,256

Barclays Premier League
Stamford Bridge, 02.03.13, 3pm

CHELSEA 1

Ba 28

WEST BROM 0

Chelsea made it three home league wins in a row thanks to Demba Ba's close-range finish in the first half. It could have been a resounding victory for the Blues, though, had it not have been for an inspired display by West Bromwich Albion keeper Ben Foster.

At times the game appeared to be a personal duel between Oscar and the Baggies No1, Foster's numerous stops including an excellent point-blank reaction save after the Brazilian had been picked out by Ba's low centre.

However, Oscar did have a hand in the game's only goal after playing a neat short corner routine with Frank Lampard. Having worked a yard of space, the former delivered a deep

Demba Ba celebrates after getting the only goal of the game

cross that David Luiz headed back into the danger zone for Ba to tap in.

The second half once again featured Foster denying Oscar, this time from a powerful volley and then an angled strike which was arrowing towards the far corner. However, Petr Cech was also called into action, making two quality saves in as many minutes.

The Blues kept their clean sheet,

though, despite the Baggies applying some late pressure.

Chelsea (4-2-3-1): Cech; Azpilicueta, Ivanovic, David Luiz, Cole; Ramires, Lampard (c); Hazard (Moses 80), Mata (Mikel 90+4), Oscar; Ba (Torres 87) **Unused subs:** Turnbull, Cahill, Terry, Bertrand **Booked:** Hazard

West Bromwich Albion (4-2-3-1): Foster; Reid, McAuley, Olsson (c), Ridgewell; Mulumbu, Yacob (Rosenberg 82); Fortune (Odemwingie 61), Morrison, Dorrans (Thomas 70); Long **Unused subs:** Myhill, Jones, Tamas, Brown **Booked:** McAuley, Odemwingie

Referee: Kevin Friend **Att:** 41,548

Barclays Premier League
Stamford Bridge, 17.03.13, 4pm

CHELSEA 2
Lampard 18, Hazard 49

WEST HAM UNITED 0

Eden Hazard rounded off a great display with a goal of his own

Frank Lampard became just the second player to score 200 goals for Chelsea as the Blues dazzled the Stamford Bridge faithful in a 2-0 victory over West Ham United.

Our No8 opened the scoring with just 18 minutes on the clock, but his goal owed much to the good work of Eden Hazard.

Having seen his left-footed thunderbolt repelled by Jussi Jaaskelainen, the Belgian regained possession and clipped a delightful cross onto the head of Lampard, who directed a well-placed header past the keeper. How it remained 1-0 at the half-time whistle is anybody's guess, as Demba Ba, Juan Mata, Victor Moses and David Luiz all went close, the latter with a fierce left-footed volley that would have been a contender for goal of the season.

However, Hazard continued his excellent recent scoring form with another fine strike. His trickery was simply too much for West Ham to handle and an exchange of passes with Mata and a quick burst of pace gave him a shooting lane – and it was an opportunity he simply wasn't about to pass up.

Chelsea (4-2-3-1): Cech; Azpilicueta, Cahill, David Luiz (Terry 77), Cole; Ramires, Lampard (c); Hazard, Mata (Mikel 85), Moses (Oscar 69); Ba **Unused subs:** Turnbull, Ivanovic, Bertrand, Torres

West Ham United (4-5-1): Jaaskelainen; Demel, Collins (Tomkins 60), Reid (c), O'Brien; Vaz Te (C Cole 79), Collison, O'Neil, Diame (Taylor h/t), Jarvis; Carroll **Unused subs:** Spiegel, McCartney, Pogatetz, Chamakh **Booked:** Reid, Demel

Referee: Michael Oliver **Att:** 41,639

Barclays Premier League
St Mary's, 30.03.13, 3pm

SOUTHAMPTON 2
Rodriguez 23, Lambert 34

CHELSEA 1
Terry 32

John Terry puts away one of his trademark headers

A disappointing display at Southampton saw Chelsea drop out of the top three in the Barclays Premier League.

Faced with the prospect of two games in 72 hours, the Blues shuffled our pack for the trip to the South Coast, with Marko Marin among those drafted into the starting line-up.

The home side went ahead as Jay Rodriguez played a one-two with Steven Davis before sliding the ball past Petr Cech with a side-footed finish.

However, Chelsea drew level within 10 minutes courtesy of a trademark header from John Terry. Marin delivered a superb corner into the danger zone and the Blues skipper evaded his marker to deliver a powerful downward header past Artur Boruc's despairing dive.

The Saints soon responded, though, through a curling Rickie Lambert free-kick from 35 yards.

The Blues rallied in the second half, but an increase in intensity was not enough to bring about an equalising goal.

Southampton (4-2-3-1): Boruc (K Davis h/t); Clyne, Yoshida, Hooiveld, Shaw; Cork, Schneiderlin; Puncheon (Ward-Prowse 61), S Davis (Fox 84), Rodriguez; Lambert (c) **Unused subs:** Fonte, Ramirez, Forren, Do Prado **Booked:** Lambert, Schneiderlin

Chelsea (4-2-3-1): Cech; Azpilicueta, Ivanovic, Terry (c), Bertrand; Mikel (Ramires 71), Lampard; Moses, Oscar (Benayoun 75), Marin (Hazard 60); Torres **Unused subs:** Turnbull, Cole, David Luiz, Ba **Booked:** Torres

Referee: Jonathan Moss **Att:** 31,779

John Mikel Obi congratulates Branislav Ivanovic on getting Chelsea's second goal

Barclays Premier League
Stamford Bridge, 07.04.13, 3pm

CHELSEA 2
Kilgallon (og) 46, Ivanovic 54

SUNDERLAND 1
Azpilicueta (og) 45

Chelsea turned around a one-goal deficit in a scrappy match against Sunderland to seal three points.

The visitors opened the scoring on the stroke of half-time. However, the goal was actually credited to Cesar Azpilicueta, as his attempted clearance only succeeded in finding the back of the Chelsea net after John O'Shea flicked on Sebastian Larsson's corner at the near post.

Chelsea's equaliser just after the interval was also an own goal.

Fernando Torres, who replaced Demba Ba at the break, showed his marker a clean pair of heels before laying off to Oscar. Although the Brazilian's touch was heavy, the ball rebounded off Simon Mignolet into Matt Kilgallon to find the net.

There was a touch of good fortune about the winner from Branislav Ivanovic, although the defender deserves credit for his improvisation.

Sunderland's failure to clear a corner allowed David Luiz to fire in a shot, but his effort looked to be missing the target until Ivanovic flicked the ball through his legs and past Mignolet.

Chelsea (4-2-3-1): Cech (c); Azpilicueta, Ivanovic, David Luiz, Bertrand; Ramires, Mikel; Oscar, Mata (Lampard 89), Hazard (Benayoun 84); Ba (Torres h/t) **Unused subs:** Turnbull, Ferreira, Terry, Marin

Sunderland (4-4-1-1): Mignolet; Bardsley, O'Shea (c), Kilgallon, Rose; Johnson, Gardner (Colback 81), N'Diaye, Larsson (McClean 70); Sessegnon; Wickham **Unused subs:** Westwood, Mangane, Laidler, Mandron, Graham **Booked:** Gardner, Rose

Referee: Neil Swarbrick **Att:** 41,500

Barclays Premier League
Craven Cottage, 17.04.13, 8pm

FULHAM 0

CHELSEA 3
David Luiz 30, Terry 42, 71

A world-class strike from David Luiz and two goals from John Terry helped Chelsea to a convincing win over Fulham.

The Blues hadn't won at Craven Cottage since 2009, but our Brazilian centre-back set about putting that right with a stunning effort from more than 30 yards out.

It was also his first Premier League goal away from Stamford Bridge, coming on his 100th appearance for the club.

Fulham had perhaps enjoyed the better of the opening exchanges, but their hopes of winning a first west London derby since 2006 evaporated

David Luiz fires home from more than 30 yards out

when John Terry headed home twice. The first, just before half-time, came from a precise Juan Mata cross and the second, which was midway through the second half, owed much to Fernando Torres' flick-on at the near post.

Fulham (4-4-1-1): Schwarzer; Riether, Senderos, Hangeland (c), Riise (Rodallega 67); Ruiz, Karagounis (Frimpong 76), Enoh, Emanuelson; Berbatov; Petric (Frei 81) **Unused subs:** Etheridge, Richardson, Hughes, Manolev **Booked:** Ruiz, Senderos

Chelsea (4-2-3-1): Cech; Ivanovic, David Luiz, Terry (c), Bertrand; Ramires (Mikel 75), Lampard; Hazard (Oscar 68), Mata (Ba 80), Moses; Torres **Unused subs:** Turnbull, Azpilicueta, Ake, Benayoun **Booked:** Ivanovic

Referee: Mike Dean **Att:** 25,002

Oscar after opening the scoring with a header

Barclays Premier League
Anfield, 21.04.13, 4pm

LIVERPOOL 2

Sturridge 51, Suarez 90+6

CHELSEA 2

Oscar 25, Hazard 57 (pen)

Chelsea were denied victory at Anfield and a return to third place in the table by a goal deep into stoppage time.

Oscar gave us a deserved lead midway through the first half with a delightful near-post header from Juan Mata's corner.

Then, the second period was only six minutes old when substitute Daniel Sturridge found the back of the net against his former club, slotting home Luis Suarez's cross from close range.

It did not take long for Chelsea to respond, when Eden Hazard coolly stroked home from the penalty spot following Suarez's handball.

The Blues defended stoutly for the final half an hour and appeared to have done enough to earn a valuable victory, until Suarez headed a last-gasp equaliser from Sturridge's cross.

Liverpool (4-2-3-1): Reina; Johnson, Carragher, Agger, Enrique; Gerrard (c), Lucas; Downing (Shelvey 79), Henderson, Coutinho (Sturridge h/t); Suarez **Unused subs:** Jones, Coates, Skrtel, Coady, Assaidi **Booked:** Henderson, Lucas, Suarez, Carragher, Shelvey

Chelsea (4-2-3-1): Cech (c); Azpilicueta, Ivanovic, David Luiz, Bertrand; Ramires, Mikel; Hazard (Benayoun 78), Mata (Lampard 90), Oscar (Moses 83); Torres **Unused subs:** Turnbull, Ferreira, Terry, Ba **Booked:** Torres, Azpilicueta, Cech

Referee: Kevin Friend **Att:** 45,009

Barclays Premier League
Stamford Bridge, 28.04.13, 3pm

CHELSEA 2

Oscar 43, Lampard 45+1 (pen)

SWANSEA CITY 0

Frank Lampard puts away a penalty against Swansea City

Oscar and Frank Lampard were on target on the stroke of half-time as Chelsea eased past Swansea City to move back into third place in the Barclays Premier League.

The visitors were proving to be a frustrating opponent in the early stages of the contest. However, the turning point in the match came shortly before the interval, when skipper John Terry burst forward from defence to instigate a neat exchange with Frank Lampard, which saw the Blues No8 slip in Oscar for a drilled low finish into the far corner.

Things were about to get even better for Chelsea as referee Mark Clattenburg pointed to the penalty spot when a clumsy challenge went in on Juan Mata. Lampard stepped up to drill home from 12 yards, moving him up to 201 Chelsea goals – just one behind Bobby Tambling.

The margin of victory could have been greater in the second half, with Mata twice firing inches wide of the target and Demba Ba continually denied by Michel Vorm, but our first-half double was more than enough to see off the Swans.

Chelsea (4-2-3-1): Cech; Azpilicueta, Cahill, Terry (c), Cole; Ramires (Lampard 24), David Luiz; Oscar, Mata, Hazard; Ba **Unused subs:** Turnbull, Ivanovic, Bertrand, Mikel, Benayoun, Torres **Booked:** Azpilicueta

Swansea City (4-2-3-1): Vorm; Rangel, Chico, Williams (c), Davies (Taylor 81); Britton (Shechter 69), Ki Sung-Yueng; Hernandez, De Guzman, Routledge (Dyer 66); Michu **Unused subs:** Tremmel, Monk, Tiendalli, Moore **Booked:** Williams, Britton, Davies

Referee: Mark Clattenburg **Att:** 41,780

Barclays Premier League
Old Trafford, 05.05.13, 4pm

MANCHESTER UNITED 0

CHELSEA 1
Mata 86

Juan Mata crowned his great display with the only goal of the game

Chelsea struck late to earn a first victory at Old Trafford since April 2010.

Despite looking the sharper side and enjoying lengthy spells of possession in United's half, opportunities were few and far between against a dogged defence.

Oscar fashioned arguably the best of the lot when he drove at the United rearguard before unleashing a swerving low drive which Anders Lindegaard pushed onto the post.

The second period featured few chances at either end until the game's outstanding performer, Juan Mata, had the final say.

Ramires' superb challenge on Wayne Rooney kick-started a counter-attack which ended with the Brazilian back-heeling the ball for Oscar to tee up Mata.

The Spaniard's drilled finish took a touch off Phil Jones before nestling in the far corner via the post, giving us a crucial victory.

The home side finished the game with 10 men when Rafael saw red for kicking out at David Luiz.

Manchester United (4-3-3): Lindegaard; Rafael, Evans, Vidic (c), Evra; Anderson (Rooney 68), Jones, Cleverley (Buttner 68); Valencia (Hernandez 89), Van Persie, Giggs **Unused subs:** De Gea, Ferdinand, Scholes, Kagawa **Booked:** Vidic, Jones **Sent off:** Rafael (88) serious foul play

Chelsea (4-2-3-1): Cech; Azpilicueta, Ivanovic, David Luiz, Cole; Ramires, Lampard (c); Moses (Torres 76), Mata (Ake 90), Oscar; Ba **Unused subs:** Turnbull, Ferreira, Cahill, Terry, Benayoun **Booked:** David Luiz

Referee: Howard Webb
Att: 75,500

Barclays Premier League
Stamford Bridge, 08.05.13, 7.45pm

CHELSEA 2
Oscar 10, Ramires 38

TOTTENHAM HOTSPUR 2
Adebayor 26, Sigurdsson 80

Ramires slides to his knees after grabbing our second goal

Chelsea were twice pegged back by Tottenham Hotspur in a pulsating encounter at the Bridge.

It was a perfect start for the home side as Oscar took advantage of slack marking at the back post to head home after Gary Cahill had won the ball in the air from Juan Mata's corner.

The Blues were looking the more likely side to grab the game's second goal, but Spurs landed a sucker punch with their first meaningful attack.

Emmanuel Adebayor was allowed too much time and space to run the ball deep into Chelsea territory and curl an unstoppable shot past Petr Cech.

We restored our advantage before half-time through Ramires, who met a Fernando Torres slide-rule pass and toe-poked the ball past Hugo Lloris.

Further chances went begging and we were punished by substitute Gylfi Sigurdsson, who fired home after being teed up by Adebayor.

Chelsea (4-2-3-1): Cech (c); Azpilicueta, Cahill, Ivanovic, Cole; Ramires, David Luiz; Oscar (Benayoun 84), Mata, Hazard (Moses 73); Torres **Unused subs:** Turnbull, Terry, Ake, Lampard, Ba **Booked:** Ramires

Tottenham (4-2-3-1): Lloris; Walker, Dawson (c), Vertonghen, Assou-Ekotto; Huddlestone, Parker; Lennon (Sigurdsson 61), Holtby (Dempsey 70), Bale; Adebayor **Unused subs:** Friedel, Caulker, Naughton, Carroll, Defoe **Booked:** Vertonghen, Bale

Referee: Mike Dean **Att:** 41,581

Frank Lampard after breaking Chelsea's all-time scoring record

Barclays Premier League
Villa Park, 11.05.13, 12.45pm

ASTON VILLA 1
Benteke 14

CHELSEA 2
Lampard 60, 88

A Frank Lampard brace gave Chelsea a hard-fought victory over Aston Villa and saw the midfielder set a new all-time goalscoring record for the Blues.

However, it was the home side who took the lead early on thanks to Christian Benteke's near-post finish after a powerful run.

The game would turn on two red cards either side of half-time, though. Firstly, Ramires was dismissed for a second bookable offence and, then,

Benteke was condemned to the same fate. Just moments after Benteke walked, Chelsea were back on level terms through a Lampard goal. All the Blues No8 required was a yard of space on the edge of the box and, once he got it, a piledriver of a left-footed drive beat Brad Guzan.

Although Gary Cahill and Demba Ba were denied a winner after a goalmouth scramble, Lampard later took advantage of good work by Eden Hazard to tap in his 203rd Blues goal,

which also all but sealed our spot in the Champions League, barring a 16-goal swing with Spurs on the final day of the season.

Aston Villa (4-3-3): Guzan; Lichaj, Vlaar (c), Baker, Bennett; Sylla, Westwood, Delph; Weimann, Benteke, Agbonlahor **Unused subs:** Given, Gardner, N'Zogbia, Williams, Holman, Bent, Bowery **Booked:** Baker **Sent off:** Benteke (58) two yellows

Chelsea (4-2-3-1): Cech; Azpilicueta, Cahill, Terry (c) (Ivanovic 76), Cole; Ramires, Lampard; Moses (David Luiz h/t), Mata, Hazard; Ba (Torres 87) **Unused subs:** Turnbull, Ake, Benayoun, Oscar **Booked:** Terry, Lampard **Sent off:** Ramires (44) two yellows

Referee: Lee Mason **Att:** 42,084

Barclays Premier League,
Stamford Bridge, 19.05.13, 4pm

CHELSEA 2
Mata 7, Torres 76

EVERTON 1
Naismith 14

Fernando Torres hit the winner in our final league game of the season

Chelsea secured third place in the Barclays Premier League with a hard-fought win over Everton thanks to goals from our two leading scorers for the 2012/13 campaign.

Juan Mata struck early on after Tim Howard could only parry Demba Ba's low drive, taking his tally for the season up to an impressive 20.

However, Steve Naismith replied for the Toffees soon after and they could have gone ahead in David Moyes' last game as manager when Darron Gibson's shot rebounded off both posts.

Instead, the winning goal came from our other Spaniard to breach the 20-goal mark for the season, Fernando Torres. It was a superb finish

with just 14 minutes remaining, as the Blues No9 smashed a first-time shot past Howard after being teed up by Victor Moses.

There was also a late cameo for Paulo Ferreira, making his final appearance for the Blues, and the Portuguese right-back addressed the fans after bringing on the Europa League trophy ahead of the traditional lap of appreciation.

Chelsea (4-2-3-1): Cech; Ivanovic, Cahill, David Luiz, Cole; Lampard (c), Ake; Oscar (Ferreira 88), Mata (Azpilicueta 82), Torres; Ba (Moses 65) **Unused subs:** Turnbull, Christensen, Benayoun, Marin **Booked:** Torres, David Luiz

Everton (4-2-3-1): Howard; Coleman, Jagielka (c), Distin, Baines; Gibson, Fellaini; Naismith (Heitinga 66), Pienaar, Mirallas; Anichebe (Jelavic 66) **Unused subs:** Mucha, Hibbert, Duffy, Oviedo, Barkley **Booked:** Fellaini, Heitinga

Referee: Anthony Taylor **Att:** 41,794

FIFA Club World Cup, semi-final,
International Stadium Yokohama, 13.12.12,
7.30pm local (10.30am UK time)

MONTERREY 1
De Nigris 90+1

CHELSEA 3
Mata 17, Torres 46, Chavez (og) 47

Juan Mata started the scoring

Chelsea cruised into the Club World Cup final with a 3-1 victory over Mexican side Monterrey in Japan.

It was a dominant display by the Blues from the off and it came as no surprise when we took the lead.

Juan Mata was in the perfect position to receive Ashley Cole's cut-back, after the England international had been played in by a majestic Oscar backheel, and slot home with his trusted left foot.

That goal took Mata level at the top of the Blues' scoring chart. However, he remained there for less than 30 minutes, as Fernando Torres made it 12 for the season in the first minute of the second half. Eden Hazard was the creator, tearing through the Monterrey back-line to square for the Spaniard, who fired home via a deflection.

A minute later, an own goal from full-back Darvin Chavez, after Mata had found himself in plenty of space in the box, made it 3-0. Aldo de Nigris did, however, pull back a consolation goal in injury time.

Monterrey (4-3-3): Orozco; Perez (Osorio 57), Mier, Basanta (c), Chavez; Ayovi, Meza (Solis 82), Cardozo; Corona, De Nigris, Delgado (Carreno 82) **Unused subs:** Dautt, Ibarra, Garcia, Lopez, Moreno, Morales, Madrigal

Chelsea (4-2-3-1): Cech (c); Azpilicueta, Cahill, Ivanovic, Cole; Mikel, David Luiz (Lampard 63); Mata (Ferreira 74), Oscar, Hazard; Torres (Moses 79) **Unused subs:** Turnbull, Hilario, Bertrand, Saville, Ramires, Marin, Piazon

Referee: Carlos Vera (Ecuador) **Att:** 36,648

FIFA Club World Cup final,
International Stadium Yokohama, 16.12.12,
7.30pm local (10.30am UK time)

CORINTHIANS 1
Guerrero 69

CHELSEA 0

Victor Moses on the ball during the final

Paolo Guerrero scored the only goal of the game as Corinthians denied us the chance of becoming Club World Cup winners in Japan.

There was little to separate the sides for much of the game, although Chelsea could argue that we had the better opportunities.

Indeed, Corinthians goalkeeper Cassio was named player of the tournament after a superb display in which he spectacularly denied Gary Cahill, Victor Moses and Fernando Torres. Then, when a chance came the way of his side, they took it with both hands, as a shot deflected off Gary Cahill and into the path of Guerrero, who directed his header past three Blues players on the line.

There was still to be late drama, though. Torres thought he had forced extra-time when he got in front of the keeper to head home, only for the offside flag to be raised.

The Blues were also reduced to 10 men when Cahill was sent off, before Juan Mata was denied an equaliser by the post.

Corinthians (4-2-3-1): Cassio; Alessandro (c), Chicao, Paulo Andre, Fabio Santos; Paulinho, Ralf; Jorge Henrique, Danilo, Emerson (Wallace 90); Guerrero (Martinez 86) **Unused subs:** Julio Cesar, Fernandes, Douglas, Polga, Arao, Edenilson, Andrade, Felipe, Giovanni, Romarinho **Booked:** Jorge Henrique

Chelsea (4-2-3-1): Cech; Ivanovic (Azpilicueta 82), Cahill, David Luiz, Cole; Lampard (c), Ramires; Moses (Oscar 72), Mata, Hazard (Marin 86); Torres **Unused subs:** Turnbull, Hilario, Ferreira, Bertrand, Saville, Mikel, Piazon **Booked:** David Luiz **Sent off:** Cahill (89) violent conduct

Referee: Cuneyt Cakir (Turkey) **Att:** 68,275

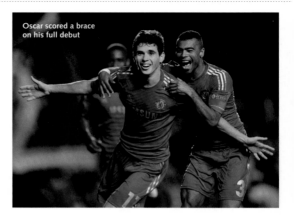

Oscar scored a brace on his full debut

UEFA Champions League, Group E,
Stamford Bridge, 19.09.12, 7.45pm

CHELSEA 2
Oscar 31, 33

JUVENTUS 2
Vidal 37, Quagliarella 80

Chelsea opened up our defence of the Champions League with a 2-2 draw against Juventus, although a superb brace from Oscar had put us on course to take all three points in this Group E tussle.

The Brazilian marked his full debut for the Blues spectacularly, scoring two goals in the space of as many first-half minutes.

His opener may have had a touch of good fortune about it, as it took a deflection off a Juventus player, but the second was a beauty.

Receiving the ball on the edge of the area, the midfielder executed a sublime turn to lose his marker before unleashing a curling effort that left keeper Gianluigi Buffon grasping at thin air. However, Juventus pulled a goal back shortly after through a low drive from Arturo Vidal.

It looked to be in vain, though, until substitute Fabio Quagliarella slipped a neat finish past Petr Cech to earn his side a share of the spoils late on.

Chelsea (4-2-3-1): Cech; Ivanovic, David Luiz, Terry (c), Cole; Mikel, Lampard; Ramires (Bertrand 68), Oscar (Mata 74), Hazard; Torres **Unused subs:** Turnbull, Azpilicueta, Cahill, Romeu, Moses **Booked:** Ramires

Juventus (3-5-2): Buffon (c); Barzagli, Bonucci, Chiellini; Lichtsteiner (Isla 76), Vidal, Pirlo, Marchisio, Asamoah; Vucinic (Matri 87), Giovinco (Quagliarella 74) **Unused subs:** Storari, Lucio, Giaccherini, Marrone **Booked:** Vidal

Referee: Pedro Proenca (Portugal) **Att:** 40,918

UEFA Champions League, Group E,
Parken (Copenhagen), 02.10.12, 7.45pm

FC NORDSJAELLAND 0

CHELSEA 4
Mata 33, 81, David Luiz 79, Ramires 88

Juan Mata slots home the opening goal in Denmark

A late flurry of goals ensured Chelsea recorded a win against FC Nordsjaelland, moving us to the top of Group E after Shakhtar Donetsk and Juventus played out a draw.

The Danish champions were playing their first-ever home game in the group stages at the stadium of FC Copenhagen and Juan Mata set Chelsea on course for victory by finishing off a slick passing move involving Fernando Torres and Frank Lampard.

Nordsjaelland rallied after the break, though, and it took a wonderful save from Petr Cech to deny Joshua John and keep us ahead going into the final stages – which proved to be most entertaining for Blues fans.

David Luiz made the victory secure with a remarkable free-kick that cannoned in via the post and Mata grabbed another goal after pouncing on a loose ball to fire home.

Ramires put the icing on the cake with his first of the season, tapping in a cross from Oscar.

FC Nordsjælland (4-2-3-1): Hansen; Parkhurst, Okore, Runje, Mtiliga; Stokholm (c), Adu; Lorentzen (Laudrup 84), Nordstrand (Ticinovic 64), John; Beckmann (Christensen 74) **Unused subs:** Villadsen, Christiansen, Gundelach, Petry **Booked:** Runje

Chelsea (4-2-3-1): Cech; Ivanovic, Cahill, David Luiz, Cole; Ramires, Lampard (c); Mata (Mikel 82), Oscar, Moses (Hazard 64); Torres **Unused subs:** Turnbull, Azpilicueta, Terry, Bertrand, Romeu

Referee: Marijo Strahonja (Croatia) **Att:** 25,120

UEFA Champions League, Group E,
Donbass Arena, 23.10.12, 7.45pm

SHAKHTAR DONETSK 2
Teixeira 3, Fernandinho 51

CHELSEA 1
Oscar 88

Ramires and Fernandinho battle for the ball

The trip to the Ukraine saw Chelsea defeated for the first time in the 2012/13 Champions League.

Shakhtar Donetsk scored with virtually their first attack as, after a couple of fortunate ricochets in the box, the ball fell for Teixeira to slot home through Ashley Cole's legs and past Petr Cech.

Chelsea were then forced into an early change when Frank Lampard, playing his 100th European game for the Blues, had to go off through injury and was replaced by Eden Hazard. However, for all our possession, the better chances were coming the way of the home side and Cech had to

be on top form to keep them out. There was little he could do to prevent Fernandinho doubling Shakhtar's advantage, though, six minutes into the second half.

Then, with two minutes remaining, Branislav Ivanovic surged down the right and sent a low pass towards Hazard, who stepped over the ball to allow Oscar a simple finish.

Shakhtar Donetsk (4-2-3-1): Pyatov; Srna (c), Kucher, Rakitskiy, Rat; Fernandinho, Hubschman; Teixeira (Ilsinho 82), Mkhitaryan, Willian (Costa 87); Luiz Adriano **Unused subs:** Kanibolotskiy, Kryvtsov, Stepanenko, Gai, Eduardo **Booked:** Kucher, Hubschman

Chelsea (4-2-3-1): Cech; Ivanovic, David Luiz, Terry (c) Cole; Mikel, Lampard (Hazard 17); Ramires, Oscar, Mata; Torres (Sturridge 70) **Unused subs:** Turnbull, Azpilicueta, Cahill, Bertrand, Romeu **Booked:** Cole, David Luiz

Referee: Damir Skomina (Slovenia) **Att:** 51,435

UEFA Champions League, Group E,
Stamford Bridge, 07.11.12, 7.45pm

CHELSEA 3
Torres 5, Oscar 39, Moses 90+3

SHAKHTAR DONETSK 2
Willian 8, 47

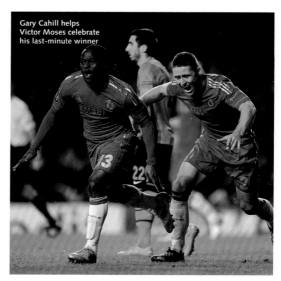

Gary Cahill helps Victor Moses celebrate his last-minute winner

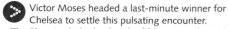

Victor Moses headed a last-minute winner for Chelsea to settle this pulsating encounter.

The Blues took the lead in the fifth minute through a defensive error by the Ukranian side. Keeper Andriy Pyatov was sold a little short with a back pass and his attempted clearance cannoned off Fernando Torres and into the back of the net.

The lead was short-lived, though, as Fernandinho picked out Willian for a composed finish past Petr Cech. However, Chelsea were ahead again before half-time, Oscar taking the keeper's headed clearance on his chest and then curling home a great half-volley from the best part of 45 yards.

Shakhtar drew level again just after the break with a goal that was almost identical to their first. However, substitute Moses met Juan Mata's corner with a powerful header to hand us a dramatic victory with the last kick of the game.

Chelsea (4-3-3): Cech (c); Ivanovic, Cahill, David Luiz, Bertrand; Oscar (Moses 80), Mikel, Ramires; Mata, Torres (Sturridge 89), Hazard **Unused subs:** Turnbull, Terry, Azpilicueta, Romeu, Marin **Booked:** David Luiz

Shakhtar Donetsk (4-2-3-1): Pyatov; Srna (c), Kucher, Rakitskiy, Rat; Fernandinho, Hubschman; Teixeira (Ilsinho 77), Mkhitaryan, Willian; Luiz Adriano **Unused subs:** Kanibolotskiy, Shevchuk, Chygrynskiy, Stepanenko, Douglas Costa, Eduardo **Booked:** Teixeira

Referee: Carlos Velasco Carballo (Spain) **Att:** 41,067

Juan Mata shields the ball from Andrea Barzagli

UEFA Champions League, Group E, Juventus Stadium, 20.11.12, 7.45pm

JUVENTUS 3
Quagliarella 37, Vidal 61, Giovinco 90

CHELSEA 0

The Blues suffered a 3-0 defeat against Juventus in what proved to be Roberto Di Matteo's final game as Chelsea manager.

We did have an early chance to seize the initiative when Eden Hazard went one-on-one with Gigi Buffon, only for the custodian to keep it out with his leg.

Juve went ahead shortly before the interval, Fabio Quagliarella diverting Andrea Pirlo's shot past Petr Cech. It was cruel on our No1, who had been exceptional throughout the opening period.

A deflection proved to be our undoing for the second goal, too, as Cech looked to have Arturo Vidal's shot covered, only for the ball to cannon off Ramires and into the opposite corner.

The defeat was confirmed in the final minute when substitute Sebastian Giovinco ran clear and slipped the ball underneath Cech.

To qualify for the knockout phase of the competition from this point, Chelsea would require a win at home to Nordsjaelland and hope Shakhtar Donetsk did the same against Juventus.

Juventus (3-5-2): Buffon (c); Barzagli, Bonucci, Chiellini, Lichtsteiner (Caceres 67), Vidal, Pirlo, Marchisio, Asamoah; Quagliarella (Pogba 89), Vucinic (Giovinco 82) **Unused subs:** Storari, Pepe, Giaccherini, Matri **Booked:** Bonucci, Marchisio, Giovinco

Chelsea (4-2-3-1): Cech (c); Ivanovic, Cahill, David Luiz, Cole; Mikel (Torres 70), Ramires; Azpilicueta (Moses 59), Oscar, Mata; Hazard **Unused subs:** Turnbull, Bertrand, Romeu, Marin, Piazon **Booked:** Ramires

Referee: Cuneyt Cakir (Turkey) **Att:** 39,670

UEFA Champions League, Group E, Stamford Bridge, 05.12.12, 7.45pm

CHELSEA 6
David Luiz 38 (pen), Torres 45+1, 56, Cahill 50, Mata 63, Oscar 70

FC NORDSJAELLAND 1
John 46

Chelsea recorded our biggest-ever Champions League win, but it wasn't enough to keep us in the competition.

The Blues were indebted to a Petr Cech penalty save to keep it goalless early on, though. There was a saved spot-kick up the other end, too, as Eden Hazard was denied by Jesper Hansen, while a third attempt from 12 yards after another Nordsjaelland handball allowed David Luiz to score.

The lead was doubled before half-time courtesy of Fernando Torres, but the visitors struck immediately after the interval thanks to Joshua John's smart finish.

That proved to be the start of a goal-filled half, as Gary Cahill directed home a superb header and then Torres was the recipient of a run and assist from Eden Hazard.

Juan Mata got the goal his performance deserved after a quick exchange of passes and he then teed up Oscar, who also found the net. However, a win in Donetsk for

FINAL STANDINGS
UEFA CHAMPIONS LEAGUE GROUP E

	P	W	D	L	F	A	PTS
Juventus	6	3	3	0	12	4	12
Shakhtar Donetsk	6	3	1	2	12	8	10
Chelsea	6	3	1	2	16	10	10
Nordsjaelland	6	0	1	5	4	22	1

Fernando Torres gets our second goal in a record-breaking game

Juventus in the other Group E match saw the Blues go into the Europa League.

Chelsea (4-2-3-1): Cech (c); Ivanovic, Cahill, David Luiz, Cole (Bertrand 60); Ramires (Oscar 64), Romeu; Moses, Mata (Ferreira 74), Hazard; Torres **Unused subs:** Turnbull, Azpilicueta, Mikel, Marin **Booked:** David Luiz

FC Nordsjaelland (4-2-3-1): Hansen; Ticinovic (Issah 64), Parkhurst, Runje (Beckmann 9), Mtiliga; Stokholm (c), Adu; Gundelach, Christiansen (Kildentoft 60), John; Lorentzen **Unused subs:** Jensen, Maxso, Laudrup, Lindberg **Booked:** Christiansen, Parkhurst, Mtiliga

Referee: Bas Nijhuis (Netherlands) **Att:** 40,084

UEFA Europa League, round of 32, first leg,
Stadion Letna, 14.02.13, 6pm

SPARTA PRAGUE 0

CHELSEA 1
Oscar 82

Oscar found the net after just 33 seconds on the pitch

Oscar came off the bench to score the only goal of the game as Chelsea defeated Sparta Prague in the first leg of our Europa League round of 32 tie.

Our opponents from the Czech capital proved to be a well-organised unit and it took until the final 10 minutes for the breakthrough to be made.

That outcome seemed far from likely in the early stages, as interim manager Rafael Benitez's side threatened to run riot after fashioning a series of chances. However, an open and engaging start soon gave way to a slow-paced tie in which neither side was able to show their best attacking play.

That is, until Oscar's introduction in place of Juan Mata. The Brazilian was on the field for just 33 seconds when he produced a moment of magic. Having exchanged passes with Eden Hazard, he danced past the challenge of one defender before confidently slotting past the goalkeeper.

It was Oscar's sixth European goal of his maiden campaign with the Blues and it put us in good shape to book a place in the last 16, where we would face the winners of the tie between Ajax and Steaua Bucharest.

Sparta Prague (4-3-3): Vaclik; Zapotocny, Svejdik, Holek, Hybs; Husbauer (Bednar 84), Vacha, Matejovsky (c); Kadlec, Lafata (Kweuke 75), Krejci (Pamic 81)
Unused subs: M Cech, Vidlicka, Polom, Janos
Booked: Husbauer

Chelsea (4-2-3-1): Cech; Azpilicueta, Cahill, Ivanovic, Bertrand; Ramires, Lampard (c); Hazard, Mata (Oscar 81), Marin (Benayoun 67); Torres
Unused subs: Turnbull, Cole, Ferreira, Terry, Ake
Booked: Cahill

Referee: Daniele Orsato (Italy) **Att:** 18,952

UEFA Europa League, round of 32, second leg,
Stamford Bridge, 21.02.13, 8.05pm

CHELSEA 1
Hazard 90+1

SPARTA PRAGUE 1
Lafata 16

Chelsea win 2-1 on aggregate

Eden Hazard unleashes his injury-time winner

Eden Hazard smashed home a goal with the last kick of the game to send Chelsea into the last 16 of the Europa League.

The Blues were defending a one-goal lead from the first leg of this tie, but that advantage was quickly wiped out through David Lafata's goal.

Chelsea could have been out of sight before the visitors struck, but a valiant rearguard effort by the Reds made life tough for us.

Ramires looked like he might put us back ahead on aggregate when he was sent clear by Oscar, but Tomas Vaclik got a touch to his shot and turned it onto the post.

The goalkeeper continued to defy our best attacks, but there was little he could do to stop Hazard netting a spectacular goal with extra-time looming.

The Belgian received the ball on the left-hand side and took on his man before sending a fierce drive past Vaclik. It earned the Blues a meeting with Steaua Bucharest after the Romanian side beat Ajax in a penalty shoot-out.

Chelsea (4-2-3-1): Cech; Azpilicueta, Cahill, Terry (c), Bertrand; Ramires, Mikel; Moses, Mata, Oscar (Hazard 67); Torres **Unused subs:** Turnbull, Cole, David Luiz, Ferreira, Marin, Benayoun **Booked:** Bertrand

Sparta Prague (4-2-3-1): Vaclik; Zapotocny, Svejdik, Holek, Hybs; Matejovsky (c), Vacha; Prikryl, Kadlec (Bednar 90+3), Krejci; Lafata (Kweuke 82) **Unused subs:** M Cech, Pamic, Vidlicka, Polom, Janos **Booked:** Lafata, Hybs, Prikryl, Matejovsky, Kwueke

Referee: Aleksandar Stavrev (Macedonia) **Att:** 38,642

Frank Lampard has a shot in Bucharest

UEFA Europa League, round of 16, first leg, National Arena, 07.03.13, 6pm

STEAUA BUCHAREST 1

Rusescu 34 (pen)

CHELSEA 0

The Blues were left having to overturn a one-goal deficit in the second leg of this Europa League last 16 tie as Steaua Bucharest emerged victorious at the National Arena.

The game's decisive moment came just past the half-hour mark when Ryan Bertrand conceded a penalty for a foul on Raul Rusescu as they challenged for an aerial ball. The Romanian top-flight's leading scorer didn't need a second invitation to smash home his penalty and give Steaua the lead.

There had been little in the way of attacking intent from the Blues until the goal but, suddenly, we came to life and a neat passing move culminated in Eden Hazard slipping in Yossi Benayoun for a shooting chance that was brilliantly turned away by Ciprian Tatarusanu.

The second half proved to be equally frustrating, with the best chance falling to Hazard after good work from Frank Lampard and Bertrand. However, when the ball bounced to the Belgian inside the box, he smashed his shot over the bar.

Steaua Bucharest (4-2-3-1): Tatarusanu; Rapa, Szukala, Chiriches, Latovlevici; Pintilii (Prepelita 57), Bourceanu (c); Popa, Chipciu, Tanase (Tatu 81); Rusescu (Gardos 90+1) **Unused subs:** Stanca, Filip, Iancu, Sobrinho. **Booked:** Pintilii

Chelsea (4-2-3-1): Cech; Ivanovic, Terry (c), David Luiz, Bertrand; Mikel, Lampard; Benayoun (Mata 64), Oscar, Hazard (Marin 74); Torres **Unused subs:** Turnbull, Ferreira, Azpilicueta, Cole, Cahill. **Booked:** Bertrand, Mikel

Referee: Sergei Karasev (Russia) **Att:** 50,016

UEFA Europa League, round of 16, second leg, Stamford Bridge, 14.03.13, 8.05pm

CHELSEA 3

Mata 33, Terry 58, Torres 71

STEAUA BUCHAREST 1

Chiriches 45

Chelsea win 3-2 on aggregate

Chelsea booked a spot in the quarter-finals of the Europa League with a stunning 3-1 victory in the second leg of our tie against Steaua Bucharest.

The visitors arrived with a one-goal lead from the first leg, but the Blues were on level terms after 33 minutes through Juan Mata, after the Spaniard was played in by Ramires.

However, our task became tougher when Steaua grabbed a crucial away goal on the stroke of half-time – meaning the Blues had to win by two clear goals to progress.

The job was half done early in the second period thanks to John Terry's bullet header from Mata's free-kick.

Then, when the Blues grabbed a third, it came as little surprise that Mata was again the architect, clipping a pass into the path of Eden Hazard, whose step-over allowed Fernando Torres space to produce a neat finish.

The Spanish striker had a late chance from the spot to put

Juan Mata puts away the opening goal of the game

the game beyond Steaua's reach, but his effort hit the top of the crossbar; it mattered little, however, as we held out to secure the win.

Chelsea (4-2-3-1): Cech; Azpilicueta, Terry (c), David Luiz, Cole; Ramires, Mikel; Oscar, Mata (Moses 90), Hazard (Benayoun 90+3); Torres **Unused subs:** Turnbull, Ferreira, Cahill, Bertrand, Lampard **Booked:** Mikel, Cole

Steaua Bucharest (4-2-3-1): Tatarusanu; Rapa (Adi Sobrinho 83), Szukala, Chiriches, Latovlevici; Pintilii, Bourceanu (c); Popa, Chipciu, Tanase (Tatu 78); Rusescu **Unused subs:** Stanca, Gardos, Filip, Prepelita, Iancu **Booked:** Bourceanu, Rapa

Referee: Stephane Lannoy (France) **Att:** 28,817

UEFA Europa League, quarter-final, first leg,
Stamford Bridge, 04.04.13, 8.05pm

CHELSEA 3
Torres 16, 69, Moses 32

RUBIN KAZAN 1
Natcho 41 (pen)

Yossi Benayoun congratulates Fernando Torres on his second goal

Fernando Torres scored twice to help Chelsea to a 3-1 victory over Rubin Kazan in the first leg of our quarter-final tie.

It was a scintillating opening against our Russian opponents. Torres got the first after controlling a superb long pass from David Luiz and, despite losing his footing, the Blues No9 somehow turned the ball past the keeper from close range.

The dominant attacking display soon got even better thanks to a stunning strike by Victor Moses, who controlled the ball with his chest on the edge of the box before unleashing a half-volley into the top corner. Rubin got back into the game shortly before the interval after John Terry was deemed to have handled a shot in the area, Natcho converting from the spot.

Our victory was made safe in the second half, though, when Juan Mata crossed for Torres to send a powerful header past the keeper for his 18th goal of the season.

Chelsea (4-2-3-1): Cech; Azpilicueta, David Luiz, Terry (c), Bertrand; Ramires, Lampard; Moses (Hazard 65), Mata (Oscar 77), Benayoun (Marin 82); Torres
Unused subs: Turnbull, Ferreira, Ivanovic, Mikel
Booked: Terry, Benayoun, Marin

Rubin Kazan (4-4-1-1): Ryzhikov; Kaleshin, Sharonov (c), Navas, Ansaldi; Kuzmin (Kasaev 82), Orbaiz, Natcho, Karadeniz; Eremenko; Dyadyun (Rondon h/t)
Unused subs: Arlauskis, Marcano, Ryazantsev, Kislyak, Tore
Booked: Orbaiz

Referee: Gianluca Rocchi (Italy)
Att: 32,994

UEFA Europa League, quarter-final, second leg,
Luzhniki Stadium, Moscow, 11.04.13, 5pm

RUBIN KAZAN 3
Marcano 50, Karadeniz 62, Natcho 74 (pen)

CHELSEA 2
Torres 4, Moses 55

Chelsea win 5-4 on aggregate

John Terry tackles Vladimir Dyadyun

Chelsea may have slipped to a 3-2 defeat against Rubin Kazan, but the Blues' excellent first-leg showing was enough to seal a 5-4 win on aggregate over the Russian side.

Fernando Torres' double had given us a 3-1 lead following the game at Stamford Bridge and the Spaniard enjoyed a perfect start in the Luzhniki Stadium as he scored a superb opening goal after just four minutes. Frank Lampard supplied the pass for the Blues No9 to lob the ball over the oncoming keeper.

Ivan Marcano gave his side a lifeline with a headed goal early in the second half, but Victor Moses quickly restored our three-goal aggregate cushion with a superb finish after a neat one-two with Ramires.

However, Gokdeniz Karadeniz headed home to make it 2-2 on the night before Bebras Natcho converted a penalty after a foul by Cesar Azpilicueta inside the area. Rubin still required two goals to progress, but they couldn't find a way past Petr Cech.

Rubin Kazan (4-2-3-1): Ryzhikov; Kuzmin (Kaleshin h/t), Navas, Marcano, Ansaldi; Natcho, Orbaiz (Dyadyun 65); Karadeniz (c), Eremenko, Kasaev (Ryazantsev 71); Rondon **Unused subs:** Arlauskis, Kislyak, Tore, Sharonov **Booked:** Marcano

Chelsea (4-1-4-1): Cech; Azpilicueta, Terry (c), David Luiz, Ferreira; Ake; Benayoun (Oscar 76), Lampard (Ivanovic 90+1), Ramires (Mikel 59), Moses; Torres **Unused subs:** Turnbull, Mata, Marin, Hazard **Booked:** Oscar

Referee: Firat Aydinus (Turkey) **Att:** 18,410

David Luiz
after curling in
a late free-kick

David Luiz scored with the last kick of the game to give Chelsea a crucial 2-1 lead in the first leg of our Europa League semi-final against Basel.

The Swiss side were formidable in this competition at their St Jakob-Park home, as they showed by eliminating Tottenham Hotspur in the previous round.

However, it was the visiting Blues who struck first, Frank Lampard's corner being headed home by Victor Moses.

Basel were handed a lifeline late in the game, though, when the referee awarded them a penalty for an alleged foul by Cesar Azpilicueta. Fabian Schar placed the resultant spot-kick past Petr Cech.

The Blues rallied and we eventually got our reward when David Luiz, a week on from his wonder strike against Fulham, curled home a free-kick at the end of stoppage time to give us the advantage ahead of next week's second leg at Stamford Bridge.

UEFA Europa League, semi-final, first leg,
St Jakob-Park, 25.04.13, 8.05pm

BASEL 1
Schar 87 (pen)

CHELSEA 2
Moses 12, David Luiz 90+4

Basel (4-3-3): Sommer; P Degen, Schär, Dragovic, Park Joo Ho; Elneny (Zoua 65), F Frei, Serey Die (Diaz 61); Salah (D Degen 78), Streller (c), Stocker **Unused subs:** Vailati, Sauro, Cabral, Steinhofer **Booked:** Dragovic, D Degen, Schar

Chelsea (4-2-3-1): Cech; Azpilicueta, Ivanovic, Terry (c), Cole; Lampard (Oscar 79), David Luiz; Ramires, Hazard (Mata 70), Moses; Torres **Unused subs:** Turnbull, Cahill, Bertrand, Mikel, Benayoun **Booked:** Cole, David Luiz, Azpilicueta

Referee: Pavel Kralovec (Czech Republic) **Att:** 36,000

UEFA Europa League, semi-final, second leg,
Stamford Bridge, 02.05.13, 8.05pm

CHELSEA 3
Torres 49, Moses 51, David Luiz 58

BASEL 1
Salah 45

Chelsea win 5-2 on aggregate

Chelsea scored three goals in nine second-half minutes to see off Basel in the second leg of our semi-final tie.

The Blues took a 2-1 lead to Stamford Bridge, but the Swiss side got themselves back on level terms on the stroke of half-time when Mohamed Salah curled a shot past Petr Cech.

However, a magnificent start to the second period put us 5-2 up on aggregate. Fernando Torres levelled on the night from close range with his 20th goal of the season before Victor Moses scored in similar fashion to give us the lead.

However, goal of the night came from David Luiz. The Brazilian curled an unstoppable shot into the top corner of the goal from 25 yards out, sending the Stamford Bridge crowd wild.

In the other semi-final, Benfica overturned a 1-0 first-leg

Victor Moses
controls the ball

defeat against Fenerbache to book their place in the final courtesy of a 3-1 win at the Stadium of Light.

Chelsea (4-2-3-1): Cech; Azpilicueta, Cahill, Ivanovic, Bertrand; David Luiz (Ake 81), Lampard (c); Ramires (Oscar 66), Hazard (Mata 74), Moses; Torres **Unused subs:** Turnbull, Ferreira, Terry, Benayoun **Booked:** Azpilicueta

Basel (4-2-3-1): Sommer; Steinhofer, Schar, Sauro, Voser; Elneny, F Frei (Diaz 74); Stocker (D Degen 61); Streller (c) (Zoua 61), Salah, Serey Die **Unused subs:** Vailati, Ajeti, Park Joo Ho, Cabral **Booked:** Schar, Steinhofer, Serey Die

Referee: Jonas Eriksson (Sweden) **Att:** 39,403

Branislav Ivanovic
heads the winner

Branislav Ivanovic scored a last-gasp winner as Chelsea became the first British side to have won all three of UEFA's major club competitions.

While Portuguese opponents Benfica enjoyed the better of the first half, it was Frank Lampard who came closest to scoring with a swerving drive that Artur did well to keep out.

Benfica did have the ball in the back of the net early in the second half, though, only for the assistant referee to flag for offside, but the first legitimate goal wasn't far away – and it came from Fernando Torres.

The Spanish striker showed great pace and strength to beat two defenders before rounding the keeper and slotting home from a tight angle.

The lead was short-lived, though, as Oscar Cardozo converted a penalty after Cesar Azpilicueta had handled in the area and extra-time looked to be on its way after Frank Lampard's late strike cannoned back off the bar.

However, the Blues won a corner in stoppage time and Juan Mata's deep set-piece was met by the head of Ivanovic, the ball looping into the far corner of the net.

UEFA Europa League final,
Amsterdam ArenA, 15.05.13, 7.45pm

BENFICA 1
Cardozo 67 (pen)

CHELSEA 2
Torres 59, Ivanovic 90+2

Benfica (4-1-3-2): Artur; Almeida, Luisao (c), Garay (Jardel 77), Melgarejo (John 65); Matic; Salvio, Perez, Gaitan; Cardozo, Rodrigo (Lima 65) **Unused subs:** Paulo Lopes, Urreta, Andre Gomes, Aimar **Booked:** Garay, Luisao

Chelsea (4-2-3-1): Cech; Azpilicueta, Cahill, Ivanovic, Cole; David Luiz, Lampard (c); Ramires, Mata, Oscar; Torres **Unused subs:** Turnbull, Ferreira, Ake, Mikel, Benayoun, Marin, Moses **Booked:** Oscar

Referee: Bjorn Kuipers (Netherlands) **Att:** 46,163

Chelsea players and staff with the Europa League trophy

WINNERS
UEFA EUROPA LEAGUE 2013

Demba Ba hit a brace on his Chelsea debut

FA Cup with Budweiser, third round
St Mary's Stadium, 05.01.13, 3pm

SOUTHAMPTON 1
Rodriguez 21

CHELSEA 5
Ba 35, 61, Moses 45+1, Ivanovic 51,
Lampard 82 (pen)

Chelsea were comfortable winners at Southampton to continue our impressive record of qualifying for the fourth round of the FA Cup in every season since 1999.

The Blues suffered an early setback when Jay Rodriguez opened the scoring. However, the lead proved to be short-lived, thanks to a debut goal from Demba Ba. The new arrival from Newcastle was in the right place at the right time to finish from close range.

Victor Moses ensured we went in at half-time 2-1 ahead when he powered home a shot from Ashley Cole's pass and the advantage was extended just after the interval through Branislav Ivanovic.

There was to be a second strike for Ba, once again from close range, after superb build-up play. Moses and Ramires were involved, but the killer pass was played by Eden Hazard from the right-hand side.

Then, Frank Lampard got the fifth from the penalty spot, which moved him level with Kerry Dixon as our second-highest scorer of all time.

Southampton (4-2-3-1): Boruc; Cork, Fonte (c) (Hooiveld 63), Yoshida, Shaw; Schneiderlin (De Ridder 54), S Davis; Puncheon (Lee 77), Ward-Prowse, Do Prado; Rodriguez **Unused subs:** K Davis, Reeves, Mayuka, Lambert
Booked: De Ridder, Ward-Prowse.

Chelsea (4-2-3-1): Turnbull; Azpilicueta, Cahill, Ivanovic (Lampard 65), Cole (c); Ramires, David Luiz; Hazard, Mata (Oscar 78), Moses (Marin 72); Ba **Unused subs:** Hilario, Ferreira, Bertrand, Torres.

Referee: Mike Dean **Att:** 27,813

A Fernando Torres goal earned us a replay

FA Cup with Budweiser, fourth round
Griffin Park, 27.01.13, 12pm

BRENTFORD 2
Trotta 42, Forrester 72 (pen)

CHELSEA 2
Oscar 55, Torres 82

Chelsea twice came from behind at Brentford to force a replay, with the winners set to face Middlesbrough in round five.

It had been 63 years since the previous west London derby between the sides and this one didn't disappoint as a frenetic encounter with twists and turns entertained a packed Griffin Park.

The Bees went ahead shortly before the break thanks to Marcello Trotta, but the Blues drew level through Oscar, the Brazilian evading two challenges with some fancy footwork before curling home a sumptuous effort.

The Blues looked the more likely side to grab a winner, but the Bees landed a sucker punch with 18 minutes remaining, winning a penalty that was expertly tucked home by Harry Forrester.

There was still time for some late drama, though, and a replay was earned through Fernando Torres, the striker curling home confidently after good work from substitute Demba Ba.

Brentford (4-5-1): Moore; Hodson, Dean, Craig, Logan; Donaldson, Forshaw (Saunders 84), Diagouraga, Douglas (c), Forrester (Barron 79); Trotta (Adeyemi 70) **Unused subs:** Lee, Dallas, Reeves, Hayes

Chelsea (4-2-3-1): Turnbull; Ivanovic (Azpilicueta 79), Cahill, Terry (c), Cole; Ramires, Lampard; Marin (Mata h/t), Oscar, Bertrand (Ba 81); Torres **Unused subs:** Hilario, Ferreira, Ake, Benayoun
Booked: Cahill, Turnbull.

Referee: Jonathan Moss **Att:** 12,146

FA Cup with Budweiser, fourth round replay,
Stamford Bridge, 17.02.13, 12pm

CHELSEA 4
Mata 54, Oscar 67, Lampard 71, Terry 81

BRENTFORD 0

John Terry got the fourth goal against the Bees

Chelsea booked an FA Cup fifth-round trip to Middlesbrough after four second-half goals finally saw off Brentford.

Just as they had done in the first meeting between the teams, the League One side proved to be a tough nut to crack and the opening period was largely a frustrating affair for the Blues with a series of near misses. Oscar went closest to breaking the deadlock when his shot came back off the woodwork.

However, just nine second-half minutes had elapsed before Rafael Benitez's side took the lead, the decisive moment coming from the boot of Juan Mata.

A long ball upfield found its way to the Spanish ace and his shot from just outside the area was perfectly placed into the far corner.

Substitute Eden Hazard and Branislav Ivanovic combined to tee up Oscar for an improvised close-range finish before Frank Lampard became our all-time leading scorer in the FA Cup with a volleyed effort from Mata's clipped centre.

There was still time for John Terry to mark his first-team comeback with a back-post header from a cross delivered by Oscar, ensuring the Blues cruised into the next round.

Chelsea (4-2-3-1): Cech; Ivanovic, Cahill, Terry (c), Cole; David Luiz, Lampard (Bertrand 80); Moses (Hazard 65), Mata (Benayoun 76), Oscar; Ba **Unused subs:** Turnbull, Azpilicueta, Ramires, Torres **Booked:** Ivanovic, David Luiz

Brentford (4-5-1): Moore; Logan, Dean, Craig, Bidwell; Forshaw (Saunders 78), Adeyemi, Diagouraga (Reeves 72), Douglas (c), Donaldson; Trotta (Forrester 55) **Unused subs:** Lee, Barron, Hodson, Hayes

Referee: Neil Swarbrick **Att:** 40,961

FA Cup with Budweiser, fifth round
Riverside Stadium, 27.02.13, 7.45pm

MIDDLESBROUGH 0

CHELSEA 2
Ramires 50, Moses 72

Victor Moses finished off a great move to secure a quarter-final spot

Second-half goals from Fernando Torres and Victor Moses secured a 2-0 win over Middlesbrough to continue our progress in the FA Cup.

The match also saw a first senior start for youngster Nathan Ake, who lined up at the base of the midfield alongside Ramires and put in an assured display.

It was the Brazilian, however, who would have a crucial role to play in the game's opening goal, which came after a first half offering little by way of entertainment or goalmouth activity.

Just five minutes into the second period, Ramires struck a peach of a shot past keeper Jason Steele. His effort had slightly deflected off the back of Torres, but the goal was awarded to the Brazilian by the club's management team.

Victor Moses then got the game-clinching goal after a slick move left Boro's defenders chasing shadows.

Substitute Eden Hazard showed his marker a clean pair of heels before exchanging passes with Oscar and, with Steele committed, the Belgian squared for Moses to tap in. It secured a quarter-final tie against Manchester United the following Sunday.

Middlesbrough (4-4-2): Steele; Bailey, Bikey (Hines 35), McManus, Friend; Haroun, R Williams (c), Leadbitter, Carayol (Zemmama 73); Main (Miller 62), McDonald **Unused subs:** Leutwiler, Emnes, Ledesma, Smallwood **Booked:** McManus, Bailey

Chelsea (4-2-3-1): Cech; Ferreira, Ivanovic, Terry (c), Bertrand; Ramires, Ake; Moses (David Luiz 75), Oscar (Marin 79), Benayoun (Hazard 58); Torres **Unused subs:** Turnbull, Cole, Lampard, Ba

Referee: Martin Atkinson **Att:** 27,856

Ramires puts away our second

FA Cup with Budweiser, quarter-final
Old Trafford, 10.03.13, 4.30pm

MANCHESTER UNITED 2
Hernandez 4, Rooney 10

CHELSEA 2
Hazard 58, Ramires 67

Eden Hazard and Ramires struck second-half goals as Chelsea fought back against Manchester United to keep our FA Cup defence alive.

Only 10 minutes had elapsed when Javier Hernandez's looping header was swiftly followed up by a Wayne Rooney free-kick.

However, the introduction of Hazard and John Mikel Obi early in the second half proved to be the catalyst for the comeback. Just six minutes after entering the fray, the former's brilliant right-footed curler saw the ball find the net.

Just as in the first half, one goal quickly became two, Ramires applying the finishing touch to a swift counter-attack with a neat drag-back before slotting home with his left foot. Juan Mata almost won it for the Blues after he took the ball out of the sky with one touch and teed himself up for a curled finish, but David de Gea's outstretched boot kept it out.

It meant the two sides would go to Stamford Bridge to battle for the chance to take on Manchester City in the semi-finals.

Manchester United (4-4-2): De Gea; Rafael, Ferdinand, Evans, Evra (c); Nani (Valencia 45+1), Carrick, Cleverley, Kagawa (Welbeck 75); Rooney, Hernandez (Van Persie 62) **Unused subs:** Amos, Vidic, Anderson, Young

Chelsea (4-2-3-1): Cech; Azpilicueta, Cahill, David Luiz, Cole; Ramires, Lampard (c) (Mikel 52); Moses (Hazard 52), Mata, Oscar, Ba (Torres 77) **Unused subs:** Turnbull, Terry, Ivanovic, Bertrand **Booked:** Azpilicueta, David Luiz, Hazard

Referee: Howard Webb
Att: 75,196

Demba Ba's spectacular finish against Manchester United

FA Cup with Budweiser, quarter-final replay
Stamford Bridge, 01.04.13, 12.30pm

CHELSEA 1
Ba 48

MANCHESTER UNITED 0

Demba Ba scored a breathtaking volley to seal Chelsea's progress to the last four of the FA Cup.

Quality football was at a premium in the opening half at the Bridge, though, and it took a moment of brilliance from Ba to bring the game to life.

Shortly after the interval, Juan Mata found himself with time and space to pick out a sumptuous pass over the shoulder of our Senegalese striker. The weight of the ball was perfect, but it still required a spectacular finish from Ba to loop it over David de Gea and into the net.

Brilliance wasn't restricted to the attacking third, though, as Petr Cech made a remarkable save to deny Javier Hernandez. Danny Welbeck's whipped cross found the Mexican striker completely unmarked, but his diving header was diverted over the bar by Cech's outstretched left hand.

That was as good as it got for the visitors, as Chelsea looked the more likely side to score again, but the 1-0 victory sealed a return to Wembley for a meeting with Manchester City.

Chelsea (4-2-3-1): Cech (c); Azpilicueta, Ivanovic, David Luiz, Cole (Bertrand 21); Ramires, Mikel; Oscar (Moses 90+1), Mata, Hazard; Ba (Torres 90+3) **Unused subs:** Turnbull, Terry, Lampard, Benayoun **Booked:** Bertrand, Azpilicueta, Mata, Oscar

Manchester United (4-4-1-1): De Gea; Valencia, Smalling, Ferdinand, Evra (c); Nani (Giggs 65), Jones, Carrick, Cleverley (Van Persie 60); Welbeck (Young 79); Hernandez **Unused subs:** Lindegaard, Vermijl, Powell, Kagawa **Booked:** Cleverley

Referee: Phil Dowd **Att:** 40,704

FA Cup with Budweiser, semi-final
Wembley Stadium, 14.04.13, 4pm

CHELSEA 1
Ba 66

MANCHESTER CITY 2
Nasri 34, Aguero 47

Chelsea saw our defence of the FA Cup come to an end at the semi-final stage against Manchester City.

The Blues were two goals down shortly after the half-time interval, Samir Nasri's fortuitous goal before the break followed up by a header from Sergio Aguero.

However, a spirited fightback began with Demba Ba scoring a spectacular goal that was reminiscent of his effort against Manchester United in the sixth-round replay.

What followed was complete dominance by the Blues and we were unfortunate not to equalise when Costel Pantilimon pulled off a superb reflex save to deny Ba a second. Referee Chris Foy turned away calls from

Branislav Ivanovic holds off Samir Nasri

Fernando Torres for a penalty after the striker felt he was held back by Vincent Kompany in the box, and with it went our chances of winning consecutive FA Cups.

Chelsea (4-2-3-1): Cech (c); Azpilicueta, Ivanovic, David Luiz, Bertrand; Ramires, Mikel (Torres 65); Hazard, Mata, Oscar; Ba **Unused subs:** Turnbull, Terry, Ake, Lampard, Benayoun, Moses **Booked:** Ramires, Torres

Manchester City (4-4-2): Pantilimon; Zabaleta, Kompany (c), Nastasic, Clichy; Milner, Y Toure, Barry, Nasri (Lescott 86); Tevez (Javi Garcia 72), Aguero **Unused subs:** Hart, Kolarov, K Toure, Sinclair, Dzeko **Booked:** Barry, Y Toure, Kompany

Referee: Chris Foy **Att:** 85,621

Capital One Cup, third round
Stamford Bridge, 25.09.12, 7.45pm

CHELSEA 6
Cahill 3, Bertrand 7, Mata 17, Romeu 52 (pen), Torres 57, Moses 70

WOLVERHAMPTON WANDERERS 0

Chelsea hit Wolverhampton Wanderers for six in the Capital One Cup to cruise into the fourth round of the competition.

The Blues dominated our Championship opponents from the start and two quick-fire goals from Gary Cahill and Ryan Bertrand – the latter a smart finish from Lucas Piazon's assist – put us in control.

The goal of the match came after 17 minutes, when Juan Mata's pass into Fernando Torres was superbly turned around the corner by the Blues No9 for a crisp finish by 2011/12's Chelsea Player of the Year.

After the break, Oriol Romeu – who had turned 21 the previous day – stepped up to confidently slot home a penalty after Victor Moses was felled by Dorus de Vries, while a powerful header from Torres gave him the goal his performance deserved. The icing on the

Ryan Bertrand was among the scorers in the rout

cake came from Moses, who marked his full debut for Chelsea with an excellent header from a precise Oscar cross.

Chelsea (4-2-3-1): Turnbull; Azpilicueta, Cahill, Terry (c), Bertrand; Romeu, Ramires (Oscar 59); Moses, Mata (Marin 69), Piazon; Torres (Hazard 78) **Unused subs:** Hilario, Ferreira, David Luiz, Mikel

Wolverhampton Wanderers (4-4-2): De Vries; Stearman, Batth, Margreitter, Zubar; Peszko (Ismail 83), Edwards (c), Davis, Hunt (Forde h/t); Sigurdarson, Boukari (Nouble 63) **Unused subs:** Ikeme, Jonsson, Price, Foley

Referee: Neil Swarbrick **Att:** 32,569

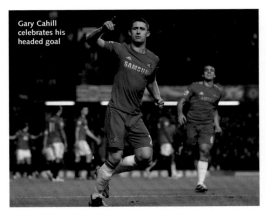

Gary Cahill celebrates his headed goal

Capital One Cup, fourth round
Stamford Bridge, 31.10.12, 7.45pm

CHELSEA 5
David Luiz 31 (pen), Cahill 52, Hazard 90+4 (pen),
Sturridge 97, Ramires 115

MANCHESTER UNITED 4
Giggs 21, 120 (pen), Hernandez 43, Nani 58

After extra-time

Chelsea won a Capital One Cup thriller against
Manchester United to progress to the quarter-finals.
David Luiz cancelled out a Ryan Giggs opener,
converting a penalty after Alex Buttner's foul on Victor
Moses. Javier Hernandez put the visitors back in front just
before half-time, but Gary Cahill replied shortly after the
interval, heading home from Juan Mata's corner.

A Nani goal appeared to have won it for United
until the referee pointed to the spot in the final minute
of stoppage time after Scott Wootton bundled Ramires
over in the penalty area. Eden Hazard sent the tie to
extra-time with the coolest of spot kicks. Daniel Sturridge
put the Blues ahead, slotting home after rounding
goalkeeper Anders Lindegaard following Wootton's
soft header. Hazard then teed up Ramires for our
fifth. Ryan Giggs scored a late penalty, but it was
the Blues who booked a spot in the quarters against
Leeds United.

Chelsea (4-2-3-1): Cech (c); Azpilicueta, Cahill, David Luiz, Bertrand; Romeu
(Oscar 71), Mikel (Ramires h/t); Moses, Mata, Piazon (Hazard 55); Sturridge **Unused subs:**
Hilario, Ferreira, Saville, Marin **Booked:** Romeu, Mikel, David Luiz, Oscar, Ramires

Manchester United (4-2-3-1): Lindegaard; Rafael, M Keane, Wootton, Buttner (Powell h/t);
Fletcher, Giggs (c); Nani, Anderson (Tunnicliffe 81), Welbeck (Macheda 98); Hernandez
Unused subs: Johnstone, Lingard, Vermijl, Brady **Booked:** Wootton, Nani, M Keane, Giggs

Referee: Lee Mason **Att:** 41,126

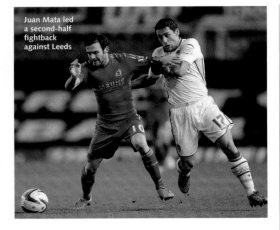

Juan Mata led a second-half fightback against Leeds

Capital One Cup, quarter-final
Elland Road, 19.12.12, 7.45pm

LEEDS UNITED 1
Becchio 36

CHELSEA 5
Mata 46, Ivanovic 64, Moses 66,
Hazard 80, Torres 83

An inspired second-half performance against Leeds
United secured Chelsea's spot in the League Cup
semi-finals.

The Blues went behind when Luciano Becchio finished
off a counter-attack.

However, we emerged from the half-time break with
renewed confidence and an early Juan Mata goal got
the ball rolling for a highly impressive performance in the
second period.

Branislav Ivanovic became our 11th different scorer in
the 2012/13 Capital One Cup when he headed home
from a corner, before the lead was consolidated by a
powerful drive from Victor Moses.

Substitute Eden Hazard had helped to inspire the
turnaround, so it was fitting that he should get a
goal, taking advantage of a superb through ball by
David Luiz to comfortably finish.

The Belgian turned provider soon after, setting up
Fernando Torres for our fifth goal of the evening.

Leeds United (4-4-2): Ashdown; Byram, Lees, Pearce, Peltier (c); Green, Brown (Norris 72),
Tonge, Thomas (White 68); Becchio, Diouf (McCormack 72) **Unused subs:** Kenny, Gray,
Somma, Varney

Chelsea (4-2-3-1): Cech; Azpilicueta, Ivanovic, David Luiz, Bertrand (Cole 74); Lampard (c),
Oscar, Marin (Hazard 60); Mata (Ferreira 85); Moses; Torres **Unused subs:** Turnbull, Ake,
Saville, Piazon **Booked:** Lampard, Bertrand

Referee: Andre Marriner **Att:** 33,816

Cesar Azpilicueta goes for the ball against Swansea City

Capital One Cup, semi-final, first leg
Stamford Bridge, 09.01.13, 7.45pm

CHELSEA 0
SWANSEA CITY 2
Michu 38, Graham 90+1

Chelsea were left having to overturn a two-goal deficit in the second leg of our Capital One Cup semi-final tie with Swansea City.

The Blues lined up with an attacking side and dominated possession throughout the game. However, chances were not taken, although credit must also go to Swans keeper Gerhard Tremmel, who was in excellent form.

The German shot-stopper kept out first-half efforts from Ramires and Juan Mata, while Michu then delivered

a sucker punch to the Blues seven minutes before the interval. Branislav Ivanovic was caught in possession and the Spaniard didn't need a second invitation to curl an effort past Ross Turnbull.

The Serbian defender almost made up for his mistake with a vicious drive that Tremmel did well to keep out, and the keeper was at it again in the second half with a good stop from David Luiz.

Substitute Demba Ba came close with two headers, but a slip-up by Ivanovic allowed Danny Graham to score during stoppage time.

There was still time for Ba to slot home what would have been a crucial goal, but it was deemed offside.

Chelsea (4-2-3-1): Turnbull; Azpilicueta, Cahill, Ivanovic, Cole (c); Ramires (Lampard 70), David Luiz; Oscar (Marin 82), Mata, Hazard; Torres (Ba 80) **Unused subs:** Hilario, Ferreira, Bertrand, Ake **Booked:** Ba

Swansea City (4-2-3-1): Tremmel; Rangel, Chico, Williams (c), Davies; Britton, Ki Sung-Yueng; Hernandez, De Guzman, Routledge (Tiendalli 62); Michu (Graham 83) **Unused subs:** Vorm, Monk, Agustien, Dyer, Shechter **Booked:** Hernandez, Chico

Referee: Anthony Taylor **Att:** 40,172

Capital One Cup, semi-final, second leg
Liberty Stadium, 23.01.13, 7.45pm

SWANSEA CITY 0
CHELSEA 0
(Swansea win 2-0 on aggregate)

A goalless draw was enough to see Swansea City progress to the Capital One Cup final after their 2-0 victory in the first leg.

Following a slow start to the contest, during which time Petr Cech was forced into a superb save by Michu, Chelsea looked like making inroads as the opening half progressed and Gerhard Tremmel kept out efforts from Eden Hazard and Ramires.

The best opportunity, however, fell to Demba Ba when the ball found him in the penalty area after ricocheting off two defenders. Unfortunately, the Senegalese striker couldn't find the target, so the deficit remained at two going into the half-time break.

Ba went close again when he sent a curling, low effort just past the far post, but chances were proving hard to come by.

The Blues' task got even tougher with 10 minutes

Ramires tries to find a way through in the second leg

remaining as Hazard was dismissed following an altercation with a ball boy and the game finished scoreless.

Swansea City (4-2-3-1): Tremmel; Rangel, Chico, Williams (c), Davies; Ki Sung-Yueng, Britton; Hernandez, De Guzman, Routledge (Dyer 65); Michu **Unused subs:** Vorm, Monk, Tiendalli, Lamah, Shechter, Graham

Chelsea (4-2-3-1): Cech; Azpilicueta, Cahill, Ivanovic (David Luiz 67), Cole (Bertrand 85); Ramires, Lampard (c); Hazard, Mata, Oscar (Torres 81); Ba **Unused subs:** Turnbull, Ferreira, Terry, Marin **Sent off:** Hazard (80) violent conduct

Referee: Chris Foy **Att:** 19,506

FIXTURES & RESULTS

Date	Opposition	Res	Att	Pts	Pos	Line-up
August						
Sun 12	Manchester City (CS)	VP 2-3	36,394	-	-	Cech · Ivanovic■ · D Luiz · Terry(c) · Cole · Mikel · Lampard · Ramires · Mata■
Sun 19	Wigan Athletic	A 2-0	19,738	3	4	Cech · Ivanovic 1 · D Luiz · Cole · Mikel · Lampard 1 · Mata■ · Hazard
Wed 22	Reading	H 4-2	41,733	6	1	Cech · Ivanovic 1 · Cahill 1 · Terry(c) · Cole · Mikel■ · Lampard 1 · Ramires■ · Hazard
Sat 25	Newcastle United	H 2-0	41,718	9	1	Cech(c) · Ivanovic · Cahill · D Luiz · Cole · Meireles■ · Mikel · Mata■ · Hazard
Fri 31	Atlético Madrid (USC)	M 1-4	14,312	-	-	Cech · Ivanovic · Cahill 1 · D Luiz · Cole■ · Mikel · Lampard(c) · Ramires · Mata■
September						
Sat 15	Queens Park Rangers	A 0-0	18,271	10	1	Cech · Ivanovic · D Luiz · Terry(c) · Cole · Mikel · Lampard · Ramires · Mata
Wed 19	Juventus (UCL Group E)	H 2-2	40,918	-	-	Cech · Ivanovic · D Luiz · Terry(c) · Cole · Mikel · Lampard · Ramires■ · Oscar 2■
Sat 22	Stoke City	H 1-0	41,112	13	1	Cech(c) · Ivanovic · Cahill · D Luiz · Cole 1 · Ramires · Mikel■ · Mata · Oscar
Tue 25	Wolves (COC3)	H 6-0	32,569	-	-	Turnbull · Azpilicueta · Cahill 1 · Terry(c) · Bertrand 1 · Romeu 1 · Ramires · Moses 1 · Mata 1
Sat 29	Arsenal	A 2-1	60,101	16	1	Cech · Ivanovic · D Luiz■ · Terry(c) · Cole · Mikel · Ramires · Mata 1■ · Mata 1
October						
Tue 2	FC Nordsjælland (UCL Group E)	A 4-0	25,120	-	-	Cech · Ivanovic · Cahill · D Luiz 1 · Cole · Ramires 1 · Lampard(c) · Mata 2■ · Oscar
Sat 6	Norwich City	H 4-1	41,784	19	1	Cech · Ivanovic 1■ · D Luiz · Terry(c) · Cole · Mikel■ · Lampard 1■ · Mata■ · Oscar
Sat 20	Tottenham Hotspur	A 4-2	36,060	22	1	Cech · Ivanovic · Cahill 1 · D Luiz · Cole · Mikel · Ramires · Mata 2■ · Oscar
Tue 23	Shakhtar Donetsk (UCL Group E)	A 1-2	51,435	-	-	Cech · Ivanovic · D Luiz · Terry(c) · Cole · Mikel · Lampard · Ramires · Oscar 1■
Sun 28	Manchester United	A 2-3	41,644	22	1	Cech · Ivanovic · Cahill 1 · D Luiz · Cole · Ramires 1 · Mikel · Mata 1■ · Oscar
Wed 31	Manchester United (COC4)	H 5-4*	41,126	-	-	Cech(c) · Azpilicueta · Cahill 1 · D Luiz 1 · Bertrand · Romeu · Mikel■ · Moses · Mata
November						
Sat 3	Swansea City	A 1-1	20,527	23	2	Cech(c) · Azpilicueta · Ivanovic · Cahill · Cole · Mikel · Romeu · Moses 1■ · Oscar■
Wed 7	Shakhtar Donetsk (UCL Group E)	H 3-2	41,067	-	-	Cech(c) · Ivanovic · Cahill · D Luiz · Bertrand · Oscar 1■ · Mikel · Ramires · Mata
Sun 11	Liverpool	H 1-1	41,627	24	3	Cech · Ivanovic · Terry(c) 1■ · Bertrand · Mikel · Ramires · Mata · Oscar
Sat 17	West Bromwich Albion	A 1-2	25,933	24	3	Cech(c) · Azpilicueta · Ivanovic · Cahill · Bertrand · Romeu · Mikel■ · Sturridge · Hazard
Tue 20	Juventus (UCL Group E)	A 0-3	39,670	-	-	Cech(c) · Ivanovic · Cahill · D Luiz · Cole · Mikel■ · Ramires · Azpilicueta■ · Oscar
Sun 25	Manchester City	H 0-0	41,792	25	4	Cech(c) · Azpilicueta · Ivanovic · Cahill · Cole · Mikel · Ramires · Mata · Oscar
Wed 28	Fulham	H 0-0	41,707	26	3	Cech(c) · Azpilicueta · Ivanovic · D Luiz · Cole · Ramires · Romeu · Hazard■ · Oscar
December						
Sat 1	West Ham United	A 1-3	35,005	26	3	Cech(c) · Azpilicueta · Cahill · Ivanovic · Cole · Mikel · Ramires · Moses■ · Mata 1
Wed 5	FC Nordsjælland (UCL Group E)	H 6-1	40,084	-	-	Cech(c) · Ivanovic · Cahill 1 · D Luiz 1 · Cole■ · Ramires■ · Romeu · Moses · Mata 1
Sat 8	Sunderland	H 3-1	39,273	29	3	Cech(c) · Azpilicueta · Cahill · Ivanovic · Cole · Ramires · Romeu■ · Moses■ · Mata 1
Thu 13	Monterrey (FCWC SF)	Y +3-1	36,648	-	-	Cech(c) · Azpilicueta · Cahill · Ivanovic · Cole · Mikel · D Luiz■ · Mata 1■ · Oscar
Sun 16	Corinthians (FCWC Final)	Y 0-1	68,275	-	-	Cech · Azpilicueta · Cahill■ · D Luiz · Cole · Lampard(c) · Ramires · Mata■ · Oscar
Wed 19	Leeds United (COC QF)	A 5-1	33,816	-	-	Cech · Azpilicueta · Ivanovic 1 · D Luiz · Bertrand■ · Lampard(c) · Oscar · Marin · Mata 1
Sun 23	Aston Villa	H 8-0	41,363	32	3	Cech · Azpilicueta · Cahill · Ivanovic 1 · Cole · D Luiz 1 · Lampard(c) 1■ · Moses · Mata 1
Wed 26	Norwich City	H 1-0	26,831	35	3	Cech · Azpilicueta · Cahill · Ivanovic · Cole · D Luiz · Mikel■ · Moses■ · Mata 1
Sun 30	Everton	A 2-1	39,485	38	3	Cech■ · Azpilicueta · Cahill · Ivanovic · Cole · Ramires · D Luiz · Lampard(c) 2■ · Mata 1
January						
Wed 2	Queens Park Rangers	H 0-0	41,634	38	4	Turnbull · Azpilicueta · Cahill · Ivanovic · Bertrand · D Luiz · Lampard(c)■ · Marin · Oscar
Sat 5	Southampton (FAC3)	A 5-1	27,813	-	-	Turnbull · Azpilicueta · Cahill · Ivanovic 1 · Cole(c) · Ramires · D Luiz · Hazard · Mata
Wed 9	Swansea City (COC SF 1st leg)	H 0-2	40,172	-	-	Cech · Azpilicueta · Cahill · Ivanovic · Cole■ · Ramires · D Luiz · Oscar■ · Mata
Sat 12	Stoke City	A ++4-0	27,348	41	3	Cech · Azpilicueta · Ivanovic · D Luiz · Cole · Lampard(c) 1 · Ramires · Hazard 1 · Mata
Wed 16	Southampton	H 2-2	38,484	42	3	Cech · Azpilicueta · Cahill · D Luiz · Cole · Ramires · Lampard(c)■ · Oscar · Mata
Sun 20	Arsenal	H 2-1	41,784	45	3	Cech · Ivanovic · Cahill · D Luiz · Cole · Ramires · Lampard(c) 1 · Hazard■ · Mata 1
Wed 23	Swansea City (COC4)	A 0-0•	19,506	-	-	Cech · Azpilicueta · Cahill · Ivanovic■ · Cole■ · Ramires · Lampard(c) · Hazard■ · Mata
Sun 27	Brentford (FAC4)	A 2-2	12,146	-	-	Turnbull · Ivanovic■ · Cahill · Terry(c) · Cole · Ramires · Lampard · Marin · Oscar 1
Wed 30	Reading	A 2-2	24,097	46	3	Turnbull · Azpilicueta · Cahill · Ivanovic · Cole · Ramires · Lampard(c) 1 · Oscar · Mata 1
February						
Sat 2	Newcastle United	A 2-3	52,314	46	3	Cech · Ivanovic · Cahill · Terry(c) · Cole · Ramires · Lampard 1 · Oscar · Mata 1
Sat 9	Wigan Athletic	H 4-1	41,562	49	3	Cech · Azpilicueta · Cahill■ · Ivanovic · Cole · D Luiz · Lampard(c) 1 · Ramires 1 · Oscar■
Thu 14	Sparta Prague (UEL Rd of 32 1st leg)	A 1-0	18,952	-	-	Cech · Azpilicueta · Cahill · Ivanovic · Bertrand · D Luiz · Lampard(c)■ · Hazard · Mata■
Sun 17	Brentford (FAC4 Replay)	A 4-0	40,961	-	-	Cech · Ivanovic · Cahill · Terry(c) 1 · Cole · D Luiz · Lampard 1■ · Moses · Mata 1
Thu 21	Sparta Prague (UEL Rd of 32 2nd leg)	H 1-1^	38,642	-	-	Cech · Azpilicueta · Terry(c) · Cole · Bertrand · Ramires · Mikel · Moses · Oscar
Sun 24	Manchester City	A 0-2	47,256	49	4	Cech · Ivanovic · Cahill · D Luiz · Cole · Mikel■ · Lampard(c)■ · Ramires · Oscar
Wed 27	Middlesbrough (FAC5)	A 2-0	27,856	-	-	Cech · Ferreira · Ivanovic · Terry(c) · Bertrand · Ramires 1 · Ake · Moses 1■ · Oscar
March						
Sat 2	West Bromwich Albion	H 1-0	41,548	52	4	Cech · Azpilicueta · Ivanovic · D Luiz · Cole · Ramires · Lampard(c) · Hazard · Mata■
Thu 7	Steaua Bucharest (UEL Rd of 16 1st leg)	A 0-1	50,016	-	-	Cech · Ivanovic · Terry(c) · D Luiz · Cole · Mikel · Lampard · Benayoun■ · Oscar
Sun 10	Manchester United (FAC QF)	A 2-2	75,196	-	-	Cech · Azpilicueta · Cahill · D Luiz · Cole · Ramires 1 · Lampard(c)■ · Mata · Mata
Thu 14	Steaua Bucharest (UEL Rd of 16 2nd leg)	H 3-1#	28,817	-	-	Cech · Azpilicueta · Terry(c) 1 · D Luiz · Cole · Ramires · Mikel · Oscar · Mata 1■
Sun 17	West Ham United	H 2-0	41,639	55	3	Cech · Azpilicueta · Cahill · D Luiz · Cole · Ramires · Lampard(c) 1 · Hazard 1 · Mata■
Sat 30	Southampton	A 1-2	31,779	55	4	Cech · Azpilicueta · Ivanovic · Terry(c) 1 · Bertrand · Mikel■ · Lampard · Moses · Oscar■
April						
Mon 1	Manchester United (FAC QF Replay)	H 1-0	40,704	-	-	Cech(c) · Azpilicueta · Ivanovic · D Luiz · Cole■ · Ramires · Mikel · Oscar■ · Mata
Thu 4	Rubin Kazan (UEL QF 1st leg)	H 3-1	32,994	-	-	Cech · Azpilicueta · D Luiz · Terry(c) · Bertrand · Ramires · Lampard · Moses 1■ · Mata 1
Sun 7	Sunderland	A +2-1	41,500	58	3	Cech · Azpilicueta · Ivanovic 1 · D Luiz · Bertrand · Ramires · Mikel · Oscar · Mata■
Thu 11	Rubin Kazan (UEL QF 2nd leg)	A 2-3°	18,410	-	-	Cech · Azpilicueta · Terry(c) · D Luiz · Ferreira · Ake · Benayoun · Lampard■ · Ramires
Sun 14	Manchester City (FA Cup SF)	W 1-2	85,621	-	-	Cech · Azpilicueta · Ivanovic · D Luiz · Cole · Bertrand · Ramires · Mikel■ · Hazard · Mata
Wed 17	Fulham	A 3-0	25,002	61	3	Cech · Ivanovic · D Luiz 1 · Terry(c) 2 · Cole · Ramires · Lampard · Hazard■ · Mata
Sun 21	Liverpool	A 2-2	45,009	62	4	Cech(c) · Azpilicueta · Ivanovic · D Luiz · Bertrand · Ramires · Mikel · Hazard 1■ · Mata 1
Thu 25	Basel (UEL SF 1st leg)	A 2-1	36,000	-	-	Cech · Ivanovic · Cahill · Terry(c) · Cole · Lampard■ · D Luiz 1■ · Ramires · Hazard■
Sun 28	Swansea City	H 2-0	41,780	65	3	Cech · Azpilicueta · Cahill · Cole · Ramires■ · D Luiz · Oscar 1 · Mata
May						
Thu 2	Basel (UEL SF 2nd leg)	H 3-1°°	39,403	-	-	Cech · Azpilicueta · Cahill · Ivanovic · Bertrand · D Luiz 1■ · Lampard(c) · Ramires■ · Hazard■
Sun 5	Manchester United	A 1-0	75,500	68	3	Cech · Azpilicueta · Ivanovic · D Luiz · Cole · Ramires · Lampard(c) · Moses■ · Mata 1■
Wed 8	Tottenham Hotspur	H 2-2	41,581	69	3	Cech(c) · Azpilicueta · Cahill · Ivanovic · Cole · Ramires 1■ · D Luiz · Oscar 1 · Mata
Sat 11	Aston Villa	A 2-1	42,084	72	3	Cech · Azpilicueta · Ivanovic · Terry(c)■ · Cole · Ramires■ · Lampard 2 · Moses · Mata
Wed 15	Benfica (UEL Final)	AA 2-1	46,163	-	-	Cech · Azpilicueta · Ivanovic 1 · Cole · D Luiz · Lampard(c) · Ramires · Mata
Sun 19	Everton	H 2-1	41,794	75	3	Cech · Ivanovic · Cahill · Cole · Ramires · D Luiz · Lampard(c) · Ake · Mata 1■

Chelsea score shown first. VP - Villa Park. M - Monaco. Y - Yokohama. W - Wembley. AA - Amsterdam ArenA. *After extra time. •Chelsea lost 0-2 on aggregate. ^Chelsea won 2-1 on aggregate. #Chelsea won 3-2 on aggregate. °Chelsea won 5-4 on aggregate. °°Chelsea won 5-2 on aggregate.
Own goals (4): Chavez, Monterrey (FCWC SF), Walters 2, Stoke (A), Kilgallon, Sunderland (H).

Key: Goalscorers in **Bold** ■ First sub ■ Second sub ■ Third sub ■ Yellow card ■ Red card + Own goal

Substitutes

Hazard	**Torres 1**	Cahill	**Bertrand 1**	Essien	Meireles	Sturridge	Piazon	Turnbull
Bertrand	Torres	Cahill	Ferreira	Essien	Meireles	Sturridge	Oscar	Turnbull
Mata	**Torres 1**	Bertrand	Essien	Romeu	Meireles	Sturridge	Oscar	Turnbull
Bertrand	**Torres 1**	Romeu	Essien	Lampard	Ramires	Oscar	Sturridge	Turnbull
Mata	Torres	Bertrand	Meireles	Romeu	Oscar	Moses	Sturridge	Turnbull
Bertrand	Torres	Azpilicueta	Cahill	Romeu	Oscar	Moses	Sturridge	Turnbull
Hazard	Torres	Azpilicueta	Cahill	Bertrand	Romeu	Mata	Moses	Turnbull
Hazard	Torres	Azpilicueta	Terry	Bertrand	Romeu	Lampard	Moses	Turnbull
Piazon	**Torres 1**	Ferreira	D Luiz	Mikel	Oscar	Marin	Hazard	Hilario
Hazard	**Torres 1**	Bertrand	Cahill	Azpilicueta	Romeu	Lampard	Moses	Turnbull
Moses	Torres	Terry	Bertrand	Azpilicueta	Mikel	Romeu	Hazard	Turnbull
Hazard 1	**Torres 1**	Cahill	Bertrand	Azpilicueta	Romeu	Ramires	Moses	Turnbull
Hazard	Torres	Azpilicueta	Bertrand	Romeu	Lampard	**Sturridge 1**	Moses	Turnbull
Mata	Torres	Cahill	Bertrand	Azpilicueta	Romeu	Hazard	Sturridge	Turnbull
Hazard	Torres	Bertrand	Azpilicueta	Romeu	Marin	Moses	Sturridge	Turnbull
Piazon	**Sturridge 1**	Ferreira	Saville	**Ramires 1**	Oscar	Marin	**Hazard 1**	Hilario
Hazard	Torres	Ferreira	Bertrand	Ramires	Marin	Sturridge	Piazon	Turnbull
Torres 1	Hazard	Terry	Azpilicueta	Romeu	Marin	Sturridge	**Moses 1**	Turnbull
Hazard	Torres	Cahill	Ferreira	Romeu	Marin	Sturridge	Moses	Turnbull
Moses	Torres	Ivanovic	Cole	Ramires	Oscar	Marin	Mata	Turnbull
Mata	Hazard	Bertrand	Romeu	Marin	Torres	Moses	Piazon	Turnbull
Hazard	Torres	Cahill	Ferreira	Bertrand	Romeu	Marin	Moses	Turnbull
Bertrand	Torres	Cahill	Ferreira	Mikel	Marin	Mata	Moses	Turnbull
Hazard	Torres	Ferreira	Bertrand	Romeu	Marin	Oscar	Piazon	Turnbull
Hazard	**Torres 2**	Ferreira	Azpilicueta	Bertrand	Mikel	**Oscar 1**	Marin	Turnbull
Hazard	**Torres 2**	Ferreira	Azpilicueta	Bertrand	Lampard	Oscar	Marin	Turnbull
Hazard	**Torres 1**	Ferreira	Bertrand	Lampard	Ramires	Saville	Marin	Moses	Piazon	Turnbull	Hilario
Moses 1	**Torres 1**	Azpilicueta	Ferreira	Bertrand	Mikel	Saville	Marin	Oscar	Piazon	Turnbull	Hilario
Moses 1	**Torres 1**	Cole	Ferreira	Ake	Saville	**Hazard 1**	Piazon	Hilario
Hazard 1	**Torres 1**	Ferreira	Ake	**Ramires 2**	**Oscar 1**	Marin	Piazon	Hilario
Oscar	Torres	Ferreira	Ake	Lampard	Hazard	Marin	Piazon	Turnbull
Torres	Hazard	Ferreira	Ake	Marin	Piazon	Oscar	Moses	Turnbull
Moses	Torres	Ferreira	Cole	Ramires	Hazard	Mata	Piazon	Hilario
Moses 1	**Ba 2**	Ferreira	Bertrand	**Lampard 1**	Oscar	Marin	Torres	Hilario
Hazard	Torres	Ferreira	Bertrand	Ake	Lampard	Marin	Ba	Hilario
Bertrand	Ba	Terry	Ferreira	Ake	Oscar	Marin	Torres	Turnbull
Hazard 1	**Ba 1**	Terry	Ivanovic	Ferreira	Bertrand	Marin	Torres	Turnbull
Oscar	Torres	Terry	Ferreira	Ake	Bertrand	Marin	Ba	Turnbull
Oscar	Ba	Terry	Ferreira	D Luiz	Bertrand	Marin	Torres	Turnbull
Bertrand	**Torres 1**	Azpilicueta	Ferreira	Ake	Benayoun	Mata	Ba	Hilario
Bertrand	Torres	Terry	Ferreira	Ake	Benayoun	Marin	Ba	Hilario
Bertrand	Ba	Azpilicueta	Ferreira	Ake	Benayoun	Marin	Torres	Turnbull
Hazard 1	Torres	Ferreira	Bertrand	Benayoun	**Marin 1**	Mata	Ba	Turnbull
Marin	Torres	Terry	Cole	Ferreira	Ake	Benayoun	**Oscar 1**	Turnbull
Oscar 1	Ba	Azpilicueta	Bertrand	Benayoun	Ramires	Hazard	Torres	Turnbull
Oscar	Torres	Cole	D Luiz	Ferreira	Benayoun	Marin	**Hazard 1**	Turnbull
Hazard 1	Ba	Terry	Azpilicueta	Bertrand	Moses	Oscar	Torres	Turnbull
Benayoun	Torres	Cole	D Luiz	Lampard	Marin	Hazard	Ba	Turnbull
Oscar	**Ba 1**	Terry	Cahill	Bertrand	Mikel	Moses	Torres	Turnbull
Oscar	Torres	Cole	Cahill	Azpilicueta	Ferreira	Marin	Mata	Turnbull
Oscar	Ba	Terry	Ivanovic	Bertrand	Mikel	**Hazard 1**	Torres	Turnbull
Hazard 1	**Torres 1**	Cahill	Ferreira	Bertrand	Lampard	Benayoun	Moses	Turnbull
Moses	Ba	Terry	Ivanovic	Ake	Mikel	Oscar	Torres	Turnbull
Marin	Torres	Cole	D Luiz	Benayoun	Ramires	Hazard	Ba	Turnbull
Hazard	**Ba 1**	Terry	Bertrand	Benayoun	Lampard	Moses	Torres	Turnbull
Benayoun	**Torres 2**	Ivanovic	Ferreira	Mikel	Marin	Oscar	Hazard	Turnbull
Hazard	**Ba 1**	Terry	Ferreira	Benayoun	Marin	Lampard	Oscar	Turnbull
Moses 1	**Torres 1**	Ivanovic	Mikel	Marin	Oscar	Mata	Hazard	Turnbull
Oscar	**Ba 1**	Terry	Ake	Lampard	Benayoun	Moses	Torres	Turnbull
Moses	Torres	Azpilicueta	Ake	Mikel	Benayoun	Oscar	Ba	Turnbull
Oscar 1	Torres	Terry	Ferreira	Benayoun	Lampard	Moses	Ba	Turnbull
Moses 1	Torres	Cahill	Bertrand	Mikel	Benayoun	Oscar	Mata	Turnbull
Hazard	Ba	Ivanovic	Bertrand	Mikel	Benayoun	**Lampard 1**	Torres	Turnbull
Moses 1	**Torres 1**	Terry	Ferreira	Ake	Benayoun	Oscar	Mata	Turnbull
Oscar	Ba	Terry	Cahill	Ferreira	Ake	Benayoun	Torres	Turnbull
Hazard	Torres	Terry	Ake	Benayoun	Lampard	Moses	Ba	Turnbull
Hazard	**Ba 1**	Ivanovic	Ake	D Luiz	Benayoun	Oscar	Torres	Turnbull
Oscar	**Torres 1**	Ferreira	Ake	Mikel	Benayoun	Marin	Moses	Turnbull
Torres 1	Ba	Azpilicueta	Ferreira	Christensen	Benayoun	Oscar	Moses	Turnbull

CS - FA Community Shield. USC - UEFA Super Cup. UCL - UEFA Champions League.
UEL - UEFA Europa League. COC - Capital One Cup. FAC - FA Cup. FCWC - FIFA Club World Cup.

FIRST-TEAM FRIENDLIES

Wednesday 18 July 2012,
CenturyLink Field, Seattle
SEATTLE 2 CHELSEA 4
4-2-3-1: Hilário (Blackman h/t); Chalobah (Hutchinson h/t); Ivanovic (c) (Kane 63), D Luiz (Cahill h/t), Ferreira (Saville 63); Mikel (Essien h/t); McEachran (Lampard h/t); Benayoun (Ramires h/t), E Hazard (Kakuta 63), Marin (De Bruyne h/t); Lukaku (Piazon 63)
Scorers: Lukaku (2, 43), Hazard (10), Marin (39)
Attendance: 53,309

Sunday 22 July 2012,
Yankee Stadium, New York
PSG 1 CHELSEA 1
4-2-3-1: Cech (Turnbull 62); Hutchinson (Chalobah 62), Cahill (Terry 62), D Luiz (Ivanovic h/t), Ferreira (Cole 62); Mikel (McEachran 62), Lampard (c) (Essien h/t); Kakuta (Ramires h/t), E Hazard (Malouda 62), De Bruyne (Marin h/t); Lukaku (Piazon 62)
Scorer: Piazon (82)
Attendance: 38,202

Wednesday 25 July 2012,
PPL Park, Philadelphia
MLS ALL-STARS 3 CHELSEA 2
4-2-3-1: Hilario (Turnbull h/t); Ivanovic, Cahill (Chalobah 74), Terry (c) (D Luiz h/t), Cole (Ferreira h/t); Essien (Mikel 60), Lampard (Meireles 60); Ramires (E Hazard 60), Marin (Piazon 60), Benayoun (Malouda h/t); Lukaku (De Bruyne 74)
Scorers: Terry (31), Lampard (58)
Attendance: 19,236

Saturday 28 July 2012,
Sun Life Stadium, Miami
AC MILAN 1 CHELSEA 0
4-2-3-1: Cech; Ivanovic (Hutchinson 76), D Luiz, Terry (c) (Cahill 58); Mikel, Lampard (Essien 76); Ramires (Malouda 76), Meireles (Marin h/t), E Hazard; Lukaku (Torres 58)
Attendance: 57,748

Saturday 4 August 2012, Amex Stadium
BRIGHTON 3 CHELSEA 1
4-3-3: Cech (Turnbull 64); Ivanovic, Cahill, Terry (c) (D Luiz 60), Cole; Meireles (Mikel h/t), Essien, Lampard; Ramires, Torres (Lukaku 78), E Hazard
Scorer: Lampard (34)
Attendance: 17,149

Thursday 23 May 2013,
Busch Stadium, St Louis
MAN CITY 4 CHELSEA 3
4-2-3-1: Cech (c) (Blackman 62); Ivanovic (Ferreira h/t), Cahill (D Luiz h/t), Christensen, Cole; Loftus-Cheek (Ake 80), Mikel; Azpilicueta (Ramires h/t), Mata (Oscar h/t), Benayoun (Marin 62); Ba (Torres h/t)
Scorers: Ba (14), Azpilicueta (44 pen), Oscar (53)
Attendance: 48,263

Saturday 25 May 2013,
Yankee Stadium, New York
MAN CITY 5 CHELSEA 3
4-4-2: Hilário (Cech h/t); Azpilicueta, Christensen, D Luiz (Mata 61), Ake; Ramires, Mikel, Loftus-Cheek (Ferreira 42), Oscar (Benayoun 66); Torres (c), Ba
Scorers: Ramires (46, 68), Mata (81)
Attendance: 39,462

CHELSEA FC HONOURS

Football League/ FA Premier League champions
1955, 2005, 2006, 2010
Runners-up
2004, 2007, 2008, 2011

UEFA Champions League winners
2012
Runners-up
2008

UEFA Europa League winners
2013

UEFA Super Cup winners
1998
Runners-up
2012, 2013

European Cup Winners' Cup winners
1971, 1998

FIFA Club World Cup runners-up
2012

FA Cup winners
1970, 1997, 2000, 2007, 2009, 2010, 2012
Runners-up
1915, 1967, 1994, 2002

Football League Cup winners
1965, 1998, 2005, 2007
Runners-up
1972, 2008

FA Charity/ Community Shield winners
1955, 2000, 2005, 2009
Runners-up
1970, 1997, 2006, 2007, 2010, 2012

Full Members' Cup winners
1986, 1990

Division Two champions
1984, 1989
Runners-up
1907, 1912, 1930, 1963, 1977

FA Premier Reserve League National champions
2011

FA Youth Cup winners
1960, 1961, 2010, 2012
Runners-up
1958, 2008, 2013

NextGen Series runners-up
2013

Chelsea won the Europa League for the first time in the club's history

FOUNDED

10 March 1905

RECORD HOME ATTENDANCE

82,905 v Arsenal, Division One, 12 October 1935

RECORD HOME ALL-SEATER ATTENDANCE

42,328 v Newcastle, Premier League, 4 December 2004

STAMFORD BRIDGE CAPACITY

41,623

PITCH SIZE

103 x 67 metres

THE DEVELOPMENT OF THE CURRENT STADIUM

East Stand 1974
Matthew Harding Stand 1994
Shed End 1997
West Stand 2001

PLAYER STATISTICS 2012/13

Additional appearances as substitute are in brackets.

PLAYER	APPEARANCES										GOALS/CLEAN SHEETS								
	FAPL	UCL	UEL	FAC	LC	CS	USC	FCWC	Total	Minutes	FAPL	UCL	UEL	FAC	LC	CS	USC	FCWC	Total
Ake	1(2)	0	1(1)	1	0	0	0	0	3(3)	302	0	0	0	0	0	0	0	0	0
Azpilicueta	24(3)	1	8	4(1)	5	0	0	1(1)	43(5)	4166	0	0	0	0	0	0	0	0	0
Ba	11(3)	0	0	5(1)	1(1)	0	0	0	17(5)	1503	2	0	0	4	0	0	0	0	6
Benayoun	0(6)	0	3(2)	1(1)	0	0	0	0	4(9)	417	0	0	0	0	0	0	0	0	0
Bertrand	14(5)	1(2)	5	3(2)	3(1)	0(1)	0(1)	0	26(12)	2709	0	0	0	0	1	1	0	0	2
Cahill	24(3)	4	4	4	4	0	1	2	43(2)	4203	2	1	0	0	2	0	1	0	6
Cech	36	6	9	5	3	1	1	2	63	5998	14	1	1	3	1	0	0	0	20
Cole	31	5	3	5	2(1)	1	1	2	50(1)	4674	1	0	0	0	0	0	0	0	1
Ferreira	0(2)	0(1)	1	1	0(1)	0	0	0(1)	2(5)	248	0	0	0	0	0	0	0	0	0
Hazard	31(3)	4(2)	5(2)	3(3)	2(3)	1	1	2	49(13)	4731	9	0	1	1	2	0	0	0	13
Ivanovic	33(1)	6	5(1)	6	3	1	1	2	57(2)	5278	5	0	1	1	1	0	0	0	8
Lampard	24(8)	3	7	3(1)	2(1)	1	1	1(1)	39(11)	3682	15	0	0	2	0	0	0	0	17
D Luiz	29(1)	6	7	5(1)	3(1)	1	1	2	54(3)	5206	2	2	2	0	1	0	0	0	7
Marin	2(4)	0	1(2)	1(2)	1(2)	0	0	0(1)	5(11)	446	1	0	0	0	0	0	0	0	1
Mata	31(4)	5(1)	5(3)	5(1)	5	1	1	2	55(9)	5149	12	3	1	1	2	0	0	1	20
Meireles	1(2)	0	0	0	0	0	0	0	1(2)	114	0	0	0	0	0	0	0	0	0
Mikel	19(3)	4(1)	3(1)	2(1)	1	1	1	1	32(6)	2939	0	0	0	0	0	0	0	0	0
Moses	12(11)	2(2)	5(1)	4(1)	3	0	0	1(1)	27(16)	2537	1	1	4	2	2	0	0	0	10
Oscar	24(10)	5(1)	4(5)	6(1)	3(2)	0	0(1)	1(1)	43(21)	4415	4	5	1	2	0	0	0	0	12
Piazon	0(1)	0	0	0	2	0	0	0	2(1)	169	0	0	0	0	0	0	0	0	0
Ramires	28(7)	6	8	6	3(1)	1	1	1	54(8)	5025	5	1	0	2	1	0	0	0	9
Romeu	4(2)	1	0	0	2	0	0	0	7(2)	505	0	0	0	0	1	0	0	0	1
Sturridge	1(6)	0(2)	0	0	1	0(1)	0(1)	0	2(10)	382	0	1	0	0	0	0	0	0	1
Terry	11(3)	2	6	3	1	1	0	0	24(3)	2247	4	0	1	1	0	0	0	0	6
Torres	28(8)	5(1)	9	2(3)	3(1)	1	1	2	51(13)	4934	8	3	6	1	2	1	0	1	22
Turnbull	2(1)	0	0	2	2	0	0	0	6(1)	620	0	0	0	0	1	0	0	0	1

USC - UEFA Super Cup. FCWC - FIFA Club World Cup.

The season summary

Barclays Premier League - third (qualified for the 2013/14 Champions League group stage)

Europa League - winners (qualified for the 2013/14 UEFA Super Cup against Bayern Munich)

FA Cup - semi-finalists

Capital One Cup - semi-finalists

FA Community Shield - runners-up

Champions League - group stage

UEFA Super Cup - runners-up

FIFA Club World Cup - runners-up

FA Youth Cup - runners-up

NextGen Series - runners-up

Trophies won in the 10 seasons of the Roman Abramovich era - 13

1 UEFA Champions League, 3 Premier Leagues, 1 UEFA Europa League, 4 FA Cups, 2 League Cups, 2 FA Community Shields.

Milestones of the 2012/13 season

• Club record number of games in a season - **69**

Beating the 64 set in 2006/07.

• Most Chelsea goals in a season - **147**

Beating the 142 set in 2009/10.

• 43 games to reach 100 goals

The second-equal fastest in our history (with 2009/10). The quickest we have achieved a ton was in 1960/61, when it took 40 games.

• The first English club, and fourth overall, to win all three major UEFA competitions: the Champions League, the Cup Winners' Cup and Europa League.

The other three clubs that have achieved it are Juventus, Ajax and Bayern Munich. (The Inter-Cities Fairs Cup was not organised by UEFA.)

• The first English club, and third overall, to complete the set of UEFA competitions - the three major cups plus the Super Cup.

The two other clubs are Juventus and Ajax.

• First-ever holders of the Champions League and Europa League at the same time.

(15 to 25 May 2013)

• 100th win in Europe - *Shakhtar Donetsk (h).*

• Club record Champions League win - 6-1 v FC Nordsjaelland (h).

• Highest scorers in the 2012/13 Champions League group stage - **16**.

• Equalled all-time record highest win in the league - 8-0 v Aston Villa (h).

• Equalled our record of six successive top-flight away wins in league and cup.

Previously achieved in 2004/05 (twice), 2005/06 and 2006/07 (twice)

• Competed in a club record number of different tournaments - **eight**.

Petr Cech, Ashley Cole, Eden Hazard, Branislav Ivanovic, Frank Lampard, David Luiz, Juan Mata, John Mikel Obi, Ramires and Fernando Torres played in all eight.

• Established a new FA Cup record for games unbeaten in open play - **29**.

• Most different goalscorers in a match, against Wolves (League Cup), since Burnley at home in the FA Cup in January 1978 - **six**.

That was also our 50th home win in the competition.

• We then equalled our club record seven different scorers against Aston Villa (h).

Previously achieved in 1971/72 against Jeunesse Hautcharage (h)

• The 6-0 win against Wolves was our biggest win at Stamford Bridge in the League Cup

• Record penalties awarded - **18**.

Surpassing the 16 set in 1988/89.

• Record penalties scored - **14**.

Surpassing the 13 set in 1988/89.

• Fourth occasion we have knocked a team out in both domestic cups in the same season - *Manchester United 2012/13.*

Previous occasions: Leeds (1969/70); Bolton (1971/72); Blackburn (2006/07).

• Six players have scored 10 or more goals in a season, equalling 2011/12's club record.

• This season has seen a club-record for different penalty takers - **seven**.

Takers: Hazard, Lampard, D Luiz, Oscar, Piazon, Romeu, Torres. Our previous record was six in 1984/85: Dixon, C Lee, Nevin, Spackman, Speedie, Thomas.

• Club record Chelsea goals - *Frank Lampard,* **203**.

• Frank Lampard became the first player ever to scorer 10 or more league goals in 10 consecutive Premier League seasons.

• Lampard also equalled Andy Cole's record of scoring against 38 different teams in the Premier League.

• Club all-time highest top-flight league scorer - *Frank Lampard,* **141**.

• Club all-time highest FA Cup scorer - *Frank Lampard,* **26**.

• Petr Cech has kept the most completed clean sheets for a single club in the Premier League era, beating the record previously held by Arsenal's David Seaman - **142**.

• Fernando Torres scored in a club-record number of different competitions - **seven**.

Beating Andriy Shevchenko's five in 2006/07.

• 600 Chelsea appearances - *Frank Lampard.*

The third highest all-time for Chelsea.

• 400 Chelsea appearances - *Petr Cech.*

The club's first overseas player to reach that milestone.

• 300 Chelsea appearances - *Ashley Cole.*

• 200 Chelsea appearances - *Branislav Ivanovic.*

• 100 Chelsea appearances - *David Luiz, Juan Mata, Ramires, Fernando Torres.*

• 100 Chelsea appearances in Europe - *Frank Lampard, John Terry.*

• 100 career appearances in Europe (for Chelsea and Arsenal) - *Ashley Cole.*

• 50 Chelsea goals - *John Terry.*

• 100 career international caps - *Fernando Torres, Ashley Cole, Petr Cech.*

• 26 players capped by their country – an equal club record

• Barclays Premier League Player of the Month (October): *Juan Mata.*

• Barclays Premier League Manager of the Month (April): *Rafael Benitez.*

• Juan Mata, Oscar, Fernando Torres and Petr Cech played more games for Chelsea in a season than any other in our history - **64**. Petr Cech made a record number of starts - **63**.

• 400th Premier League appearance - *Frank Lampard.*

Against Swansea (h), the first Chelsea player to do so, and the first non-Liverpool or Man Utd player to reach that milestone for one club.

• Nathan Ake became the youngest winner of the Europa League, at 18, and Frank Lampard the oldest winner, at 34.

Frank Lampard broke Bobby Tambling's goalscoring record

SEASON SUMMARY (ALL COMPETITIONS)

Played **69**, won **39**, drawn **14**, lost **16**, goals **147**, goals against **82**, clean sheets **21**, failed to score **10**

ASSISTS 149

Assists are judged not for the last touch but by the subjective view of the editor for a crucial part played in the goal.

Mata **37**, Hazard **25**, Oscar **16**, Torres **13**, Lampard **10**, Ramires **9**, Moses **7**, Azpilicueta **6**, D Luiz **6**, Cahill **4**, Cole **4**, Ivanovic **4**, Ba **2**, Piazon **2**, Marin **1**, Romeu **1**, Sturridge **1**, Terry **1**

PENALTIES WON 18

SCORED 14

Lampard **6** (Wigan a, Reading h, Southampton FAC, Stoke a, Arsenal h, Swansea PL h), Hazard **3** (Newcastle h, Man Utd LC, Liverpool h), D Luiz **2** (Man Utd LC, Nordsjaelland CL h), Oscar **1** (Aston Villa h), Romeu **1** (Wolves LC), Torres **1** (Sunderland a)

MISSED 4

Hazard **1** (Nordsjaelland CL h, saved), Lampard **1** (Man City a, saved), Piazon **1** (Aston Villa h, saved), Torres **1** (Steaua Bucharest UEL h, hit crossbar)

PENALTIES CONCEDED 9

CONCESSIONS 7

Cech **6** (Man Utd LC, Steaua Bucharest UEL a, Rubin Kazan UEL h and a, Basel UEL a, Benfica UEL), Turnbull **1** (Brentford FAC a)

SAVED 1

Cech **1** (Nordsjaelland CL h)

MISSED TARGET 1

Walters (Stoke a)

CAPTAIN 69

Terry **24**, Lampard **22**, Cech **21**, Cole **2**.

STRIKES ON WOODWORK 18

Lampard **3**, Torres **3**, Moses **2**, Oscar **2**, Ramires **2**, Hazard **1**, Ivanovic **1**, D Luiz **1**, Mata **1**, Evans (Man Utd) own post, Stokholm (Nordsjaelland) own crossbar

OPPONENTS' STRIKES ON WOODWORK 24

SENT OFF 6

Ivanovic **2** (Man City CS, serious foul play, Man Utd PL h, denying a goalscoring opportunity), Torres (Man Utd PL h, two yellows), Cahill (Corinthians, violent conduct), Hazard (Swansea LC a, violent conduct towards a ball boy), Ramires (Aston Villa a, two yellows)

OPPONENTS SENT OFF 2

Rafael (Man Utd PL a, serious foul play), Benteke (Aston Villa a, two yellows)

ABUSED 114

Incidents suffered leading to an opponent being booked or sent off

Hazard **20**, Oscar **17**, Ramires **16**, Torres **11**, Mata **10**, Moses **5**, Cole **3**, Ivanovic **3**, Azpilicueta **2**, Ba **2**, D Luiz **2**, Mikel **2**, Sturridge **2**, Terry **2**, Ake **1**, Bertrand **1**, Cech **1**, Lampard **1**, Romeu **1**, General **12**. Luis Suarez (Liverpool a) subsequently suspended for 10 games following a charge of violent conduct for biting Branislav Ivanovic using video evidence.

BOOKED 100

D Luiz **16**, Ramires **13**, Azpilicueta **8**, Cole **7**, Mikel **7**, Bertrand **6**, Ivanovic **6**, Oscar **6**, Torres **5**, Lampard **4**, Mata **4**, Cahill **3**, Hazard **3**, Marin **3**, Cech **2**, Romeu **2**, Terry **2**, Ba **1**, Benayoun **1**, Turnbull **1**

GAMES MISSED

INJURY AND ILLNESS 169

Romeu **43**, Terry **20**, Sturridge **14**, Lampard **12**, Marin **10**, Bertrand **9**, Cahill **9**, Cole **9**, Mikel **8**, D Luiz **7**, Cech **5**, Hilario **5**, Hazard **3**, Kakuta **3**, Blackman **2**, Mata **2**, Piazon **2**, Ramires **2**, Azpilicueta **1**, Benayoun **1**, Moses **1**, Turnbull **1**

SUSPENSION 19

Terry **5**, Hazard **3**, Mikel **3**, D Luiz **2**, Ramires **2**, Cahill **1**, Cole **1**, Ivanovic **1**, Torres **1**

INTERNATIONALS 21

Mikel **11**, Moses **9**, Oscar **1**

CUP TIED 9

Ba **9** (Europa League)

PERSONAL REASONS 2

Cahill **1**, Mata **1**

2012/13 INTERNATIONAL APPEARANCES BY BLUES

G - Goals CS - Clean sheets

FULL	Apps	G/CS
Azpilicueta (Spain)	3+1	0
Ba (Senegal)	1	0
Benayoun (Israel)	2+3	0
Bertrand (England)	0+2	0
Cahill (England)	6	0
Cech (Czech Rep)	7	5
Cole (England)	4+1	0
Courtois (Belgium)	8	5
De Bruyne (Belgium)	8+3	3
E Hazard (Belgium)	7+2	3(2p)
T Hazard (Belgium)	0+1	0
Ivanovic (Serbia)	9+1	1
Kalas (Czech Rep)	0+1	0
Lampard (England)	6+1	6(2p)
D Luiz (Brazil)	16	0
Lukaku (Belgium)	1+5	1
Mata (Spain)	5+5	2
Meireles (Portugal)	1	0
Mikel (Nigeria)	14	2(1p)
Moses (Nigeria)	9	4(2p)
Omeruo (Nigeria)	12+2	0
Oscar (Brazil)	16	5(1p)
Ramires (Brazil)	7	1
Sturridge (England)	0+2	0
Terry (England)	1	0
Torres (Spain)	6+2	5

UNDER-21s		
Bruma (Holland)	4+2	0
Chalobah (England)	4+3	0
Delac (Croatia)	0+1	0+1
Feruz (Scotland)	2+1	2
T Hazard (Belgium)	4+3	0
Kalas (Czech Rep)	3+1	0
Lalkovic (Slovakia)	4+3	1
McEachran (England)	3+2	1(p)
L Musonda (Belgium)	3+3	0
Romeu (Spain)	4	0
Van Aanholt (Holland)	4+2	0

UNDER-20s		
Delac (Croatia)	0+1	0+1
Muleba (DR Congo)	0+1	0
Pappoe (Ghana)	1	0
Wallace (Brazil)	2	0

UNDER-19s		
Affane (Sweden)	3+1	0
Ake (Holland)	8	3
Baker (England)	4+1	2(1p)
Chalobah (England)	5	1
Christensen (Denmark)	2	0
Davey (Scotland)	6+2	1
Feruz (Scotland)	5	3
Osmanovic (Sweden)	1+1	0
Swift (England)	2+2	0

UNDER-18s		
A Gordon (England)	0+1	0
Starkey (England)	1	0
Swift (England)	1	0

UNDER-17s		
Aina (England)	9+2	0
Christensen (Denmark)	10	3
Colkett (England)	5+2	2
Hunte (England)	1+2	0
Kiwomya (England)	6+2	1
Loftus-Cheek (England)	6+2	1
Ssewankambo (Sweden)	14+2	2(1p)

UNDER-16s		
Boga (France)	1+1	1
Christie-Davies (England)	3	0
Dasilva (England)	1	0
Mukhtar Ali (England)	1+1	0
Sammut (Scotland)	2+2	0
Scott (England)	0+1	0
Solanke (England)	3+3	1

CHELSEA STATISTICS ALL TIME

Up to and including the 2012/13 season and other than those mentioned in milestones of last season.

BIGGEST WIN BY COMPETITION

LEAGUE
8-0 v Wigan Athletic (h), 2009/10, Aston Villa (h), 2012/13

EUROPE
13-0 v Jeunesse Hautcharage (Luxembourg) (h), European Cup Winners' Cup, 1971/72

UEFA CHAMPIONS LEAGUE
6-1 v Nordsjaelland (h) 2012/13

FA CUP
9-1 v Worksop (h), 1907/08

LEAGUE CUP
7-0 v Doncaster Rovers (a), 1960/61

MOST APPEARANCES

Ron Harris **795**

MOST APPEARANCES BY COMPETITION

LEAGUE
Ron Harris **655**

LEAGUE, TOP FLIGHT
Ron Harris **550**

EUROPE
Frank Lampard **107**

FA CUP
Ron Harris **64**

LEAGUE CUP
John Hollins and Ron Harris **48**

FA COMMUNITY SHIELD
Frank Lampard **6**

MOST GOALS

Frank Lampard **203**

MOST GOALS BY COMPETITION

LEAGUE
Bobby Tambling **164**

LEAGUE, TOP FLIGHT
Frank Lampard **141**

EUROPE
Dider Drogba **34**

FA CUP
Frank Lampard **26**

LEAGUE CUP
Kerry Dixon **25**

FA COMMUNITY SHIELD
Dider Drogba **2**

MOST CLEAN SHEETS

Peter Bonetti **208**

MOST GAMES AS CAPTAIN

John Terry **445**

MOST CUP FINAL APPEARANCES

Frank Lampard **13**

MOST CUP FINAL GOALS

Didier Drogba **9**

MOST INTERNATIONAL CAPS WON AS A CHELSEA PLAYER

Frank Lampard (England) **95**

MOST INTERNATIONAL GOALS SCORED AS A CHELSEA PLAYER

Didier Drogba (Ivory Coast) **46**

MOST PENALTIES SCORED

Frank Lampard **48**

MOST PENALTIES SAVED

Reg Matthews **9**

MOST GAMES AS CHELSEA MANAGER

David Calderhead **966**

MOST TROPHIES WON (Manager)

José Mourinho **6**

MOST TROPHIES WON (Player)

John Terry **14**

MOST WINS IN A SEASON

42 in 2004/05 and 2006/07

MOST NUMBER OF POINTS

99 in 1988/89 (Old Second Division)

MOST NUMBER OF POINTS
(Top flight)

95 in 2004/05
Also an English top-flight record

MOST HAT-TRICKS

Jimmy Greaves **13**

MOST GOALS IN A SEASON

Jimmy Greaves **43** in 1960/61

YOUNGEST PLAYER

Ian Hamilton **16** years, **138** days

OLDEST PLAYER

Dick Spence **39** years, **57** days

QUICKEST RECORDED GOAL

Keith Weller **12** seconds v Middlesbrough (h) 1970/71

MOST GOALS IN A MATCH

George Hilsdon **6** v Worksop (h) 1907/08

TEAM CHELSEA HAVE PLAYED MOST GAMES AGAINST

Arsenal **179**

TEAM CHELSEA HAVE WON MOST GAMES AGAINST

Everton **65**

MOST LIVE GAMES ON BRITISH TV

45 in 2006/07

MOST LEAGUE DOUBLES

v Sunderland **13**

BEST MANAGER WIN RECORD

Guus Hiddink **72.7%**

LONGEST UNBEATEN SEQUENCE

23 games in 2006/07 and 2008/09 (14) + 2009/10 (9)

LONGEST UNBEATEN LEAGUE SEQUENCE

40 games in 2004/05 (29) + 2005/06 (11)
Third longest in English top-flight history

MOST LEAGUE GOALS IN A SEASON

103 in 2009/10
Also a Premier League record

FEWEST GOALS CONCEDED IN A SEASON

34 in 2004/05 and 2005/06

FEWEST LEAGUE GOALS CONCEDED IN A SEASON

15 in 2004/05
Also an English top-flight record

MOST CONSECUTIVE APPEARANCES

John Hollins **167** games from 14 August 1971 to 25 September 1974 (135 League, 10 FA Cup, 18 League Cup, 4 European Cup Winners' Cup)

ELEVEN INTERNATIONALS IN A STARTING TEAM

The first occasion 11 full internationals started a game was away at Coventry on 15 August 1998. This has now occurred on 381 occasions.

FIRST TO HAVE NUMBERS

Chelsea (and Arsenal) were the first British clubs to wear shirt numbers. The numbers trial was on 25 August 1928, when Chelsea beat Swansea Town 4-0 at Stamford Bridge. Arsenal lost at Hillsborough to Sheffield Wednesday.

TAKING THE NEXT STEP

It was a memorable debut term for the Under-21s as the Blues made the final of their first European campaign – the NextGen Series – and many players came into the squad from younger ranks

The 2012/13 campaign was the first in which the reserve team was replaced by an Under-21s side in an effort to bridge the gap between Academy football and senior football.

Dermot Drummy oversaw the squad in their first Under-21s Premier League season and it was from the same group – less those who were overage – that he selected his squad for the NextGen Under-19s Series, a continental competition that gave the young Blues their first taste of European tournament football.

It proved to be a memorable debut, as we made it all the way to the final, finishing runners-up to Aston Villa in Como, Italy. Most impressive of all was the list of teams we passed

to reach that final. Ajax, Barcelona and Juventus all failed to dispatch Chelsea's youngsters and notes were being taken by each of those giants of European football.

"The way the club has performed along the way has reverberated around the Academies," said Drummy at the conclusion of the series. "At Ajax, Frank de Boer was very complimentary about how the team played, as was the Juventus coach, and to have beaten Arsenal in the semi-final in the manner we did was very impressive.

"We are all proud of the boys and the culture of football within the Academy. On the way to the final, the performance against Juventus was the

best I have seen in my time in youth development, with goals that you could watch over and over again.

"Since the start of the tournament, six of our regular players went out on loan and we competed in the latter stages with a young squad of players."

The performances of the side were reflected in the awarding of Player of the Tournament to captain and midfield pivot Lewis Baker, who enjoyed a fine season as an influential figure in the NextGen Series and FA Youth Cup runs.

In the league, the Under-21s were significantly affected by the large numbers of players who went out on loan deals, as well as by the

Back row, left to right: Matt Birnie (Head of Academy physical fitness and Under-21s conditioning coach), Adam Nditi, Billy Clifford, Dion Conroy, Ruben Loftus-Cheek, Lewis Baker, Alex Kiwomya, Isaiah Brown, Nathan Ake, Jack Christopher (sports scientist)

Middle row, left to right: David Porter (Under-21s doctor), Gerry Harvey (head of education), Jordan Houghton, John Swift, Andreas Christensen, Tika Musonda, Mitchell Beeney, Ben Killip, Reece Mitchell, Fankaty Dabo, Islam Feruz, Simon Dickie (physiotherapist), Jack Francis (head of lifestyle and mentoring), Craig Brown (Under-21s kit manager)

Front row, left to right: Ben Smith (head of development performance systems), Kevin Wright, Isak Ssewankambo, Alex Davey, Andy Myers (Under-21s assistant coach), Dermot Drummy (Under-21s manager), Mark Beeney (Under-21s and Academy goalkeeper coach), Jeremie Boga, Ola Aina, Lamisha Musonda, Stuart Vaughan (physiotherapist)

Lewis Baker, scoring here against Juventus in the NextGen Under-19 Series, was named Player of the Tournament

FIXTURES & RESULTS 2012/13

Date	Opposition		Res
August (Group 3)			
Fri 17	Manchester City	H	0-0
Tue 28	CSKA Moscow (NextGen Grp 3)	H	1-2
September (Group 3)			
Sat 1	Wolverhampton Wanderers	H	5-0
Fri 14	Liverpool	H	1-4
Mon 24	Crystal Palace	A	2-2
Fri 28	Middlesbrough	H	1-3
October (Group 3)			
Wed 3	CSKA Moscow (NextGen Grp 3)	A	1-0
Fri 5	Fulham	A	1-3
Mon 22	Wolverhampton Wanderers	A	2-3
Wed 31	Molde (NextGen Grp 3)	A	1-1
November (Group 3)			
Sun 4	Manchester City	A	3-2
Thu 8	Molde (NextGen Grp 3)	H	6-0
Mon 12	Crystal Palace	H	4-1
Sun 18	Liverpool	A	3-3
Mon 26	Fulham	H	3-0
December (Group 3)			
Mon 3	Middlesbrough	A	3-2
Wed 12	Ajax (NextGen Grp 3)	H	0-0
January (Group 1)			
Thu 10	Fulham	H	2-0
Fri 25	Middlesbrough	H	1-0
Tue 29	Ajax (NextGen Grp 3)	A	3-3
February (Group 1)			
Sun 3	Sunderland	H	1-0
Mon 11	Blackburn Rovers	A	1-2
Wed 20	Barcelona (NextGen Rd of 16)	A	2-0
March (Group 1)			
Fri 1	Fulham	A	0-1
Mon 11	Everton	H	0-1
Sun 17	Juventus (NextGen QF)	H	4-1
Tue 19	Middlesbrough	A	0-2
Fri 29	Arsenal (NextGen SF)	N+	4-3*
April (Group 1)			
Mon 1	Aston Villa (NextGen Final)	N+	2-0
Thu 4	Aston Villa	H	1-2
Mon 8	Sunderland	A	1-0
Mon 15	Aston Villa	A	1-1
Thu 25	Everton	A	0-0
Mon 29	Blackburn Rovers	H	1-0

Chelsea score shown first. +Como, Italy.
*After extra time.

BARCLAYS U21S PREMIER LEAGUE GROUP 3 (Aug-Dec 2012)

	Team	Pld	W	D	L	GD	Pts
1	Liverpool	12	9	3	0	+19	30
2	Wolves	12	5	4	3	-2	19
3	**Chelsea**	12	5	3	4	+5	18
4	Middlesbrough	12	4	3	5	-1	15
5	Fulham	12	3	2	7	-10	11
6	Man City	12	1	7	4	-1	10
7	Crystal Palace	12	2	4	6	-10	10

BARCLAYS U21S PREMIER LEAGUE GROUP 1 (Jan-April 2013)

	Team	Pld	W	D	L	GD	Pts
1	Everton	12	6	6	0	+9	24
2	Aston Villa	12	5	4	3	+5	19
3	Fulham	12	5	4	3	+4	19
4	**Chelsea**	12	5	2	5	0	17
5	Middlesbrough	12	4	4	4	+2	16
6	Blackburn	12	4	0	8	-9	12
7	Sunderland	12	0	6	6	-11	6

NEXTGEN U19S GROUP 3

	Team	Pld	W	D	L	GD	Pts
1	CSKA Moscow	6	4	0	2	+3	12
2	Ajax	6	3	2	1	+9	11
3	**Chelsea**	6	2	3	1	+6	9
4	Molde	6	0	1	5	-18	1

aforementioned cup commitments, which left playing positions open to younger players from the Academy for Under-21s Premier League games.

In the opening stage of the campaign, we finished third in our group, before going on to take fourth place in the second half of the season.

"I would say we probably need to have a look at the Under-21s league and see if we can find a way to get a competitive edge into it at a time when some of the boys are going out on loan," explained Drummy at the end of the campaign. "Having said

that, there have been some very successful loan spells for our players and it is an aspect of our Academy that a number of boys play in a higher age group in order to bring their development on.

"We have seen several younger boys come into the Under-21s group and do a wonderful job. Jeremie Boga, who was an Under-16s player, has been outstanding for us, while there are young players such as Ruben Loftus-Cheek and Lewis Baker coming through and making the step up from the Under-18s group. They have both been superb this season, while Mitchell Beeney, as a young goalkeeper, has greatly developed mentally over the past year.

"There are many other examples, too, so we are very pleased with the progress being made by several of the younger boys stepping into the Under-21s."

Finally, it was a positive campaign for one young Blue, who began the campaign as a member of our Under-21s squad. Nathan Ake ended the season with six first-team appearances under his belt, three of which were starts, setting a good example to all the players in the Chelsea Academy of what can be achieved.

APPEARANCES 2012/13

Additional appearances as substitute in brackets.

Baker 26, Blackman 24, Davey 23(4), Feruz 20(2), Nditi 18(3), Ake 18(1), Saville 18, Christensen 15(2), Loftus-Cheek 15(1), Bamford 14, B Clifford 14, Kane 14, Deen-Conteh 13(2), Boga 12(7), Lalkovic 12, Pappoe 11(3), Kiwomya 10(3), Dabo 9(2), T Musonda 9(2), Beeney 9, Swift 8(6), L Musonda 7(5), Conroy 7(4), Piazon 7, Hunte 6(8), Ssewankambo 6(3), Wright 4(2), C Clifford 4(1), Ince 4(1), Marin 3, Starkey 2(4), Bangura 2(3), Chalobah 2, Mitchell 1(9), Gnahore 1(2), Houghton 1(2), Phillip 1(2), T Hazard 1(1), Nkumu 1, Terry 1, Walker 1, Colkett 0(5), Seremba 0(3), Ashton 0(1), Muleba 0(1), Nortey 0(1).

GOALS 2012/13

Feruz 16, Baker 10 (3 pens), Boga 6, Bamford 5, B Clifford 3, Kiwomya 3, Piazon 3 (1 pen), Saville 3, Hunte 2, Marin 2, Ake 1, Davey 1, Deen-Conteh 1, Kane 1, Lalkovic 1 (pen), Mitchell 1, Phillip 1, Ssewankambo 1.

NATHAN AKE

The 2012/13 season was one to remember for the talented Dutchman, who made six first-team appearances and figured prominently in the Under-18s' run to the FA Youth Cup final. He was voted the club's Young Player of the Year.

FACTS AND FIGURES

Born: 's-Gravenhage, Holland, 18.02.95
Height: 1.80m (5ft 11in) **Weight:** 75.5kgs (11st 12lb)
Source: Feyenoord
Chelsea scholarship: July 2011
Turned pro: July 2012
Chelsea debut: Norwich (a) 26.12.12, substitute for Juan Mata. Won 1-0
Trophies won with Chelsea: UEFA Europa League 2013, FA Youth Cup 2012
Other Chelsea honours: Chelsea Young Player of the Year 2013
International honours: 2011 and 2012 UEFA Under-17s Championship winner
International caps won with Chelsea: Holland Under-19s, Under-17s
First team appearances: 3+3 games
Reserve/U21s appearances: 16+3 games, 1 goal
U19s appearances: 4 games
U18s appearances: 28 games, 3 goals

LEWIS BAKER

Regularly asked to wear the captain's armband, Baker is comfortable in possession, with either foot, and can play a variety of midfield roles. Last season, he was instrumental in the club's runs to the FA Youth Cup and NextGen Series finals.

FACTS AND FIGURES

Born: Luton, 25.04.95
Height: 1.82m (6ft) **Weight:** 72kgs (11st 5lb)
Source: Chelsea Academy
Chelsea scholarship: July 2011
Turned pro: July 2012
Trophies won with Chelsea: FA Youth Cup 2012
International caps won with Chelsea: England Under-19s, Under-17s
Reserve/U21s appearances: 17+3 games, 6 goals (3 pens)
U19s appearances: 10 games, 4 goals
U18s appearances: 50+8 games, 12 goals (6 pens)

JEREMIE BOGA

Skilful French midfielder with an eye for the creative and a rapid burst of pace. His dribbling skills and angular runs cause even the most organised defences to wobble and he has been a key player for the youth team and Under-21s recently.

FACTS AND FIGURES

Born: Marseille, France, 03.01.97
Height: 1.73m (5ft 8in) **Weight:** 72kgs (11st 5lb)
Source: Chelsea Academy
Chelsea scholarship: July 2013
International caps won with Chelsea: France Under-16s
U21s appearances: 5+6 games, 3 goals
U19s appearances: 8+1 games, 3 goals
U18s appearances: 18 games, 5 goals

MITCHELL BEENEY

Beeney will compete with Jamal Blackman and Ben Killip for the place between the posts in the Under-21s side this term. The son of Chelsea coach and former Leeds stopper Mark, Mitchell was last season's FA Youth Cup goalkeeper.

FACTS AND FIGURES

Born: Leeds, 03.10.95
Height: 1.96m (6ft 5in) **Weight:** 86kgs (13st 8lb)
Source: Chelsea Academy
Chelsea scholarship: July 2012
Turned pro: July 2013
Trophies won with Chelsea: FA Youth Cup 2012
Reserve/U21s appearances: 2 games
U19s appearances: 7 games
U18s appearances: 38+2 games

ISAIAH BROWN

Brought in from West Bromwich Albion in the summer, Brown immediately went about proving himself as an excellent striker in pre-season. In his first year as a full-time footballer, he has been fast-tracked into the Under-21s squad.

FACTS AND FIGURES

Born: Peterborough, 07.01.97
Height: 1.82m (6ft) **Weight:** 75.5kgs (11st 12lb)
Source: West Bromwich Albion
Chelsea scholarship: July 2013
International recognition: England Under-17s, Under-16s

ANDREAS CHRISTENSEN

Cultured centre-back, whose ability to play out from the back forms the foundation for many a passing move. He is also an intelligent defender with excellent positional sense, composure and the agility to mark even the trickiest opposition forward.

FACTS AND FIGURES

Born: Allerød, Denmark, 10.04.96
Height: 1.87m (6ft 2in) **Weight:** 75.5kgs (11st 12lb)
Source: Brondby
Chelsea scholarship: July 2012
Turned pro: July 2013
International caps won with Chelsea: Denmark Under-19s, Under-17s
Reserve/U21s appearances: 9+2 games
U19s appearances: 6 games
U18s appearances: 6 games, 1 goal

BILLY CLIFFORD

An FA Youth Cup winner with Chelsea in 2010, Clifford enjoyed a successful loan with Colchester United in 2012/13, making 18 appearances and scoring one goal, against Yeovil, who he also played once for during a brief loan at the start of this season.

FACTS AND FIGURES

Born: Slough, 18.10.92
Height: 1.71m (5ft 7in) **Weight:** 67kgs (10st 8lb)
Source: Chelsea Academy
Chelsea scholarship: July 2009
Turned pro: July 2010
Loans since signing: Colchester (2012/13, 18 games, 1 goal), Yeovil (2013/14)
Trophies won with Chelsea: Premier Reserve League South 2011, National Premier Reserve League 2011, FA Youth Cup 2010
Reserve/U21s appearances: 47+5 games, 7 goals
U18s appearances: 39+3 games, 6 goals (1 pen)

DION CONROY

A confident centre-half who has come through as part of a very successful year group. Solid at the back and comfortable on the ball, he looks to get moves started from the back. One of several promising centre-halves in the Academy.

FACTS AND FIGURES

Born: Redhill, 11.12.95
Height: 1.84m (6ft) **Weight:** 84.5kgs (13st 4lb)
Source: Chelsea Academy
Chelsea scholarship: July 2012
Turned pro: July 2013
Reserve/U21s appearances: 5+2 games
U19s appearances: 2+2 games
U18s appearances: 23+5 games, 1 goal

FANKATY DABO

A full-back with natural attacking instincts, after he reverted from a midfield role in his mid-teens to play right-back, Dabo looks to get on the ball as much as he can. Solid in the challenge, his pace allows him to recover quickly defensively.

FACTS AND FIGURES

Born: Southwark, 11.10.95
Height: 1.72m (5ft 8in) **Weight:** 69.5kgs (10st 13lb)
Source: Chelsea Academy
Chelsea scholarship: July 2012
Turned pro: July 2013
International caps won with Chelsea: England Under-17s, Under-16s
Reserve/U21s appearances: 5+2 games
U19s appearances: 4 games
U18s appearances: 18+8 games, 2 goals

ALEX DAVEY

Tough, committed centre-back who organises the backline and shows fantastic defensive instincts under pressure. Good in the air and comfortable on the ball, he has an eye for a long, cutting pass to launch the quick counter-attack at the right moment.

FACTS AND FIGURES

Born: Welwyn Garden City, 24.11.94
Height: 1.92m (6ft 3in) **Weight:** 79kgs (12st 6lb)
Source: Chelsea Academy
Chelsea scholarship: July 2011
Turned pro: July 2012
Trophies won with Chelsea: FA Youth Cup 2012
International caps won with Chelsea: Scotland Under-19s
Reserve/U21s appearances: 14+7 games, 1 goal
U19s appearances: 10 games
U18s appearances: 37+4 games, 1 goal

ISLAM FERUZ

Leading the line with a mixture of direct running, excellent close control and powerful finishing, Feruz demonstrated his scoring prowess last season, finishing the campaign as top scorer in the Academy with 19 goals across all age groups.

FACTS AND FIGURES

Born: Kismayo, Somalia, 10.09.95
Height: 1.67m (5ft 6in) **Weight:** 68kgs (10st 10lb)
Source: Celtic
Chelsea scholarship: July 2012
Turned pro: September 2012
Trophies won with Chelsea: FA Youth Cup 2012
International caps won with Chelsea: Scotland Under-21s 4 caps, 2 goals, Under-20s, Under-19s, Under-17s. Scotland's youngest ever Under-21s international at 16 years, 229 days
Reserve/U21s appearances: 13+3 games, 11 goals
U19s appearances: 9+1 games, 7 goals
U18s appearances: 29 games, 15 goals

Youth training is all about developing the players

BEN KILLIP

Now in his second year as a scholar, Killip is a local lad who has been at the club since he was eight years old and who shared Under-18s goalkeeping responsibilities with Mitchell Beeney for much of the 2012/13 season.

FACTS AND FIGURES

Born: Isleworth, 24.11.95
Height: 1.85m (6ft 1in)
Weight: 82kgs (12st 13lb)
Source: Chelsea Academy
Chelsea scholarship: July 2012
U18s appearances: 14 games

ALEX KIWOMYA

Son of former Bradford winger Andy Kiwomya and nephew of Notts County manager Chris Kiwomya, Alex has scored some vital goals for Chelsea in recent seasons, playing wide right or up front and terrorising defences with his devastating pace.

FACTS AND FIGURES

Born: Sheffield, 20.05.96
Height: 1.79m (5ft 10in) **Weight:** 66.5kgs (10st 7lb)
Source: Chelsea Academy
Chelsea scholarship: July 2012
Trophies won with Chelsea: FA Youth Cup 2012
International caps won with Chelsea: England Under-17s, Under-16s
Reserve/U21s appearances: 6+3 games
U19s appearances: 5+2 games, 3 goals
U18s appearances: 19+21 games, 18 goals

RUBEN LOFTUS-CHEEK

Tall, imposing and technically gifted central midfielder whose composure on the ball is often a result of his ability to find space in which to receive possession. A playmaker – often from deep positions – with quick feet and an eye for a defence-splitting pass.

FACTS AND FIGURES

Born: Lewisham, 23.01.96
Height: 1.91m (6ft 3in) **Weight:** 80kgs (12st 8lb)
Source: Chelsea Academy
Chelsea scholarship: July 2012
Turned pro: January 2013
Trophies won with Chelsea: FA Youth Cup 2012
International caps won with Chelsea: England Under-17s, Under-16s
Reserve/U21s appearances: 8+1 games
U19s appearances: 7 games
U18s appearances: 34+1 games, 6 goals

LAMISHA MUSONDA

The oldest of the three Musonda brothers, whose father Charly was also a professional footballer in Belgium and a Zambian international. Lamisha is a skilful winger who looks to run at opponents and open up defences with runs in behind.

FACTS AND FIGURES

Born: Brussels, Belgium, 27.03.92
Height: 1.68m (5ft 6in) **Weight:** 63kgs (9st 13lb)
Previous club: Anderlecht
Signed: August 2012
International recognition: Belgium Under-21s 11 caps
International caps won with Chelsea: Belgium Under-21s 6 caps, 0 goals
Reserve/U21s appearances: 7+5 games

TIKA MUSONDA

More solidly built than his brothers, Tika is a right-back signed from Anderlecht at the beginning of the 2012/13 campaign, who featured in the club's run to the NextGen Series final in his debut season with Chelsea.

FACTS AND FIGURES

Born: Brussels, Belgium, 18.01.94
Height: 1.82m (6ft) **Weight:** 71.5kgs (11st 3lb)
Previous club: Anderlecht
Signed: August 2012
International recognition: Belgium Youth
International caps won with Chelsea: None
Reserve/U21s appearances: 8+1 games
U19s appearances: 1+1 games

ADAM NDITI

A marauding left-back who was born in Tanzania, moving to England as a young boy. Nditi has also been asked to play on the left-wing on several occasions, largely due to his crossing ability and direct running on the flank.

FACTS AND FIGURES

Born: Zanzibar, Tanzania, 18.09.94
Height: 1.73m (5ft 8in) **Weight:** 61.5kgs (9st 10lb)
Source: Chelsea Academy
Chelsea scholarship: July 2011
Turned pro: July 2012
Trophies won with Chelsea: FA Youth Cup 2012
Reserve/U21s appearances: 11+6 games
U19s appearances: 8 games
U18s appearances: 55+10 games, 2 goals

KENNETH OMERUO

Versatile defender who spent last season on loan to Dutch club ADO Den Haag. Omeruo is most comfortable at centre-back, where he excelled in the 2013 Africa Cup of Nations, as he played in every game of Nigeria's triumphant tournament.

FACTS AND FIGURES

Born: Obuohia Okike, Nigeria, 17.10.93
Height: 1.90m (6ft 3in) **Weight:** 82kgs (12st 13lb)
Previous clubs: Sunshine Stars, Standard Liege (loan)
Signed: January 2012
Loan since signing: Den Haag (2011/12, 9 games, 2 goals, 2012/13, 27+2 games)
International honours: 2013 Africa Cup of Nations winner, 2009 FIFA Under-17s World Cup runners-up
Major international tournaments: 2013 Africa Cup of Nations (5+1 games)
International recognition: Nigeria 14 caps. Nigeria Youth
International caps won with Chelsea: Nigeria 14 caps, 0 goals

ISAK SSEWANKAMBO

Strong defender who can also play as a central midfielder and has represented his native Sweden at youth level. Ssewankambo played an increasingly important role in the youth team last season and has now stepped up to Dermot Drummy's Under-21 squad.

FACTS AND FIGURES

Born: Angered, Sweden, 27.02.96
Height: 1.78m (5ft 10in) **Weight:** 74.5kgs (11st 10lb)
Source: Larje-Angereds IF
Chelsea scholarship: July 2012
Turned pro: July 2013
International caps won with Chelsea: Sweden Under-17s
Reserve/U21s appearances: 6 games
U19s appearances: 0+3 games, 1 goal
U18s appearances: 13+3 games

JOHN SWIFT

All-round midfielder who fits happily into the "box-to-box" category, with his well-timed runs forward regularly resulting in shots on goal. Talented on the ball, dogged in his attempts to win possession back and excellent at timing his runs into the opposition box.

FACTS AND FIGURES

Born: Portsmouth, 23.06.95
Height: 1.84m (6ft) **Weight:** 76kgs (11st 13lb)
Source: Chelsea Academy
Chelsea scholarship: July 2011
Turned pro: July 2012
Trophies won with Chelsea: FA Youth Cup 2012
International caps won with Chelsea: England Under-19s, Under-18s, Under-17s, Under-16s
Reserve/U21s appearances: 5+5 games
U19s appearances: 3+2 games
U18s appearances: 44+10 games, 8 goals

KEVIN WRIGHT

Shared left-back duties with Adam Nditi during last season's run to the FA Youth Cup final, during which time he demonstrated great determination with some committed defensive displays and a willingness to attack whenever the opportunity arose.

FACTS AND FIGURES

Born: Walthamstow, 28.12.95
Height: 1.70m (5ft 7in) **Weight:** 68kgs (10st 10lb)
Source: Chelsea Academy
Chelsea scholarship: July 2012
Turned pro: July 2013
Reserve/U21s appearances: 1 game
U19s appearances: 3+2 games
U18s appearances: 22+2 games

EXPERIENCES INSPIRE YOUNGSTERS

Another FA Youth Cup final, Chelsea reaching the showpiece of the NextGen Series in the Blues' debut season and players gaining first-team spots – the Academy is proving it has strength and depth

As another group of talented youngsters begin their full-time football careers at the Chelsea Academy, they will take heart from the performances of the youth team last season.

Another FA Youth Cup final – the club's fourth in the last six seasons – may have ended in defeat for Chelsea's Under-18s, but coach Adi Viveash's side can be very pleased with the standard of football they played on their way to the two-legged finale against Norwich City.

In the final itself, the Blues dominated possession in typical fashion, having enjoyed the lion's share of the ball and chances in the first leg at Carrow Road, only to lose 1-0 to a last-minute penalty.

The second leg at Stamford Bridge became a tricky affair when, after Jeremie Boga had opened the scoring on the night, Norwich once again scored against the run of play to leave Chelsea requiring two goals. In the end, it was not to be for the young Blues as the Canaries won 4-2 on aggregate.

The run to the final will be remembered for all the right reasons, particularly a sensational 4-1 aggregate win over Liverpool in the two-legged semi-final.

"I want to thank all the players and staff who have been involved with my programme throughout the season," Viveash said as the campaign drew to a close. "They have given a tremendous amount of effort and it is an outstanding achievement to reach the final of the Youth Cup in consecutive seasons.

"We now have to learn from this final, dust ourselves down and come back stronger for the experience next season."

Following an accomplished 2012/13 campaign, two of the ball players who have helped form the basis for the smart interplay and neat passing game the youth team pride themselves on were called up to join the first team on their post-season trip to the United States. Midfielder Ruben Loftus-Cheek and centre-back Andreas Christensen gained great experience as they featured in both the friendly matches we played against Manchester City in May.

The experience of playing at Anfield, Carrow Road and, of course, Stamford Bridge in front of sizeable FA Youth Cup crowds would certainly have laid the groundwork for the young duo – both 17 – to make the step up to first-team action.

Seeing Nathan Ake, who is a year older than the pair, make his first-team breakthrough in the second half of last season will also have helped the rest of the youth squad see the

Back row, left to right: Jo Clubb (sports science officer), Kasey Palmer, Ambrose Gnahore, Dominic Solanke, Chike Kandi, Ruben Loftus-Cheek, Alex Kiwomya, Isaiah Brown, George Brady, Stuart Vaughan (physiotherapist)

Middle row, left to right: Will Tullett (movement specialist), Elliot Axtell (Under-18s conditioning coach), Gerry Harvey (head of education), Bill Thompson (Under-18s goalkeeper coach), Jonathan Muleba, Charlie Colkett, Andreas Christensen, Bradley Collins, Mitchell Beeney, Ben Killip, Reece Mitchell, Fankaty Dabo, Islam Feruz, Eric Asiedu (Academy kit manager), Jack Francis (head of lifestyle and mentoring), Chris Hughes (Academy doctor)

Front row, left to right: George Cole, Kevin Wright, Jordan Houghton, Dion Conroy, Adi Viveash (youth-team manager), Joe Edwards (Under-16s coach and Under-18s assistant coach), Charly Musonda, Jeremie Boga, Ola Aina, Isak Ssewankambo

John Swift celebrates finding the net against Liverpool in the second leg of our FA Youth Cup semi-final

pathways opening up ahead of them.

In the Under-18s Premier League, Viveash's side enjoyed a blistering start to last term and, after winning their group, took part in the Elite Group for the second half of the campaign.

However, a combination of loan deals for key players and the demands of runs in the NextGen Under-19s Series and FA Youth Cup meant that the second stage of the league season was played out by a much younger Chelsea team than the first phase.

As Viveash explained, while that took its toll on results, it was certainly a fantastic way of intensifying the learning curve for the club's young prospects.

Playing among older boys in the league and with expectation to get results in the Youth Cup, the players arguably learned as much mentally and physically about themselves as they did technically.

"In the league games, we look at development, playing various Under-16s boys at a higher age level," the manager said. "However, in the Youth Cup, the emphasis is on winning and we get our best team together.

"Jeremie Boga, who is at Under-16s age, played in several Under-21s games last season in the league, but the Youth Cup is a different kind of pressure. As a schoolboy, you can go into Under-21s games and play a little bit more freely, but there is an expectation to perform in the Youth Cup.

"Charlie Colkett is another Under-16 who developed nicely over the season, Connor Hunte came on in the semi-final and probably the biggest story was Ola Aina coming in at right-back for the semi-final and the final.

"I told the boys that the experience was probably worth two years in development because you can't recreate moments like that.

"I said to them that some of the players I played with went through 20-year careers where 10,000 was the biggest crowd they played in front of. These boys have doubled that – and some of them are schoolboys – so it is fantastic for their learning."

APPEARANCES 2012/13

Additional appearances as substitute are in brackets.

Wright 22(2), Muleba 20(2), Beeney 20, Dabo 18(3), Loftus-Cheek 18, Conroy 17(4), Mitchell 17, Starkey 16(2), Swift 16(2), Kiwomya 15(2), Boga 15, Hunte 14(6), Killip 14, Ssewankambo 13(3), Houghton 13(1), Howard 11(9), Gnahore 10(11), Colkett 10(9), G Cole 10(6), Kandi 10(4), Davey 10, Baker 8(1), Feruz 8, Nditi 8, Aina 7(2), Ake 6, Christensen 6, Palmer 5, Solanke 4(6), Nortey 4(4), Seremba 3(1), Dasilva 3, Bangura 2(2), C Musonda 1(2), Mukhtar Ali 0(2), Figueira 0(2), A Gordon 0(2), Sammut 0(2), Christie-Davies 0(1).

GOALS 2012/13

Kiwomya 10, Boga 5, Hunte 5, Baker 4 (2 pens), Starkey 4 (2 pens), Swift 4, G Cole 3, Feruz 3, Gnahore 3, Houghton 3, Kandi 3, Mitchell 3, Colkett 2, Loftus-Cheek 2, Solanke 2, Ake 1, Christensen 1, Dabo 1, Figueira 1, Howard 1, own goals 1.

FIXTURES & RESULTS 2012/13

Date	Opposition		Res
August (Group 3)			
Sat 18	Manchester City	H	6-1
September (Group 3)			
Sat 1	Wolverhampton Wanderers	H	2-0
Sat 15	Liverpool	H	2-1
Sat 22	Crystal Palace	H	3-1
Sat 29	Middlesbrough	H	4-2
October (Group 3)			
Sat 6	Fulham	H	2-1
Sat 20	Wolverhampton Wanderers	A	2-2
November (Group 3)			
Sat 3	Manchester City	A	2-0
Sat 10	Crystal Palace	A	3-3
Sat 17	Liverpool	A	2-1
Sat 24	Middlesbrough	A	1-0
December (Group 3)			
Sat 1	Colchester United (FAYC 3)	A	3-2
Wed 19	Fulham	A	1-2
January (Elite Group)			
Fri 11	Southampton	A	0-0
Wed 16	Charlton Athletic (FAYC 4)	A	3-2*
February (Elite Group)			
Sat 2	Manchester United	H	1-1
Sat 9	Crystal Palace	A	5-1
Fri 15	Barnsley (FAYC 5)	H	3-0
Sat 23	Fulham	A	0-5
March (Elite Group)			
Sat 2	Southampton	H	1-3
Fri 8	Derby County (FAYC QF)	A	2-1
Sat 16	Everton	H	0-1
Sat 23	Bolton Wanderers	H	2-3
April (Elite Group)			
Sat 6	Manchester United	A	0-1
Fri 12	Liverpool (FAYC SF 1)	A	2-0
Sat 13	Reading	A	0-3
Fri 19	Liverpool (FAYC SF 2)	H	2-1•
Sat 20	Fulham	H	1-0
Tue 23	Bolton Wanderers	A	1-0
Sat 27	Everton	A	1-3
Mon 29	Norwich City (FAYC final 1)	A	0-1
May (Elite Group)			
Sat 4	Reading	H	0-3
Fri 10	Crystal Palace	H	3-1
Mon 13	Norwich City (FAYC final 2)	H	2-3#

Chelsea score shown first.
* After extra time.
• Chelsea won 4-1 on aggregate.
Chelsea lost 2-4 on aggregate.

BARCLAYS UNDER-18S PREMIER LEAGUE GROUP 3

(Aug-Dec 2012)

	Team	Pld	W	D	L	GD	Pts
1	Chelsea	12	9	2	1	+16	29
2	Fulham	12	8	1	3	+19	25
3	Crystal Palace	12	5	3	4	+6	18
4	Liverpool	12	4	2	6	0	14
5	Wolves	12	3	4	5	-6	13
6	Manchester City	12	4	1	7	-13	13
7	Middlesbrough	12	1	3	8	-22	6

BARCLAYS U18S PREMIER LEAGUE ELITE GROUP (Jan-May '13)

	Team	Pld	W	D	L	GD	Pts
1	Fulham	14	10	1	3	+19	31
2	Reading	14	10	1	3	+15	31
3	Everton	14	7	3	4	+7	24
4	Man Utd	14	7	3	4	+3	24
5	Southampton	14	6	3	5	+3	21
6	Chelsea	14	4	2	8	-10	14
7	Bolton	14	3	1	10	-16	10
8	Crystal Palace	14	1	2	11	-21	5

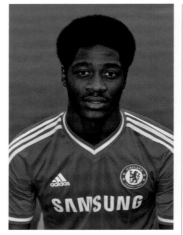

OLA AINA

Position: Central defender/right back
Born: Southwark, 08.10.96
Height: 1.82m (6ft)
Weight: 77.5kgs (12st 3lb)
Source: Chelsea Academy
Chelsea scholarship: July 2013
International caps won with Chelsea:
England Under-17s, Under-16s
U18s appearances: 7+2 games

GEORGE BRADY

Position: Central defender
Born: Gassin, France, 29.12.96
Height: 1.91m (6ft 3in)
Weight: 79.5kgs (12st 7lb)
Source: Chelsea Academy
Chelsea scholarship: July 2013

GEORGE COLE

Position: Midfield
Born: Basildon, 22.12.95
Height: 1.78m (5ft 10in)
Weight: 78kgs (12st 4lb)
Source: Chelsea Academy
Chelsea scholarship: July 2012
International caps won with Chelsea:
England Under-16s
U18s appearances: 11+8 games, 3 goals

CHARLIE COLKETT

Position: Midfield
Born: Hackney, 04.09.96
Height: 1.77m (5ft 10in)
Weight: 67kgs (10st 8lb)
Source: Chelsea Academy
Chelsea scholarship: July 2013
Turned pro: September 2013
International caps won with Chelsea:
England Under-17s, Under-16s
U19s appearances: 0+5 games
U18s appearances: 10+10 games, 2 goals

BRADLEY COLLINS

Position: Goalkeeper
Born: Southampton, 18.02.97
Height: 1.89m (6ft 2in)
Weight: 80kgs (12st 8lb)
Source: Chelsea Academy
Chelsea scholarship: July 2013

AMBROSE GNAHORE

Position: Midfield
Born: Lewisham, 11.12.95
Height: 1.76m (5ft 9in)
Weight: 77.5kgs (12st 3lb)
Source: Chelsea Academy
Chelsea scholarship: July 2012
U21s appearances: 1+1 games
U19s appearances: 0+1 game
U18s appearances: 11+13 games, 3 goals

JORDAN HOUGHTON

Position: Defender/midfield
Born: Chertsey, 05.11.95
Height: 1.82m (6ft)
Weight: 77.5kgs (12st 3lb)
Source: Chelsea Academy
Chelsea scholarship: July 2012
Turned pro: July 2013
International caps won with Chelsea:
England U17s, Under-16s
U19s appearances: 1+2 games
U18s appearances: 18+6 games, 3 goals

CHIKE KANDI

Position: Striker
Born: Hammersmith, 06.10.95
Height: 1.80m (5ft 11in)
Weight: 84kgs (13st 3lb)
Source: Birmingham City
Chelsea scholarship: July 2012
Turned pro: July 2013
International recognition:
Wales Under-17s, Under-16s
U18s appearances: 10+4 games, 3 goals

REECE MITCHELL

Position: Striker
Born: Westminster, 19.09.95
Height: 1.69m (5ft 6in)
Weight: 68kgs (10st 10lb)
Source: Chelsea Academy
Chelsea scholarship: July 2012
Turned pro: July 2013
Trophies won with Chelsea:
FA Youth Cup 2012
International caps won with Chelsea:
England Under-16s
Reserve/U21s appearances: 0+4 games
U19s appearances: 1+5 games, 1 goal
U18s appearances: 24+4 games, 4 goals

JONATHAN MULEBA

Position: Central defender
Born: Bujumbura, Burundi, 04.09.95
Height: 1.78m (5ft 10in)
Weight: 75.5kgs (11st 12lb)
Source: Chelsea Academy
Chelsea scholarship: July 2012
International caps won with Chelsea:
Democratic Republic of Congo Under-20s
U21s appearances: 0+1 game
U18s appearances: 22+2 games, 1 goal

CHARLY MUSONDA

Position: Midfield
Born: Brussels, Belgium, 15.10.96
Height: 1.70m (5ft 7in)
Weight: 57kgs (9st)
Source: Chelsea Academy
Chelsea scholarship: July 2013
International recognition:
Belgium Under-17s, Under-16s
U18s appearances: 1+2 games

KASEY PALMER

Position: Midfield
Born: Lewisham, 09.11.96
Height: 1.79m (5ft 10in)
Weight: 72.5kgs (11st 6lb)
Source: Charlton Athletic
Chelsea scholarship: July 2013
International recognition: England Under-17s
U18s appearances: 5 games

SQUAD GROWS IN STRENGTH AHEAD OF LEAGUE CHANGES

A healthy mix of top internationals and players who have graduated from the Chelsea youth ranks have made a solid foundation in the Ladies side as they prepare for a two-tier league system

Chelsea Ladies made good progress in the 2013 FA Women's Super League season as the Blues built a squad of world-class players and talented youngsters who look capable of challenging for major honours.

With manager Emma Hayes and her assistant Paul Green making full use of their experience in the women's game, the off-season rebuilding of the squad saw some impressive signings. Among them was Eniola Aluko, who returned to her former club after a spell at Birmingham.

Despite exiting the cup competitions, the early league form

was solid and the Blues were in good goalscoring form, particularly at Staines Town's Wheatsheaf Park, our home ground for the second straight season.

The stand-out result came against Liverpool Ladies, who we defeated 2-1 in a thrilling encounter to briefly top the league table in the early part of the season. However, our form tailed off heading into the mid-season break for the European Championship.

The tournament, held in Sweden, didn't go well for England, but the most positive development of the break came closer to home, with the addition of Japanese star Yuki Ogimi.

"This is the calibre of player that we want to attract to Chelsea," said Hayes. "Yuki is a world-class striker and a World Cup winner who will be a great success in this country. She will also aid the development of our young players."

Among those youngsters to step up to the first-team squad were England Under-19s full-back Hannah Blundell as well as Centre of Excellence graduates Rosella Ayane and Jodie Brett.

"We're really excited about them," added Hayes. "The second half of the season gave us the opportunity to integrate them into the squad, so they

Eniola Aluko in WSL action against Arsenal

Great signings made in 2013 included Japanese star Yuki Ogimi

FIXTURES & RESULTS 2013

Date	Opposition		Res
March			
Sun 17	Lincoln Ladies (FAWC5)	A	0-1
April			
Sun 14	Birmingham City Ladies	H	1-1
Sat 20	Doncaster Rovers Belles	A	4-0
Sun 28	Doncaster Rovers Belles (CC Group 2)	A	1-1
May			
Sun 5	Everton Ladies (CC Group 2)	A	1-2
Sun 12	Liverpool Ladies	H	2-1
Thu 16	Bristol Academy	A	0-2
Sun 19	Liverpool Ladies (CC Group 2)	H	0-4
Tue 28	Birmingham City Ladies	A	1-2
June			
Thu 6	Arsenal Ladies	A	1-2
Sun 9	Everton Ladies	H	1-4
August			
Sun 4	Doncaster Rovers Belles	H	4-0
Sun 11	Lincoln Ladies	A	0-2
Sat 17	Liverpool Ladies	A	3-4
Thu 29	Arsenal Ladies	H	0-1
September			
Sun 1	Everton Ladies	A	2-3
Thu 5	Bristol Academy	H	1-3
Sun 29	Lincoln Ladies	H	-

Chelsea score shown first.
Women's Super League unless stated.
CC - Continental Cup. FAWC - FA Women's Cup.

could feel the benefit of that going into next year's campaign."

The future certainly looks bright for the Ladies heading into next season, which sees a shake-up to the WSL set-up.

A new-look two-tier system will come into play in 2014 and we were selected as one of the eight teams who will take part in the top flight of the FA Women's Super League. Ten new teams have joined, with nine of them lining up in WSL2 alongside Doncaster Rovers Belles, whose place in the top tier will be taken by Manchester City Ladies.

"We've got a competitive squad now that can push on and, hopefully, challenge for the WSL title in the future," said Hayes. "We have a playing style that's very clear – we want to possess the ball and have a lot of rotation and good movement."

Danielle Buet has made 16 starts

APPEARANCES 2013

Additional appearances as substitute are in brackets.

Aluko 17, Buet 16+1, Jakobsson 15, Holtham 14+1, Ward 13+4, Susi 12+2, Ester 10+3, Vidarsdottir 10+1, K Davies 10, Ingle 10, Gardarsdottir 9, Coombs 6+5, Spence 6+5, Lynn 6, Telford 6, Bleazard 5+5, Blundell 5+3, Ogimi 4, Hourihan 3, Brett 2+2, C Rafferty 2+1, N Davies 2, Longhurst 1+7, Ayane 1+2, Cole 1+1, Fogarty 1+1, Muya 0+3, L Rafferty 0+1.

GOALS 2013

Jakobsson 7, Aluko 6, Ward 3, Ayane 1, Blundell 1, Muya 1, Spence 1, Vidarsdottir 1, own goal 1.

THE FA WOMEN'S SUPER LEAGUE 2013

	Team	Pld	W	D	L	GD	Pts
1	Liverpool Ladies	13	11	0	2	+25	33
2	Bristol Academy Women	13	10	1	2	+12	31
3	Arsenal Ladies	13	9	3	1	+19	30
4	Everton Ladies	13	4	3	6	-6	15
5	Birmingham City Ladies	13	4	3	6	-8	15
6	**Chelsea Ladies**	13	3	1	9	-5	10
7	Lincoln Ladies	13	1	4	8	-7	7
8	Doncaster Rovers Belles	13	1	3	9	-30	6

THE FA WSL CONTINENTAL CUP 2013 – GROUP 2

	Team	Pld	W	D	L	GD	Pts
1	Liverpool Ladies	3	2	1	0	+5	7
2	Everton Ladies	3	2	1	0	+3	7
3	Doncaster Rovers Belles	3	0	1	2	-3	1
4	**Chelsea Ladies**	3	0	1	2	-5	1

Stats correct up to and including 15.09.13

All eyes were on Stamford Bridge when the Women's Champions League final took place at the home of the Blues in May.

Almost 20,000 people – including the Chelsea Ladies squad and members of the coaching team – attended an exciting game in which Wolfsburg ended Lyon's incredible 118-match unbeaten run to ensure there would be a German clean sweep of the year's Champions League titles.

INCLUSIVE WORK
IMPROVING LIVES

Working at home and abroad, the scope of the Chelsea Foundation is testament to the commitment of both those who run its schemes and the participants

The Chelsea Foundation was launched in July 2010 to continue the club's own charity and community commitments and oversee all aspects of the Blues' award-winning social responsibility work.

Since then, the Foundation has gone from strength to strength, working to support underprivileged communities, supporting our global charity partner Right To Play and working alongside club partners Samsung, adidas, Sauber F1 Team, Digicel, Audi and Gazprom to deliver an exciting range of sporting activities.

The Foundation is committed to improving the lives of people in our local communities and throughout the world by tackling issues such as crime and anti-social behaviour, as well as encouraging children and adults to engage in positive activities and lead healthier lives.

The key to the Foundation's work is harnessing the popularity of sport, football and Chelsea in particular to benefit communities. That is helped greatly by the invaluable contribution of the Blues players themselves, including the first-team squad's annual Christmas visit to the paediatric wards of Chelsea and Westminster Hospital and hosting community days at Cobham, where seriously and terminally ill young fans are able to watch training before meeting their heroes.

DISABILITY

The Chelsea Foundation promotes disability football both by arranging their own teams and introducing disabled people to sport.

The Foundation has become increasingly involved in the running of disability football, taking on responsibility for both the Player Development Centre – to identify and improve promising young talent eligible for the national team – and the top-level Cerebral Palsy Centre of Excellence for the Surrey FA, as well as representing the entire South-East region in the FA National Cerebral Palsy Football League.

The work of the Chelsea Foundation in promoting disability sport was recognised last year when development manager Rob Seale and Chelsea Community FC players Sami El-Kasef, Gareth Canning, Jay Beckford and Matt Slough were invited to take part in the torch relay ahead of the London 2012 Paralympic Games.

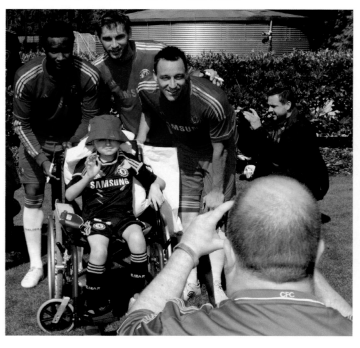

Above: Chelsea-run courses help develop young players at all levels

Left: Chelsea players at a Community Day at Cobham training ground in August 2012

Soccer Schools offer a safe environment for children to enjoy their football

SOCCER SCHOOLS

As well as charity work, the Chelsea Foundation holds Soccer Schools for those who want to learn to play football like the Blues.

Soccer School courses are specifically designed to cater for all abilities and combine the fun of playing football with keeping children active and healthy in a safe environment. All of the Chelsea Foundation's coaches hold valid and up-to-date CRB, FA Coaching, Safeguarding Children and first aid certificates.

They run during the school holidays throughout the year and are available for children aged four to 15 throughout Surrey, London, Essex, Hampshire, Berkshire and Sussex.

Chelsea Soccer Schools also offer specialised courses for goalkeepers. This involves smaller groups and focuses on the skills needed for keepers to excel between the posts.

As well as helping to develop footballing skills and levels of fitness, soccer schools are also dedicated to promoting the Chelsea Foundation's values of fair play, respect and discipline.

UNLOCKING POTENTIAL

The Chelsea Foundation works with the Premier League, the Professional Footballers' Association and Essex County Council to deliver the Unlocking Potential programme.

Working with young people, the groundbreaking initiative delivers football coaching and prison visits to reduce both re-offending and first-time offending, while also increasing participants' employability and providing them with new opportunities, either within the Chelsea Foundation or at local colleges.

Young people considered at risk of offending are taken to Chelmsford prison to receive football coaching from inmates who have been educated by the Foundation, an approach that has proved mutually beneficial. Jeremy Wright, Minister for Prisons and Rehabilitation, joined Gary Cahill and participants at Cobham to celebrate the programme's success.

Gary Cahill meets participants at the Unlocking Potential launch

ASIAN STAR

The annual Asian Star event works to level the playing field for the under-represented Asian communities when it comes to starting a career in professional football.

Young players from Asian backgrounds are welcomed to Cobham and given the chance to impress the Chelsea coaches, with the best from each age group receiving a year-long place at our Football Development Centre.

Almost 400 children aged between Under-9s and Under-12s took part in the fifth edition in 2013, with the medals being handed out by businessman and philanthropist

Peter Virdee, Pakistan international defender Kashif Siddiqi and 2011 winner Sam Khan, who now plays in the Birmingham City Academy.

All the players taking part in the day were put through their paces by Chelsea Foundation coaches, who assessed those in each age group using the same methods as the club's Academy.

Parents attending were also encouraged to take part, with a number of organisations, including the Zesh Rehman Foundation, providing coaching classes and advice on how to get involved in the sport off the pitch.

Our Asian Star initiative has provided a boost to young football players in a community which historically has been under-represented in the sport

"ALIVE AND KICKING" SENIOR GROUP FANS

The award-winning project for over-75s offers weekly IT classes at the Hub, supplemented by talks, social events and educational visits.

Members of the group visit local schools to give talks and, having grown up during World War Two, many of the senior fans share their invaluable memories, helping bring history to life for the children.

MEAL OR NO MEAL

The Meal Or No Meal project started in early 2013 and has seen Chelsea Foundation staff joining Stamford the Lion to give special assemblies on healthy eating at schools in Sutton.

Based on the popular Deal Or No Deal TV show, pupils are taught to identify which foods are good for them and how to maintain a nutritious diet.

The children are also encouraged to discuss why certain foods are healthy, helping them to understand what they should be eating.

EDUCATION THROUGH FOOTBALL

The Education Through Football programme works in schools, focusing on maths, literacy and IT skills, while also putting on anti-discrimination workshops.

The scheme has reached more than 6,000 children in Westminster, Hammersmith & Fulham, Kensington and Chelsea, Wandsworth and Cobham since it began, with teachers reporting that more than 90 per cent of pupils taking part achieved a better-than-expected rise in their attainment levels.

To celebrate the continued success of Education Through Football, Chelsea star Juan Mata met pupils from the Servite Primary School at Stamford Bridge, a treat for the pupils of the nearby school.

"Education is really important and I'm really proud the club is using the pull of Chelsea to help these children learn," said our No10.

Juan Mata meets children at an Education Through Football celebration event

England star Rachel Yankey and ex-Blues player Paul Canoville at the Show Racism the Red Card and Kick It Out School Competition Awards at Stamford Bridge

KICKSTART AFTER-SCHOOL PROGRAMME

Kickstart Maths and IT is funded by the club with support from the Premier League.

It sees up to 300 children attend our after-school study support sessions each year, the focus of which is on using football to help improve maths and ICT skills.

The engaging scheme, which is delivered at the Hub, supports the National Curriculum and helps address the Every Child Matters agenda.

BUILDING BRIDGES

Chelsea's Building Bridges initiative was launched in 2010 to promote equality in our club, our stadium and throughout our communities.

The club actively celebrates our diversity and takes the strongest possible action, including a lifetime ban, against any fan who does not share our vision of a Chelsea free of discrimination.

Any fans entering Stamford Bridge, visiting our website or reading our club programme will be instantly aware that we are a club proud of our multi-ethnic and religious make-up.

The club has undertaken numerous projects to engage with fans and our communities in aspects of our equality work. Thousands of young people in south-west London participate in the club's anti-discrimination education campaign every year. The programme is supported by Chelsea's first black player, Paul Canoville.

Chelsea has a close working relationship with a number of equality organisations, including Kick It Out, Show Racism the Red Card, FARE and the Black and Asian Coaches Association.

The Premier League meeting with Manchester United last October was our 2012/13 One Game, One Community fixture to mark the Kick It Out Weeks of Action. The two sides were led out by youngsters from Chelsea Foundation programmes and the players from both sides showed their support by wearing special T-shirts during the warm-up.

To coincide with Kick It Out's Weeks of Action, our Cobham training ground hosted a Black and Asian Coaching Association Workshop, allowing participants to learn about non-playing roles in football and take the first steps to gaining sports qualifications.

Stamford Bridge was the venue for the Show Racism the Red Card and Kick It Out School Competition Awards in April, with former Blues Paul Canoville and Ken Monkou helping present the trophies alongside England women's international Rachel Yankey.

Further details about all the Chelsea Foundation's projects can be found at www.chelseafc.com/foundation

SPREADING THE MESSAGE OF HOPE

Chelsea have proudly displayed the Right To Play logo on shirts to highlight the work of our global charity partner as we both strive to help underprivileged young people everywhere

Last season was the sixth since Chelsea began working with our global charity partner Right To Play and it saw the Blues agree a further three-year extension of the partnership.

Since joining forces in 2007, more than £2million has been raised to support Right To Play's work, as well as Chelsea players, staff and facilities also contributing to help the charity improve young people's lives in locations across Africa, Asia, Latin America, the Middle East and North America.

Right To Play and Chelsea both believe in using sport as a tool to provide positive changes in young people's lives, with the former working with more than one million children in 20 different countries every week.

"Chelsea Football Club understands the significance that sport can play in communities around the world and we are delighted to be extending our partnership with Right To Play, who are continuing to change lives across the globe," said Chelsea Chief Executive Ron Gourlay. "We believe in the power of football and sport to reach people at home and abroad and look forward to working with Right To Play over the next three years to help hundreds of thousands of children play, learn and inspire each other."

The partnership has also given Right To Play even more valuable exposure internationally since the Blues added their logo to the back of their shirts for all European games. That has seen the charity's name taking prominent position during our Champions League and Europa League triumphs in the last two seasons.

Right To Play founder and Chief Executive Johann Olav Koss added: "I am excited about our relationship with Chelsea Football Club. The club has consistently shown their dedication to Right To Play since we first started working together in 2007 and we have achieved great things.

"Our partnership has helped spread the message that sport and play have the power to improve the lives of children in some of the most disadvantaged areas of the world. We're proud of what we have already achieved and now we look forward to the future."

Another scheme between Chelsea and Right To Play was also launched in 2013, asking fans to recycle their old football kits for underprivileged children.

Demba Ba, Branislav Ivanovic and Marko Marin announced the start of the project on a visit to the Chelsea Store in Kingston, where they donated the first shirts to Right To Play's kit bin.

"It's important for all of us to do what we can," said Ba. "An old kit that you may not use or that may be too small could make a real difference to young people who have never had a football shirt before."

All the kits donated to the collections, which are taking place at both the Chelsea Store in Kingston and the Stadium Megastore at Stamford Bridge, will be handed over at Right To Play projects working with some of the world's most marginalised groups in countries throughout Africa, Asia and South America.

Ivanovic added: "This is a great new programme and I hope the community and our fans get behind this scheme and donate their old shirts to this great cause."

For the first time, Chelsea and Right To Play offered Chelsea fans

Gary Cahill celebrates the £2million Chelsea and Right To Play have raised since the partnership began in 2007

Right To Play's logo appeared on Chelsea's shirts in the successful 2013 Europa League final

Right To Play events have even been held on the pitch at Stamford Bridge

Eden Hazard holding one of the iconic Right To Play Red Balls in Seattle

the chance to bid for their chance to play at Stamford Bridge in a unique 11-a-side match. Thousands of bids were placed on eBay in a special store containing signed shirts and the opportunity to play in the match.

This inaugural match finished 8-2, with Chelsea Blue beating Chelsea White, and was played in a great spirit, with fans even flying in from the USA to play. The initiative raised £25,000 and the match will hopefully become an annual highlight.

Right To Play's symbolic Red Balls have become a common sight during the past six years at Chelsea's pre-season matches in Asia and the USA, with the players carrying them on to the pitch before games and kicking them into the crowd to raise awareness among our fans throughout the world and symbolise our shared belief that every child has the right to play.

All of Right To Play's programmes give children a chance to become constructive participants in society regardless of gender, disability, ethnicity, social background or religion. Through games and sport, Right To Play helps create social change in communities affected by war, poverty and disease.

ENHANCING OUR LEGACY THROUGHOUT THE WORLD

Be it returning to Asia on our pre-season tour or working with sponsors on a campaign that crosses continents, Chelsea is committed to sending out a positive message to children everywhere

The Chelsea first-team squad spent the early part of pre-season preparing for the 2013/14 campaign in the Far East during our Here To Play, Here To Stay tour of Asia.

Thailand, Malaysia and, for the first time, Indonesia all received a visit from the Blues in July as returning manager José Mourinho got his players ready for another busy season.

The Thai capital of Bangkok was Chelsea's first port of call, being greeted by the large crowds of fans we have come to expect when travelling to that part of the world. The Blues announced our arrival in the country as Mourinho was joined by Chelsea Chief Executive Ron Gourlay, captain John Terry and vice-captain Frank Lampard on a trip to the Siriraj Hospital, residence of Thailand's king.

On the pitch, things started well with a 1-0 victory over the Singha All-Stars in the Singha 80th Anniversary Cup. That success continued throughout the tour as we went on to maintain our 100 per cent record by beating a Malaysia XI 4-1 in Kuala Lumpur and flying back to England on a high after finishing the trip with an 8-1 win against the BNI Indonesia All-Stars.

The Chelsea fans in all three countries were also able to get closer to their favourite team in the build-up to the matches by attending open training sessions where the players handed out gifts to the crowd and signed autographs. Supporters could also soak up the pre-match atmosphere in the Fanzones outside the stadium. Even shopping centres were turned Blue during the visits, with Chelsea Foundation coaches on hand to provide advice and fun games for youngsters.

As always, our Here To Play, Here To Stay tour also saw the club reiterating our commitment to helping the development of grassroots football in the region.

Coaches from the Chelsea Foundation were working in all three locations throughout the tour, showing youngsters how they can improve their skills as well as teaching fellow coaches from around Asia about the methods and philosophy of the Blues.

The Soccer Schools put on in all three countries also received visits from the first-team players themselves, with no less than

Kevin De Bruyne gets involved at a coaching clinic in Bangkok

Ryan Bertrand, Marco van Ginkel and Andre Schurrle during an adidas coaching clinic at the Malaysian Blue Pitch

13 joining the children for training sessions during the tour.

In Thailand and Malaysia, the Foundation coaches were able to use the Blue Pitch facilities created by Chelsea during previous tours, while a Blue Pitch is set to open in Indonesia in the near future.

"It's great to spend time with the kids when we are here. However, when we leave, there is also a legacy that lives on for many years to come," said Gary Cahill. "These kids can come and get some good coaching and improve their football, that's the main thing."

Romelu Lukaku added: "The facilities are great and I think the kids can develop a lot of technical qualities on those pitches because the surface is perfect, they have good coaches, good balls and equipment to train with."

Some of our club sponsors were also involved at the Soccer Schools, with children invited to the Bangkok session through charities linked to global beer partner Singha, while official club sponsors adidas and Samsung hosted the events in Thailand and Malaysia respectively.

The preparations for the 2013/14 season also saw the Blues travel to the USA, holding a training camp in Washington, DC, while competing in the inaugural Guinness International Champions Cup.

That tournament featured some of football's biggest clubs, with Chelsea finishing in second place after 2-0 wins over Inter Milan and AC Milan, before succumbing to Real Madrid in the final.

The Blues also played a friendly before flying back to London, beating Roma 2-1.

It was the senior side's second US trip in 2013, having previously played two matches against Manchester City in May.

Our Under-21s also spent time in America over the summer, coinciding with the announcement of a partnership between the Chelsea Foundation and FC Harlem.

The Young L.I.O.N.S (Leaders In Our Neighbourhoods) initiative works with young people in New York to create exciting opportunities, provide positive activities and develop social and leadership skills.

The two organisations previously collaborated during Chelsea's visits to New York in the summer of 2012 and spring of 2013.

Chelsea Foundation staff, Chelsea youth players and FC Harlem players in New York

Home kit

Goalkeeper's home kit

BLUE BOLDLY GOES WHERE NO BLUE HAS GONE BEFORE

To view all the kits and to buy online,
go to www.chelseafc.com/allin

In the 2013/14 season, Chelsea's stylish play will once again be matched on the pitch by a striking range of kits from official kit supplier and sponsor adidas.

There is definitely a nod to the club's heritage with the new home kit, as the simple colour scheme with a classic white V-neck collar and cuffs brings back memories of iconic shirts of the 1960s.

The new goalkeeping kit signals a return to the eye-catching designs

Away kit

Third kit

that have often been sported by Petr Cech in previous campaigns, with a bright yellow to make sure he commands attention as well as his penalty area.

There is also a significant nod to the Sixties with the 2013/14 away kit, as the white design with a red and a blue stripe across the chest is reminiscent of some classic shirts of that era.

In contrast, the third strip has a much more modern look with its silver trim. Although its main colour of black

had never been used for a Chelsea kit before 2002, it has appeared in nine out of the 12 seasons since.

All of the Chelsea kits have a touch of the modern about them, though, incorporating the very latest in adidas technology to give the players an edge on the pitch, with TechFit designed to help improve speed, endurance and awareness.

Fans also receive a helping hand for remaining comfortable in the stands thanks to adidas' ClimaCool

technology in the replica shirts, which improves air flow to the skin in key heat zones.

It isn't just this season's kit designs that have proven to be striking, either, thanks to adidas' teaser campaign "it's blue, what else matters?" ahead of revealing the home kit. That saw the Chelsea players covering themselves in blue paint from head to toe, showing themselves going "all in" for the Blues.

Left: Support for Chelsea now stretches from England to Asia and, as seen here, America

Below: Platinum tier membership gives fans the chance to present the Supporters' Clubs Player of the Year award at the Bridge, just as these Ennis Blues did in 2012/13, when the honour went to Juan Mata

BECOMING A BLUE IS SO EASY

Our world-class status is reflected in our ever-growing fanbase both at home and abroad, so why not add your voice by joining – or even setting up – a supporters' club?

The number of official Chelsea supporters' clubs has regularly surpassed 100 in recent seasons, with fans throughout the world coming together to show their love for the Blues.

The number of supporters' clubs is growing all the time, with new groups in Indonesia, Mongolia and Macau all joining in 2012/13, while clubs from Costa Rica, Sri Lanka and Afghanistan have already signed up for this season.

Of course, not all the supporters' clubs have such a long journey to Stamford Bridge, with a large number of local groups within the UK as well as their overseas comrades in Europe, Asia, Africa and the Americas.

With such a range of locations, the requirements of supporters' clubs obviously vary. To accommodate individual needs, different options and

benefits are available to all clubs when they register.

The Facebook and Bronze supporters' club tiers are designed for fans who want to be officially affiliated with the Blues without fees or access to match tickets. However, the creators/administrators of those clubs do receive invitations to the supporters' clubs end of season dinner, plus priority purchase of tickets for Chelsea's Player of the Year event at Stamford Bridge.

The Silver through to Platinum supporters' club tiers can choose different added benefits, such as priority ticketing access for games in the Premier League, domestic cups and the Champions League group stage as well as signed merchandise.

Platinum tier representatives also receive the opportunity to present

their Player of the Year award to the chosen player on the Stamford Bridge pitch. There is also an overall Supporters' Clubs Player of the Year award, with every club getting a vote and the representatives of one getting to hand over the trophy before a game. Fans from the Ennis Supporters' Club in the Republic of Ireland had the honour of presenting the prize to Juan Mata in 2013.

The Fans' section of the official Chelsea website contains details on how to start an official supporters' club before this season's deadline of 31 December 2013, as well as further information on the different tier options and their benefits.

If you want to get in touch with, or join, a Chelsea supporters' club, a list of locations and contact details is available on the site.

Stamford the Lion meets some young Blues on the pitch

JOIN US AND PLAY YOUR PART

Chelsea FC membership for the 2013/14 season offers fantastic choice and a variety of benefits, with tiers of membership suitable for every Blues supporter

TRUE BLUE TICKET ONLY

If it is just priority access to match tickets for every Chelsea game you want, this is the tier of membership for you. Members pay £5 less than non-members for match tickets, so you only need to watch Chelsea five times and you will have recouped your membership fee!
£25 one season/£48 two seasons

TRUE BLUE MAGAZINE

As well as those vital tickets, if you want Chelsea magazine delivered to your door each month during the season, then this is the option for you. With the magazine retailing at £3.25, this tier offers unbelievable value. **£35**

TRUE BLUE ORIGINAL

If you want the full works – including the specially designed membership collectors' box with the 2013/14 Chelsea Yearbook, an exclusive DVD from our 2013 Asia tour and a Chelsea calendar, not to mention the magazine and ticket access – go for this tier. **£45**

TRUE BLUE INTERNATIONAL

True Blue International members get vital ticket access. In addition, as well as your membership card and a range of discount vouchers for use outside the UK, you will receive full access to Chelsea TV online throughout the 2013/14 season with unlimited access to our online video centre and live streaming service.
Members also get full access to premium content, including match highlights, within the official Chelsea FC mobile application, meaning you will never miss a moment of the Blues' 2013/14 campaign. **£30**

TRUE BLUE DIGITAL

If you rarely get the opportunity to visit the Bridge but don't want to miss a minute of the action, then True Blue Digital is the new membership tier for you.
You will receive full access to Chelsea TV online throughout the 2013/14 season, meaning unlimited access to our online video centre and live streaming service.
Members also get full access to premium content, including match highlights, within the official Chelsea FC mobile application, so you will never miss a moment of the Blues' 2013/14 campaign. **£30**

CHELSEA JUNIOR MEMBERSHIP

Chelsea's young fans are our future and we want to make it as easy and as cheap as possible for them to get close to their club. In addition to offering the opportunity to watch the Blues play live, CFC junior membership offers many other great benefits. **£15**

To purchase membership, visit www.chelseafc.com/membership or call 0871 984 1905.

KEEP UP TO SPEED WITH BLUES NEWS

Be it through the official club website, publications, TV channel or social media platforms, there are plenty of ways to get involved with your club and hear the latest from the Bridge

OFFICIAL WEBSITE

Chelsea's website gives easy access to the latest news, ticket and booking details, player info, Chelsea TV streamed live with video on demand, the online Megastore and much more.

Prior to games, media conferences are streamed live and, on matchdays, we have extensive previews followed by live text updates and radio commentary throughout the game as well as post-match reaction.

Insightful thoughts come from columnists Pat Nevin and Giles Smith, while supporters blog on the site and have their say on chat forums in The Shed section – dedicated to fan-generated content.

With versions available in the English, Chinese, Japanese, Korean, Indonesian, Russian and Thai languages as well as a mobile site and app, chelseafc.com is the first port of call for any Blues fans.

CHELSEA TV

Chelsea TV has unrivalled access to the players and provides must-see content for Blues fans around the world. With the service available on Sky, online and via your smartphone, you can watch wherever you may be.

Some of our most popular features include:
• Behind the scenes footage from Cobham with daily news bulletins broadcast live from Stamford Bridge;
• Phone-in shows giving fans the chance to speak to the players live;
• Matchday Live brings you exclusive build-up, live commentary, post-match reaction and extended highlights from all first-team fixtures;
• Full re-runs of every first-team game plus exclusive live coverage of

first-team friendlies, Under-21s and Under-18s fixtures as well as exclusive first interviews with new signings.

To join via Sky, call 08442 410 203 or visit www.sky.com/chelseatv. To sign up online, visit www.chelseafc.com/chelseatv. To join via you mobile, download the free official Chelsea FC app on selected smartphones.

SOCIAL MEDIA

Each of our social media platforms provides its own exclusive content, meaning that however you choose to interact with the Blues you can enjoy all the latest news, behind the scenes videos, competitions and much more.

Fans are engaging with us on social media, with our regular Q&A sessions with first-team players proving extremely popular and helping us become the most followed Premier League club on Twitter. Also, with a growing number of our stars utilising the likes of Twitter and Instagram, what better way to get closer to your heroes? Try one of the services listed in the bar below.

PUBLICATIONS

Chelsea's official publications provide an all-encompassing insight into life at the club.

Our award-winning matchday programme is packed with exclusive player interviews, extended historical coverage, a detailed look at our opponents and regular columns from the manager, captain and celebrity fans. It is available at all home games, price £3, while seasonal subscriptions start from £70 and can be purchased by calling 0845 241 6210.

The revamped Chelsea magazine is packed full of new additions, including a monthly fans' Q&A with José

Mourinho. In-depth player features are accompanied by exclusive photo shoots and we look at the history of the Blues in retrospective articles.

The magazine is available in the Megastore and newsagents for £3.25, with subscriptions available on certain membership packages (see page 119). Back copies of the magazine and programme can be purchased at www.chelseafc.com/shop.

• The matchday programme is also available to download during the 2013/14 season. You can buy individual copies for £2.99 or get a season subscription for £39.99 and have the latest edition downloaded to your tablet when it goes on sale.

Chelsea magazine is also available digitally, with individual issues costing £2.99 and an annual subscription £29.99. For more information, go to www.chelseafc.com/mobile.

Facebook facebook.com/chelseafc Twitter @ChelseaFC #CFC Instagram @ChelseaFC #CFC
Foursquare foursquare.com/chelseafc YouTube youtube.com/chelseafc Google+ +ChelseaFC

120 | CHELSEA FOOTBALL CLUB YEARBOOK 2013/14

TOUR OUR HOME, TAKE IN OUR HISTORY

Immerse yourself in more than a century of memories and silverware with the Chelsea Museum and a stadium tour

The Chelsea Museum and Stadium Tours let you get an insider's look at the Blues' past and present.

The museum at Stamford Bridge opened in the summer of 2011 and covers events at the club from our formation in 1905 right up to the recent successes at home and in Europe.

Located behind the Matthew Harding Stand, it tells the story of the Blues' most famous moments as well as charting the culture of football at the Bridge.

There is also a modern touch with plenty of interactive exhibits to enjoy, such as controlling the display of shirts worn by some of our biggest legends, watching a collection of our greatest games and viewing a life-size 3D hologram featuring actor and fan Phil Daniels, and former players Ron Harris and Marcel Desailly.

Visitors can also test their skills against Chelsea stars of past and present with the adidas Shooting Gallery and Beat the Cat batak game.

Plus, of course, there's the chance to take in all the silverware acquired in the Blues' 108 years of history in the trophy cabinet.

A stadium tour is another great opportunity to get closer than ever to the club, with the chance to get inside some of the otherwise inaccessible areas of Stamford Bridge.

Led by one of our knowledgeable tour guides, visitors can enjoy a truly memorable trip and see the areas of the stadium usually reserved for players and officials.

You can go to the press room and sit where the manager addresses the media, before getting a look inside the home and away changing rooms.

Fans can also experience the thrill of walking down the players' tunnel with the sound of a crowd ringing in their ears before sampling the view from the dugout.

SPECIAL OCCASIONS

Further options are available to make your visit to Stamford Bridge even more memorable.

A Museum Party or Football Party caters specifically for children, both starting with a private tour of the stadium before enjoying fun and games in the museum or a football match on a special inflatable pitch.

Private tours can also be arranged for small or large groups in a VIP Platinum package, which includes lunch at the on-site Frankie's Sports Bar and Grill.

Additionally, the Chelsea Museum specialises in educational visits for Key Stage 2 art and maths pupils, harnessing the excitement of football and the Blues to make learning fun.

For more information and prices on any of these packages, please visit www.chelseafc.com/tours or call 0871 984 1955.

OPENING TIMES AND PRICES

The Chelsea Museum is open seven days a week from 9.30am-5pm, with last entry at 4pm.

Entrance is £11 for adults and £9 for children. Family tickets allow two adults and two children entry for £36.

For a small additional fee you can also get a museum audio guide, which is available in four languages, as well as souvenir photos with your favourite Chelsea star.

Stadium Tours also operate every day of the week and begin every 30 minutes from 10am until 3pm, lasting one hour.

Tickets cost £20 for adults and £13 for children, including entry to the museum.

To book tickets in advance, go to www.chelseafc.com/tours, where a pre-booking discount is available, or call 0871 984 1955.

Please note that the museum is closed and there are no tours on the day of, or the day before, European fixtures.

FIXTURES 2013/14

Date	Opposition		Result
August			
Sun 18	Hull City (4pm)	H	-
Wed 21	Aston Villa (7.45pm)	H	-
Mon 26	Manchester United (8pm) Sky	A	-
Fri 30	Bayern Munich (UEFA Super Cup)	N	-
September			
Sat 14	Everton (5.30pm) Sky	A	-
Wed 18	Basel (UCL Group E)	H	-
Sat 21	Fulham (5.30pm) Sky	H	-
Tue 24	Swindon Town (COC3, 7.45pm) Sky	A	-
Sat 28	Tottenham Hotspur (12.45pm) BT	A	-
October			
Tue 1	Steaua Bucharest (UCL Group E)	A	-
Sun 6	Norwich City (1.30pm) Sky	A	-
Sat 19	Cardiff City	H	-
Tue 22	Schalke (UCL Group E)	A	-
Sun 27	Manchester City (1.30pm) Sky	H	-
29/30	Capital One Cup fourth round	-	-
November			
Sat 2	Newcastle United (12.45pm) BT	A	-
Wed 6	Schalke (UCL Group E)	H	-
Sat 9	West Bromwich Albion	H	-
Sat 23	West Ham United (5.30pm) Sky	A	-
Tue 26	Basel (UCL Group E)	A	-
December			
Sun 1	Southampton (4pm) Sky	H	-
Wed 4	Sunderland (7.45pm)	A	-
Sat 7	Stoke City	A	-
Wed 11	Steaua Bucharest (UCL Group E)	H	-
Sat 14	Crystal Palace	H	-
17/18	Capital One Cup quarter-final	-	-
Sat 21	Arsenal	A	-
Thu 26	Swansea City	H	-
Sat 28	Liverpool	H	-
January			
Wed 1	Southampton	A	-
4/5	FA Cup third round	-	-
7/8	Capital One Cup semi-final, first leg	-	-
Sat 11	Hull City	A	-
Sat 18	Manchester United	H	-
21/22	Capital One Cup semi-final, second leg	-	-
25/26	FA Cup fourth round	-	-
Wed 29	West Ham United (7.45pm)	H	-
February			
Sat 1	Manchester City	A	-
Sat 8	Newcastle United	H	-
Tue 11	West Bromwich Albion (7.45pm)	A	-
15/16	FA Cup fifth round	-	-
18/19	UCL round of 16, first leg	-	-
Sat 22	Everton	H	-
25/26	UCL round of 16, first leg	-	-
March			
Sat 1	Fulham	A	-
Sun 2	Capital One Cup final	N	-
Sat 8	Tottenham Hotspur	H	-
8/9	FA Cup quarter-final	-	-
11/12	UCL round of 16, second leg	-	-
Sat 15	Aston Villa	A	-
18/19	UCL round of 16, second leg	-	-
Sat 22	Arsenal	H	-
Sat 29	Crystal Palace	A	-
April			
1/2	UCL quarter-final, first leg	-	-
Sat 5	Stoke City	H	-
8/9	UCL quarter-final, second leg	-	-
Sat 12	Swansea City	A	-
12/13	FA Cup semi-final	N	-
Sat 19	Sunderland	H	-
22/23	UCL semi-final, first leg	-	-
Sat 26	Liverpool	A	-
29/30	UCL semi-final, second leg	-	-
May			
Sat 3	Norwich City	H	-
Sun 11	Cardiff City (4pm)	A	-
Sat 17	FA Cup final	N	-
Sat 24	UCL final	N	-

Fixtures correct at time of going to press and are
subject to change.
All games kick-off at 3pm unless stated.
N - Neutral venue. UCL - UEFA Champions League.